Primary Source

DOCUMENTS IN WESTERN CIVILIZATION

VOLUME ONE: TO 1700

JONATHAN S. PERRY
University of South Florida

SARA E. CHAPMAN
Oakland University

DEREK HASTINGS
Oakland University

Upper Saddle River, New Jersey 07458

© 2009 by PEARSON EDUCATION, INC.
Upper Saddle River, New Jersey 07458

10 9 8 7 6 5 4 3 2 1

ISBN-10: 0-13-175583-8
ISBN-13: 978-0-13-175583-3

Table Of Contents

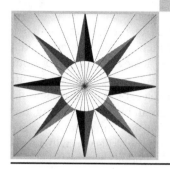

Introduction

In the year 24 CE, in the city of Rome, an important government official reportedly threw his wife out of a window—'for some unknown reason', according to our only source for the incident. Documenting the case nearly a century later, in a short paragraph in his *Annals*, P. Cornelius Tacitus passed along the bizarre circumstances surrounding this event. Unconvinced by the murderer's claim that his wife must have killed herself, the Emperor Tiberius went to the room from which the wife had been ejected and personally investigated the murder scene. Discovering signs of violence, Tiberius referred the matter to the Senate, but, before the trial could begin, the man stabbed himself to death in prison. A further shocking detail: the man's grandmother, a close friend of the Emperor's mother, had reportedly sent the dagger to her grandson, hinting rather pointedly that he should use it, to maintain a shred of the family's tattered dignity. And there is one final element here: soon after the suicide, the man's first wife was acquitted on the charge of making her husband insane…by means of various magic potions and spells.

Within this little story is encapsulated all the joys—and all the frustrations—of utilizing 'primary sources'. Tacitus tells us a great deal of interesting detail here, but is it reliable? Does his account even begin to tell us all that we would like to know about this incident? Historians, like the authors of your course textbooks, ultimately build their accounts on primary sources—those documents, written, physical, or in some other form, that survive from the period under investigation. Primary sources can be written accounts, but they are by no means only textual documents. Regardless of its appearance, however, each primary source is only as trustworthy as the person or persons who created it—and even then, we must factor in the unique perspective of its creator. Even a photograph, which seems to be a straightforward depiction of "reality," frozen in a moment of time, must be contextualized by the investigator. If we could see what was positioned just *outside* the frame, would we interpret the moment differently? To what or to whom is the person in the photograph reacting, and is that information essential for making sense of the person's expression?

This book is designed to aid you in the process of interpreting sources, which is the cornerstone of the "craft" we historians practice. We have adopted a number of approaches and organizational methods to achieve this goal, but our main hope is that you will never accept any source—even one provided by your instructor—simply at face value. Everything you read, see, or experience should be subjected to rigorous and critical examination. This can be an exhausting, but also a very exciting, habit, like exercising muscles that are infrequently used. Whether you decide to continue studying history or not, the skills you will develop by using this book will be of value to you, both as a student and as a resident in "the real world."

Jonathan S. Perry
University of South Florida

How to Read Primary Sources

Primary source accounts, like the ones in this collection, are invaluable tools for historians as they work to interpret past events. This collection of documents invites you to practice the historian's craft, just as professional historians do, by using primary sources.

Primary Sources

Anything that was produced or written by someone who directly participated in or observed a historical event can be considered a primary source. Traditionally, historians have used a wide array of written primary sources such as trial transcripts, contracts, financial records, correspondence, diaries, memoirs, edicts, laws, philosophical treatises and works of literature. Historians of older periods, especially those in the ancient and medieval worlds, have a broader definition of primary sources that encompasses anything produced or written in the general time-frame of their study. Increasingly, they now also use visual materials, such as pictures, photographs, and maps. Choosing what primary sources to use to study a historical event or trend is important because different sources provide different perspectives on the event. An official newspaper account, for example, would present a very different version of an incident than a diary entry written by a person directly involved.

If read carefully and analytically against their historical backdrops, primary sources clarify not only *what* happened, but more importantly, they also shed light on the underlying beliefs, assumptions and ideas that informed *why* people acted as they did. Because most primary sources offer one particular view of an event or trend, it is important to use them in conjunction with secondary sources (overview histories of the period under study, such as a textbook) to place them in the larger context of historical trends, linking them to larger ideas and events that were happening at the same time in history.

There are no precise rules or procedures that dictate how to read or analyze historical documents—no two historians would interpret a primary source document in the same way. Also, each period of historical study poses unique problems in this regard. There are, however, some general approaches and methods that can help guide you as you work with the documents in this collection. Reading primary sources involves carefully considering and exploring several key aspects of a document. Which will be discusses below. These include:

- Analyzing Authorship
- Determining the Audience
- Identifying the Argument
- Historical Significance: Making Links to Larger Ideas, Trends, and Events

Analyzing Authorship

When reading primary sources, a good starting point is to consider the author's background in order to determine, at least to some degree, the factors that shaped his or her account of the historical era, issue or event. Knowing something about the author helps to analyze his or her argument and tie it to larger political, social, intellectual and economic trends occurring at the same time.

Several factors are key to understanding an author's viewpoint. Consider what kind of education the author received. The author's religious and political beliefs are also often relevant, as well as his or her social status or place in the society. Other factors that can shape an author's approach are gender and race.

In analyzing authorship, it is also important to think about the author's reliability as a source. In some cases, they participated directly in the event under study, while in other scenarios, they were observers or bystanders. While both types of accounts can be credible sources, the different vantage points might yield different versions of what transpired. For example, a judge writing about his verdict on a trial would likely explain and justify his decision, while an observer who was sympathetic to the accused would be more likely to question the judge's decision and offer a more critical view of his verdict. Analyzing authorship means thinking about the author's interests and how they affect his or her version of events.

Determining when the author wrote or created a document also helps to analyze the authors' viewpoint. An account of an event written or recorded immediately after, is usually a dependable source for the detailed sequence of events. Likewise, an account written long after the event transpired might not get the details of what happened just right, but might better explain its long-term consequences or ramifications. Some questions to consider when analyzing authorship are:

- What kind of education did the author have?
- Where can you place the author in terms of social and economic status? Are they from a marginalized group or the elite?

- Was the author a female or male? How might gender shape how the author experienced and understood the event?
- What were the author's political views?
- What were the author's religious beliefs and views?
- When was the document written or created in relation to the event described?

Determining the Audience

Sometimes the main audience or intended receptions of the document are clearly indicated, as for example, with letters or correspondence. For other documents, it is necessary to use other methods to establish, in more general terms, the groups and individuals targeted by the author.

Literacy rates, which estimate what groups and people could read during any given historical period, are often helpful in determining the audience. Using your textbook or other secondary source, research what groups of people were likely, or not likely, to be able to read during the time the document appeared. Using estimated literacy rates and gauging the level of difficulty of the vocabulary used in the document, can provide a rough estimate of its audience. Another important factor is where the document appeared and what kind of access people had to it. For example, if it was published in a newspaper or a pamphlet, it would likely have a larger and broader audience, than if it appeared in a limited run of hardback books which were expensive to print and purchase. Finally, one should consider in what language the source was originally created, and how many people in the writer's society would have been familiar with that language.

Knowing the intended audience for a document is important, because authors persuade or inform by appealing to their audience's interests. The author, audience, and argument of any given document, then, are tightly intertwined. In trying to determine the audience of a document, consider the following questions:

- Did the author write or create the document for publication, or was it written only for friends or family members?
- What groups or individuals might have been expected to see it beyond those who were explicitly addressed?
- Did the choice of language that the documents was originally written in limit or expand the size of the document's potential audience?
- Where was the document published or where did it first appear?
- Based on cost, literacy rates, and availability, who would have had access to it?

Identifying the Argument

For some documents, it is easy to determine the author's argument, but in others it takes the form of a more subtle message. Likewise, authors writing about the same event or trend often have conflicting arguments or messages which depend on their own perspectives, backgrounds, and interests. All arguments or versions of the event might be equally valid, all might be "true." It is our job, as historians, to identify their main arguments and analyze the underlying ideas, viewpoints, and interests that informed their different perspectives or arguments. To use a modern example, imagine that a fender-bender takes place in a parking lot. The drivers of the two vehicles that collided would no doubt have very different accounts of what actually transpired. Bystanders who saw the crash take place might also have yet other points of view. The drivers of the cars would presumable filter the exact sequence of events through their own "argument" about what took place, intentionally or unintentionally distorting them for a purpose. When reading primary source documents, we have to consider and analyze the arguments and information offered by the author or authors, taking into consideration their interests and perspectives.

- What main idea or concept was the author trying to convey?
- What were the author's primary motivations for creating the document? Was the author trying to instruct or persuade? How?
- What groups' or individuals' political, economic, religious or social interests were directly addressed by the author in the document? How?

Historical Significance: Making Links to Larger Ideas, Trends, and Events

A good analysis of a primary source document takes into consideration the author, the author's audience, and his or her argument, and then links these to larger, significant historical events, trends, and changes happening at the same time.

Reading primary sources often means wrestling with the idea that people in the past viewed and understood their own lives, events, and the world around them in very different ways than we do today. In the words of English writer L.P. Hartley (1895–1972) "the past is a foreign country; they do things differently there." The actions of people in the past can often be attributed to assumptions, beliefs, feelings, or attitudes, but these are often very different than the ones we hold today. For example, people in medieval and early modern Europe believed that illnesses stemmed from an imbalance of fluids or humors in the body, and so they treated the sick by bleeding or cutting to release a small amount of blood. They believed this practice readjusted the humors in the body and returned a person to good health. From our vantage point of the twenty-first century, this practice seems absurd, counterproductive, and even potentially lethal. By placing these practices into historical context and understanding the medical and philo-sophical traditions grounded in ancient and medieval theories about how the body functioned that informed them, it is possible to understand why and how this approach to curing illnesses made perfect sense to people at that time. Dismissing those who came before us as ignorant or irrational is a barrier to thinking historically. A good analysis of a historical document seeks to deter-mine how their beliefs, ideas, and approaches were linked to larger ideas and tra-ditions that informed people's actions and shaped how they saw the world. This allows us, as historians, to link particular events to larger historical trends and identify periods where they began to shift or change. To make links to larger his-torical trends, consider the following questions:

- What other important events or trends were occurring at the same time the document was written (for example, wars, intellectual movements, religious movements)? What does the primary source tell us about these larger historical issues?
- In what ways was the author's argument connected to larger trends, events, or issues happening at the same time?
- What kinds of symbols or images were depicted in the document, how were they linked to larger issues or trends, and what did they represent or mean to the author and his or her audience?

Sara E. Chapman
Oakland University

Primary Source
DOCUMENTS IN WESTERN
CIVILIZATION
VOLUME ONE: TO 1700

JONATHAN S. PERRY
University of South Florida

SARA E. CHAPMAN
Oakland University

DEREK HASTINGS
Oakland University

Upper Saddle River, New Jersey 07458

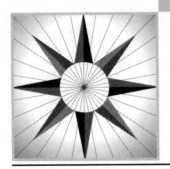

PART 1

The Ancient World
(5000 B.C.E. — 500 C.E.)

CHAPTER 1

The Ancient Middle East

Hittite Law Code:
Excerpts from *The Code of the Nesilim*

The Hittites emerged as a major power in the Near East around 1520 BCE, when King Telipinus seized the throne and unified his people. In time, Hittite power grew to rival that of Egypt, and their wars and treaties have been preserved in a remarkable series of documents. Like most ancient peoples, the Hittites also enshrined their beliefs in law codes, expressing their society's values, structure, and priorities. This document is translated from two surviving tablets of a series called "If anyone." Notice the tone of the text, and the sliding scales of punishment.

Source: Ancient History Sourcebook: The Code of the Nesilim, c. 1650–1500 BCE

FOCUS QUESTIONS:

1. What general principles inform the laws stated here?
2. When was a financial punishment appropriate and when a capital punishment?
3. Is the principle applied consistently?

1. If anyone slay a man or woman in a quarrel, he shall bring this one. He shall also give four persons, either men or women, he shall let them go to his home.

2. If anyone slay a male or female slave in a quarrel, he shall bring this one and give two persons, either men or women, he shall let them go to his home.

3. If anyone smite a free man or woman and this one die, he shall bring this one and give two persons, he shall let them go to his home.

4. If anyone smite a male or female slave, he shall bring this one also and give one person, he shall let him or her go to his home.

5. If anyone slay a merchant of Hatti, he shall give one and a half pounds of silver, he shall let it go to his home.

6. If anyone blind a free man or knock out his teeth, formerly they would give one pound of silver, now he shall give twenty half-shekels of silver.

8. If anyone blind a male or female slave or knock out their teeth, he shall give ten half-shekels of silver, he shall let it go to his home.

10. If anyone injure a man so that he cause him suffering, he shall take care of him. Yet he shall give him a man in his place, who shall work for him in his house until he recovers. But if he recover, he shall give him six half-shekels of silver. And to the physician this one shall also give the fee.

17. If anyone cause a free woman to miscarry, if it be the tenth month, he shall give ten half-shekels of silver, if it be the fifth month, he shall give five half-shekels of silver.

18. If anyone cause a female slave to miscarry, if it be the tenth month, he shall give five half-shekels of silver.

20. If any man of Hatti steal a Nesian slave and lead him here to the land of Hatti, and his master discover him, he shall give him twelve half-shekels of silver, he shall let it go to his home.

21. If anyone steal a slave of a Luwian from the land of Luwia, and lead him here to the land of Hatti, and his master discover him, he shall take his slave only.

24. If a male or female slave run away, he at whose hearth his master finds him or her, shall give fifty half-shekels of silver a year.

31. If a free man and a female slave be fond of each other and come together and he take her for his wife and they set up house and get children, and afterward they either become hostile or come to close quarters, and they divide the house between them, the man shall take the children, only one child shall the woman take.

32. If a slave take a woman as his wife, their case is the same. The majority of the children to the wife and one child to the slave.

33. If a slave take a female slave their case is the same. The majority of children to the female slave and one child to the slave.

34. If a slave convey the bride price to a free son and take him as husband for his daughter, nobody dare surrender him to slavery.

36. If a slave convey the bride price to a free son and take him as husband for his daughter, nobody dare surrender him to slavery.

40. If a soldier disappear, and a vassal arise and the vassal say, "This is my military holding, but this other one is my tenancy," and lay hands upon the fields

of the soldier, he may both hold the military holding and perform the tenancy duties. If he refuse the military service, then he forfeits the vacant fields of the soldier. The men of the village shall cultivate them. If the king give a captive, they shall give the fields to him, and he becomes a soldier.

98. If a free man set a house ablaze, he shall build the house, again. And whatever is inside the house, be it a man, an ox, or a sheep that perishes, nothing of these he need compensate.

99. If a slave set a house ablaze, his master shall compensate for him. The nose of the slave and his ears they shall cut off, and give him back to his master. But if he do not compensate, then he shall give up this one.

158. If a man go for wages, bind sheaves, load it into carts, spread it on the straw barn and so forth "till they clear the threshing floor, for three months his wages are thirty pecks of barley. If a woman go for wages in the harvest, for two months he shall give twelve pecks of barley.

159. If anyone harness a yoke of oxen, his wages are one-half peck of barley.

160. If a smith make a copper box, his wages are one hundred pecks of barley. He who makes a copper dish of two-pound weight, his wages are one peck of emmer.

164. If anyone come for borrowing, then make a quarrel and throw down either bread or wine jug, then he shall give one sheep, ten loaves, and one jug of beer. Then he cleanses his house by the offering. Not until the year has elapsed may he salute again the other's house.

170. If a free man kill a serpent and speak the name of another, he shall give one pound of silver; if a slave, this one shall die.

173. If anyone oppose the judgment of the king, his house shall become a ruin. If anyone oppose the judgment of a lord, his head shall be cut off. If a slave rise against his master, he shall go into the pit.

176. If anyone buy an artisan's apprentice, buy either a potter, a smith, a carpenter, a leatherworker, a tailor, a weaver, or a lace-maker, he shall give ten half-shekels.

178. A plow-ox costs fifteen half-shekels of silver, a bull costs ten half-shekels of silver, a great cow costs seven half-shekels of silver, a sheep one half-shekel of silver, a draft horse twenty half shekels of silver, a mule one pound of silver, a horse fourteen half-shekels of silver.

181-182. Four pounds of copper cost one half-shekel of silver; one tub of lard, one half-shekel of silver; two cheese one half-shekel of silver; a gown twelve half-shekels of silver; one blue woolen garment costs twenty half-shekels of silver; breeches cost ten half-shekels of silver...

187. If a man have intercourse with a cow, it is a capital crime, he shall die. They shall lead him to the king's hall. But the king may kill him, the king may grant him his life. But he shall not approach the king.

188. If a man have intercourse with his own mother, it is a capital crime, he shall die. If a man have intercourse with a daughter, it is a capital crime, he shall die. If a man have intercourse with a son, it is a capital crime, he shall die.

190. If a man and a woman come willingly, as men and women, and have intercourse, there shall be no punishment. And if a man have intercourse with his stepmother, there shall be no punishment; except if his father is living, it is a capital crime, the son shall die.

191. If a free man picks up now this woman, now that one, now in this country, then in that country, there shall be no punishment if they came together sexually willingly.

192. If the husband of a woman die, his wife may take her husband's patrimony.

194. If a free man pick up female slaves, now one, now another, there is no punishment for intercourse. If brothers sleep with a free woman, together, or one after the other, there is no punishment. If father and son sleep with a female slave or harlot, together, or one after the other, there is no punishment.

195. If a man sleep with the wife of his brother, while his brother is living, it is a capital crime, he shall die. If a man have taken a free woman, then have intercourse also with her daughter, it is a capital crime, he shall die. If he have taken her daughter, then have intercourse with her mother or her sister, it is a capital crime, he shall die.

197. If a man rape a woman in the mountain, it is the man's wrong, he shall die. But if he rape her in the house, it is the woman's fault, the woman shall die. If the husband find them and then kill them, there is no punishing the husband.

199. If anyone have intercourse with a pig or a dog, he shall die. If a man have intercourse with a horse or a mule, there is no punishment. But he shall not approach the king, and shall not become a priest. If an ox spring upon a man for intercourse, the ox shall die but the man shall not die. One sheep shall be fetched as a substitute for the man, and they shall kill it. If a pig spring upon a man for intercourse, there is no punishment. If any man have intercourse with a foreign woman and pick up this one, now that one, there is no punishment.

200. If anyone give a son for instruction, be it a carpenter, or a potter, or a weaver, or a tailor, or a smith, he shall give six half-shekels of silver for the instruction.

The Code of Hammurabi

In order to "establish law and justice in the language of the land" and to "promote the welfare of the people," the Amorite King Hammurabi (C. 1728–1686 BCE), who had made Babylon his capital and conquered Mesopotamia, issued a comprehensive code of laws. He caused them to be inscribed on stones that were erected at cross-roads and in marketplaces throughout his kingdom, so that all his sub-jects would understand the penalties that their actions might incur. This document survives on one of these stones, topped by an illustration showing Hammurabi receiving the order to write the laws from the sun-god Shamash. The stone was discovered by French archaeologists in 1901–1902, and it remains one of the treasures of the Louvre in Paris.

Source: Robert Francis Harper, trans., The Code of Hammurabi, King of Babylon, Chicago: University of Chicago Press, 1904.

Focus Questions:

1. What general principles inform the laws stated here?
2. When was a financial punishment appropriate, and when a capital punishment? Is the principle applied consistently?
3. What does the document reveal about the status of women in this society?

When the lofty Anu, king of the Anunnaki, and Bel, lord of heaven and earth; he who determines the destiny of the land, committed the rule of all mankind to Marduk, the chief son of Ea; when they pronounced the lofty name of Babylon: when they made it famous among the quarters of the world and in its midst established an everlasting kingdom whose foundations were firm as heaven and earth—at that time, Ann and Bel called me, Hummurabi, the exalt-ed prince, the worshiper of the gods, to cause justice to prevail in the land, to destroy the wicked and the evil, to prevent the strong from oppressing the weak…to enlighten the land and to further the welfare of the people. Hammurabi, the governor named by Bel, am I, who brought about plenty and abundance… …the ancient seed of royalty, the powerful king, the Sun of Babylon, who caused light to go forth over the lands of Sumer and Akkad; the king, who caused the four quarters of the world to render obedience; the favorite of Nana, am I. When Marduk sent me to rule the people and to bring help to the country, I established law and justice in the land and promoted the welfare of the people.

1.

If a man bring an accusation against a man, and charge him with a (capital) crime, but cannot prove it, he, the accuser, shall be put to death.

2.

If a man charge a man with sorcery, and cannot prove it, he who is charged with sorcery shall go to the river, into the river he shall throw himself and if the river overcome him, his accuser shall take to him-self his house (estate). If the river show that man to be innocent and he come forth unharmed, he who charged him with sorcery shall be put to death. He who threw himself into the river shall take to him-self the house of his accuser.

If a man has come forward to bear witness to a felony and then has not proved the statement he has made, if that case (is) a capital one, that man shall be put to death.

If a man aid a male or female slave of the palace, or a male or female slave of a freeman to escape from the city gate, he shall be put to death.

If a man seize a male or female slave, a fugitive, in the field and bring that (slave) back to his owner, the owner of the slave shall pay him two shekels of silver.

23.

If the brigand be not captured, the man who has been robbed, shall, in the presence of god, make an itemized statement of his loss, and the city and the governor, in whose province and jurisdiction the robbery was committed, shall compensate him for whatever was lost.

24.

If it be a life (that is lost), the city and governor shall pay one mana of silver to his heirs.

26.

If either an officer or a constable, who is ordered to go on an errand of the king, do not go but hire a substitute and dispatch him in his stead, that officer or constable shall be put to death; his hired substitute shall take to himself his (the officer's) house.

53.

If a man neglect to strengthen his dyke and do not strengthen it, and a break be made in his dyke and the water carry away the farm-land, the man in whose dyke the break has been made shall restore the grain which he has damaged.

127.

If a man point the finger at a priestess or the wife of another and cannot justify it, they shall drag that man before the judges and they shall brand his forehead.

128.

If a man take a wife and do not arrange with her the (proper) contracts, that woman is not a (legal) wife.

129.

If the wife of a man be taken in lying with another man, they shall bind them and throw them into the water. If the husband of the woman would save his wife, or if the king would save his male servant (he may).

130.

If a man force the (betrothed) wife of another who has not known a male and is living in her father's house, and he lie in her bosom and they take him, that man shall be put to death and that woman shall go free.

131.

If a man accuse his wife and she has not been taken in lying with another man, she shall take an oath in the name of god and she shall return to her house.

132.

If the finger have been pointed at the wife of a man because of another man, and she have not been taken in lying with another man, for her husband's sake she shall throw herself into the river.

142.

If a woman hate her husband, and say: "Thou shalt not have me," they shall inquire into her antecedents for her defects; and if she have been a careful mistress and be without reproach and her husband have been going about and greatly belittling her, that woman has no blame. She shall receive her dowry and shall go to her father's house.

143.

If she have not been a careful mistress, have gadded about, have neglected her house and have belittled her husband, they shall throw that woman into the water.

144.

If a man take a wife and that wife give a maid servant to her husband and she bear children; if that man set his face to take a concubine, they shall not countenance him. He may not take a concubine.

145.

If a man take a wife and she do not present him with children and he set his face to take a concubine, that man may take a concubine and bring her into his house. That concubine shall not rank with his wife.

146.

If a man take a wife and she give a maid servant to her husband, and that maid servant bear children and afterwards would take rank with her mistress; because she has borne children, her mistress may not sell her for money, but she may reduce her to bondage and count her among the maid servants.

196.

If a man destroy the eye of another freeman [i.e., a man in the upper class], they shall destroy his eye.

197.

If one break a man's bone, they shall break his bone.

198.

If one destroy the eye of a villein [a dependent laborer] or break the bone of a freeman, he shall pay one mana of silver.

199.

If one destroy the eye of a man's slave or break a bone of a man's slave he shall pay one-half his price.

200.

If a man knock out a tooth of a man of his own rank, they shall knock out his tooth.

201.

If one knock out a tooth of a villein, he shall pay one-third mana of silver.

203.

If a man strike another man of his own rank, he shall pay one mana of silver.

204.

If a villein strike a villein, he shall pay ten shekels of silver.

205.

If a man's slave strike a man's son, they shall cut off his ear.

253.

If a man hire a man to oversee his farm and furnish him the seed-grain and intrust him with oxen and contract with him to cultivate the field, and that man steal either the seed or the crop and it be found in his possession, they shall cut off his fingers.

254.

If he take the seed-grain and overwork the oxen, he shall restore the quantity of grain which he has hoed.

257.

If a man hire a field-laborer, he shall pay him 8 GUR of grain per year.

258.

If a man hire a herdsman, he shall pay him 6 GUR of grain per year.

The righteous laws, which Hammurabi, the wise king, established and (by which) he gave the land stable support and pure government. Hammurabi, the perfect king, am I...

The great gods proclaimed me and I am the guardian governor, whose scepter is righteous and whose beneficent protection is spread over my city...

The king, who is pre-eminent among city kings, am I. My words are precious, my wisdom is unrivaled. By the command of Shamash, the great judge of heaven and earth, may I make righteousness to shine forth on the land. By the order of [the god] Marduk, my lord, may no one efface my statues...

...Let any oppressed man, who has a cause, come before my image as king of righteousness!...

...Let him read the code and pray with a full heart before Marduk, my lord, and Zarpanit, my lady, and may the protecting deities...look with favor on his wishes (plans) in the presence of Marduk, my lord, and Zarpanit, my lady!...

If that man pay attention to my words which I have written upon my monument, do not efface my judgments, do not overrule my words, and do not alter my statues, then will Shamash prolong that man's reign, as he has mine, who am king of righteousness, that he may rule his people in righteousness.

If that man do not pay attention to my words which I have written upon my monument: if he forget my curse and do not fear the curse of god: if he abolish the judgments which I have formulated, overrule my words, alter my statues, efface my name written thereon and write his own name: on account of these curses, commission another to do so—as for that man, be he king or lord, or priest-king or commoner, whoever he may be, may the great god, the father of the gods, who has ordained my reign, take from him the glory of his sovereignty, may be break his scepter, and curse his fate!

May Ea, the great prince, whose decrees take precedence, the leader of the gods, who knows everything, who prolongs the days of my life, deprive him of knowledge and wisdom! May he bring him to oblivion, and dam up his rivers at their sources! May he not permit corn, which is the life of the people, to grow in his land!

An Egyptian Hymn to the Nile

This document survives in several copies, of varying quality, suggesting that it was a common exercise for students to copy this hymn. The original composition, presumably from ancient Thebes in Egypt, may date back to the Middle Kingdom (c. 2100-1700 bce). Notice that the Egyptians recognized that the Nile was the source and origin of their civilization, and this hymn expressed their gratitude to the god of the river itself.

Source: Adoph Erman, *The Literature of the Ancient Egyptians*, trans. A.M. Blackman (London: Methuen & Co., Ltd., 1927), 146-49, reprinted in John L. Beatty and Oliver A. Johnson, eds., *Heritage of Western Civilization*, volume 1, 7th edition (Englewood Cliffs, NJ: Prentice Hall. 1991), 19-20.

Focus Questions:

1. What values or elements of civilization does this document highlight?
2. What specific elements can be connected to ancient civilizations, in general?

Praise to thee, O Nile, that issueth from the earth, and cometh to nourish Egypt. Of hidden nature, a darkness in the daytime....

That watereth the meadows, he that R-e[1] hath created to nourish all cattle. That giveth drink to the desert places, which are fat: from water; it is his dew that falleth from heaven.

Beloved of K-eb,[2] director of the corn-god; that maketh to nourish every workshop of Ptah.[3]

Lord of fish, that maketh the water-fowl to go upstream....

That maketh barley and createth wheat, so that he may cause the temples to keep festivals.

If he be sluggish,[4] the nostrils are stopped up,[5] and all men are impoverished; the victuals of the gods are diminished, and millions of men perish.

If he be niggardly the whole land is in terror and great and small lament.... Khnum[6] hath fashioned him. When he riseth, the land is in exultation and every body is in joy. All jaws begin to laugh and every tooth is revealed.

---

1 The sun-god.
2 The earth-god.
3 Ptah, the craftsman, who fashions everything, could effect nothing without the Nile.
4 On the occasion of a deficient inundation.
5 Men no longer breathe and live.
6 The ram-headed god, who fashions all that is.

He that bringeth victuals and is rich in food, that createth all that is good. The revered, sweet-smelling .... That createth herbage for the cattle, and giveth sacrifice to every god, be he in the underworld, in heaven, or upon earth.... That illleth the storehouses, and maketh wide the granaries, that giveth things to the poor.

He that maketh trees to grow according to every wish, and men have no lack thereof; the ship is built by his power, for there is no joinery with stones....

... thy young folk and thy children shout for joy over thee, and men hail thee as king. Unchanging of laws, when he cometh forth in the presence of Upper and Lower Egypt. Men drink the water....

He that was in sorrow is become glad, and every heart is joyful. Sobk,[7] the child of Neith, laugheth, and the divine Ennead, that is in thee, is glorious.

Thou that vomitest forth, giving the fields to drink and making strong the people. He that makctl1 the one rich and loveth the other. He maketh no distinctions, and boundaries are not made for him.

... one beholdeth the wealthy as him that is full of care, one beholdeth each one with his implements .... None that (otherwise) goett clad, is clad,[8] and the children of notables are unadorned....

He that establisheth right whom men love.... It would be but lies to compare thee with the sea, that bringeth no corn.... no bird descendeth in the desert....

Men begin to play to thee on the harp, and men sing to thee with the hand.[9] Thy young folk and thy children shout for joy over thee, and deputations to thee are appointed.

He that cometh with splendid things and adorneth the earth! That causeth the ship to prosper before men; that quickeneth the hearts in them that are with child; that would fain have there be a multitude of all kinds of cattle.

When thou art risen in the city of the sovereign, then men are satisfied with a goodly list.[10] "I would like lotus flowers," saith the little one, "and all manner of things," saith the... commander, "and all manner of herbs," say the children. Eating bringeth forgetfulness ofhim.[11] Good things are scattered over the dwelling....

When the Nile floodeth, offering is made to thee, cattle are slaughtered for thee, a great oblation is made for thee. Birds are fattened for thee, antelopes are hunted for thee in the desert. Good is recompensed unto thee.

Offering is also made to every other god, even as is done for the Nile, with

7 Sobk has the form of a crocodile and will originally have been a water-god, who rejoices in the inundation.
8 For hard work, clothes are taken of.
9 It is an old custom to beat lime with the hand while singing.
10 i.e. a multitude of good things.
11 The Nile.

incense, oxen, cattle, and birds (upon) the flame. The Nile hath made him his cave in Thebes, and his name shall be known no more in the underworld....

All ye men, extol the Nine Gods, and stand in awe of the might which his son, the Lord of All, hath displayed, even he that maketh green the Two River-banks. Thou art verdant, O Nile, thou art verdant. He that maketh man to live on his cattle, and his cattle on the meadow! Thou art verdant, thou art verdant: O Nile, thou art verdant.

Excerpts from The Epic of Gilgamesh

First written down around 2000 BCE, the story of Gilgamesh is one of the oldest surviving works of world literature. Based on an actual historical figure, King Gilgamesh of Uruk (reigned c. 2700 BCE), it recounts Gilgamesh's travels, adventures, and his search for immortality. In the process, it provides evidence of ancient Mesopotamian ideas about death, the place of humanity in the universe, and societal organization. The work survives in multiple copies, and it seems to have been a compilation of several hero narratives associated with Gilgamesh, his rival-turned-friend Enkidu, and the gods and men they encountered throughout their travels. This selection draws on multiple sections of the "Epic," and it gives a flavor of the whole.

Source: N.K. Sandars., trans. The Epic of Gilgamesh. (London: Penguin Books Ltd., 1978), pp. 61,62-3,69,878,102,116-7,118.

FOCUS QUESTIONS:

1. What does the document suggest about ancient Mesopotamian beliefs about the gods and their effects on men?
2. What is the reaction of Gilgamesh to death, and how does this motivate his behavior?
3. Is any of this document familiar to you from other sources?

I will proclaim to the world the deeds of Gilgamesh. This was the man to whom all things were known; this was the king who knew the countries of the world. He was wise, he saw mysteries and knew secret things, he brought us a tale of the days before the flood. He went on a long journey, was weary, worn-out with labour, returning he rested, he engraved on a stone the whole story.

When the gods created Gilgamesh they gave him a perfect body. Shamash the glorious sun endowed him with beauty, Adad the god of the storm endowed him with courage, the great gods made his beauty perfect, surpassing all others, terrifying like a great wild bull. Two thirds they made him god and one third man.

Gilgamesh went abroad in the world, but he met \\lith none who could withstand his arms till he came to Uruk. But the men of Uruk muttered in their houses. 'Gilgamesh sounds the tocsin for his amusement, his arrogance has no bounds by day or night. No son is left with his father, for Gilgamesh takes them all, even the children; yet the king would be a shepherd to his people. His lust leaves no virgin to her lover, neither the warrior's daughter nor the wife of the noble; yet this is the shepherd of the city, wise, comely, and resolute.'

The gods heard their lament, the gods in heaven cried to the Lord of Uruk, to Anu the god of Uruk: 'A goddess made him, strong as a savage bull, none can withstand his arms. No son is left with his father, for Gilgamesh takes them all; and is this the king, the shepherd of his people? His lust leaves no virgin to her lover, neither the warrior's daughter nor the wife of the noble. 'When Anu had heard their lamentation the gods cried to Aruru" the goddess of creation, 'You made him, O Aruru, now create his equal; let it be as like him as his own reflection, his second self, stormy heart for stormy heart. Let them contend together and leave Uruk in quiet.'

So the goddess conceived an image in her mind, and it was of the stuff of Anu of the firmament. She dipped her hands in water and pinched off clay, she let it fall in the wilderness, and noble Enkidu was created. There was virtue in him of the god of war, of Ninurta himself. His body was rough, he had long hair Eke a woman's; it waved like the hair of Nisaba, the goddess of the corn. His body was covered with matted hair like Samuquan's, the god of cattle.

In Uruk the bridal bed was made, fit for the goddess of love. The bride waited for the bridegroom, but in the night Gilgamesh got up and came to the house. Then Enkidu stepped out, he stood in the street and blocked the way. Mighty Gilgamesh came on and Enkidu met him at the gate. He put out his foot and prevented Gilgamesh from entering the house, so they grappled, holding each other like bulls. They broke the doorposts and the walls shook, they snorted like bulls locked together. They shattered the doorposts and the walls shook. Gilgamesh bent his knee with his foot planted on the ground and with a turn Enkidu was thrown. Then immediately his fury died. When Enkidu was thrown he said to Gilgamesh, 'There is not another like you in the world. Ninsun, who is as strong as a wild ox in the byre. she was the mother who bore you, and now you are raised above all men, and Enlil has given you the kingship, for your strength surpasses the strength of men.' So Enkidu and Gilgamesh embraced and their friendship was sealed.

[Gilgamesh and Enkidu become great friends. Together they set out on a long journey to the Cedar Forest ill the North. They slay afire-breathing monster called Humbaba, who is the guardian of the forest. After their return, Ishtar, the goddess of love, becomes infatuated with Gilgamesh and offers to marry him. Gilgamesh, citing Ishtar's fickle nature in matters of love, refuses. Ishtar becomes incensed.]

Ishtar opened her mouth and said again, 'My father, give me the Bull of Heaven to destroy Gilgamesh. Fill Gilgamesh, I say, with arrogance to his destruction; but if you refuse to give me the Bull of Heaven I will break in the doors of hell and smash the bolts; there will be confusion of people, those above with those from the lower depths. I shall bring up the dead to eat food like the living; and the hosts of dead will outnumber the living'....

When Anu heard what Ishtar had said he gave her the Bull of Heaven to lead by the halter down to Uruk. When they reached the gates of Uruk the Bull, vent to the river; with his first snort cracks opened in the earth and a hundred young men fell down to death. With his second snort cracks opened and two hundred fell down to death.

With his third snort cracks opened. Enkidu doubled over but instantly recovered, he dodged aside and leapt on the Bull and seized it by the horns, The Bull of Heaven foamed in his face, it brushed him with the thick of its tail. Enkidu cried to Gilgamesh, 'My friend, we boasted that we would leave enduring names behind us. Now thrust the sword between the nape and the horns.' So Gilgamesh followed the Bull, he seized the thick of its tail, he thrust the sword between the nape and the horns and slew the Bull. When they had killed the Bull of Heaven they cut out its heart and gave it to Shamash, and the brothers rested.

[The death of the Bull Heaven offends the gods. As compensation, they decree that one of the two heroes must die. After an ominous dream, Enkidu passes away. Gilgamesh greatly mourns for his friend and for the fate of all mortal men. He decides to seek the secret of immortality from Utnapishtim, the Mesopotamian Noah to whom the gods granted everlasting life.]

Bitterly Gilgamesh wept for his friend Enkidu; he wandered over the wilderness as a hunter, he roamed over the plains; in his bitterness he cried. 'How can I rest, how can I be at peace? Despair is in my heart. What my brother is now, that shall I be when I am dead. Because I am afraid of death I will go as best I can to find Utnapishtim whom they call the Faraway, for he has entered the assembly of the gods.' So Gilgamesh traveled over the wilderness, he wandered over the grasslands, a long journey, in search of Utnapishtim, whom the gods took after the deluge: and they set him to live in the land of Dilmun, in the garden of the sun: and to him alone of men they gave everlasting life.

[Gilgamesh then encounters Siduri, "the woman of the vine, the maker of wine." She offers him sage advice concerning his quest.]

She answered, 'Gilgamesh, where are you hurrying to'! You will never find that life for which you are looking. When the gods created man they allotted to him death, but life they retained in their own keeping. As for you, Gilgamesh, fin your belly with good things; day and night, night and day, dance and be merry, feast and rejoice. Let your clothes be fresh, bathe yourself in water, cherish the little child that holds your hand, and make your wife happy in your embrace; for this too is the lot of man.'

[After an arduous journey, Gilgamesh finds Utnapishtim. Utnapishtim tells the hero the story of the flood: mankind's incessant activity had disturbed the rest of the gods, who thus decided to destroy the humans by flooding the earth. Ea, the god of the waters, warned Utnapishtim of the coming deluge. By building a strong ship, Utnapishtim and his family survive. The gods then repented of their action and granted immortality to the survivor. Utnapishtim also reveals another important secret to Gilgamesh.]

'Gilgamesh, I shall reveal a secret thing, it is a mystery of the gods that I am telling you. There is a plant that grows under the water, it has a prickle like a thorn, like a rose; it will wound your hands, but if you succeed in taking it, then your hands will hold that which restores his lost youth to a man.'

When Gilgamesh heard this he opened the sluices so that a sweet-water current might carry him out to the deepest channel; he tied heavy stones to his feet and they dragged him down to the water-bed. There he saw the plant growing; although it pricked him he took it in his hands; then he cut the heavy stones from his feet, and the sea carried him and threw him on to the shore. Gilgamesh said to Urshanabi the ferryman, 'Come here, and see the marvelous plant. By its virtue a man may win back all his former strength. I will take it to Uruk of the strong walls; there I will give it to the old men to eat. Its name shall be "The Old Men Are Young Again"; and at last I shall eat it myself and have back all my lost youth.'

So Gilgamesh returned by the gate through which he had come, Gilgamesh and Urshanabi went together. They traveled their twenty leagues and then they broke their fast; after thirty leagues they stopped for the night.

Gilgamesh saw a well of cool water and he went down and bathed: but deep in the pool there was lying a serpent, and the serpent sensed the sweetness of the flower. It rose out of the water and snatched it away, and immediately it sloughed its skin and returned to the well. Then Gilgamesh sat down and wept, the tears ran down his face, and he took the hand of Urshanabi; 'O Urshanabi, was it for this that I toiled with my hands, is it for this I have wrung out my heart's blood? For myself I have gained nothing; not I, but the beast of the earth has joy of it now. Already the stream has carried it twenty leagues back to the channels where I found it. I found a sign and now I have lost it. Let us leave the boat on the bank and go.'

The destiny was fulfilled which the father of the gods, Enlil of the mountain, had decreed for Gilgamesh: 'In nether-earth the darkness will show him a light: of mankind, all that are known, none will leave a monument for generations to come to compare with his. The heroes, the wise men, like the new moon have their waxing and waning. Men will say, "Who has ever ruled with might and with power like him?" As in the dark month, the month of shadows, so without him there is no light. O Gilgamesh, this was the meaning of your dream. You were given the kingship, such was your destiny, everlasting life was not your destiny. Because of this do not be sad at heart, do not be grieved or oppressed; he has given you power to hid and to loose, to be the darkness and the light of mankind. He has given unexampled supremacy over the people, victory in battle from which no fugitive returns, in forays and assaults from which there is no going back. But do not abuse this power, deal justly with your servants in the palace, deal justly before the face of the Sun.'

CHAPTER 2

Ancient Greece

Tyrtaeus
The Spartan Creed
C. 650 BCE

Tyrtaeus seems to have been a Spartan poet in the 7ᵗʰ century BCE, and a general who led the Spartans in their successful war against neighboring Messenia. It was as a result of this victory that the "Helots" (the word derives from "to seize", in Greek) were forcibly removed and taken as perpetual slaves by the Spartans, with enormous consequences for their culture's subsequent development. Tyrtaeus wrote in an epic style, echoing Homer at many points, and it is reported that his songs were sung by the Spartans while they marched.

Source: *The Norton Book of Classical Literature,* ed. Bernard Knox (New York: W. W. Norton & Co., 1993), pp. 211–212.

Focus Questions:

1. Why should a Spartan hold the line in his hoplite contingent? What benefit would he derive from doing so?
2. Compare the sentiments expressed here with those attributed by Homer to Thersites and to Odysseus.

I would not say anything for a man nor take account of him for any speed of his feet or wrestling skill he might have,
not if he had the size of a Cyclops and strength to go with it, not if he could outrun Bóreas, the North Wind of Thrace,
not if he were more handsome and gracefully formed than Tithónos, or had more riches than Midas had, or Kínyras too,
not if he were more of a king than Tantalid Pelops, or had the power of speech

and persuasion Adrastos had,

not if he had all splendors except for a fighting spirit. For no man ever proves himself a good man in war

unless he can endure to face the blood and the slaughter, go close against the enemy and fight with his hands.

Here is courage, mankind's finest possession, here is the noblest prize that a young man can endeavor to win,

and it is a good thing his city and all the people share with him when a man plants his feet and stands in the foremost spears

relentlessly, all thought of foul flight completely forgotten, and has well trained his heart to be steadfast and to endure,

and with words encourages the man who is stationed beside him. Here is a man who proves himself to be valiant in war.

With a sudden rush he turns to flight the rugged battalions of the enemy, and sustains the beating waves of assault.

And he who so falls among the champions and loses his sweet life, so blessing with honor his city, his father, and all his people,

with wounds in his chest, where the spear that he was facing has transfixed that massive guard of his shield, and gone through his breastplate as well,

why, such a man is lamented alike by the young and the elders, and all his city goes into mourning and grieves for his loss.

His tomb is pointed to with pride, and so are his children, and his children's children, and afterward all the race that is his.

His shining glory is never forgotten, his name is remembered, and he becomes an immortal, though he lies under the ground,

when one who was a brave man has been killed by the furious War God standing his ground and fighting hard for his children and land.

But if he escapes the doom of death, the destroyer of bodies, and wins his battle, and bright renown for the work of his spear,

all men give place to him alike, the youth and the elders, and much joy comes his way before he goes down to the dead.

Aging, he has reputation among his citizens. No one tries to interfere with his honors or all he deserves;

all men withdraw before his presence, and yield their seats to him, the youth, and the men his age, and even those older than he.

Thus a man should endeavor to reach this high place of courage with all his heart, and, so trying, never be backward in war.

Translated by Richmond Lattimore.

Thucydides
The Debate on the Sicilian Expedition
C. 420 BCE

Despite Pericles' confidence in the abilities of Athens' fighting force, the Peloponnesian War quickly degenerated into a stalemate. Roughly one third of Athens' population, including Pericles himself, died in a horrific plague, both Athens and Sparta suffered a series of betrayals, reversals, and incompetent forays, and there seemed no end in sight for this "war like no other". Fifteen years after Pericles had offered his oration, the Athenians contemplated expanding the war to the Greek settlements in Sicily, as a means of destabilizing Spartan alliances and "liberating" more financial assets for their own use. As they deliberated, the Athenians heard two speakers, Nicias against intervention and Alcibiades for it, and Thucydides records their speeches and the results.

Source: Thucydides, *History of the Peloponnesian War*, Translated by Rex Warner, (England: Penguin Books, 1954), pp. 414-415, 416-417, 419-420, 422, and 425.

Focus Questions:

1. What is Nicias' main fear in sending out this expeditionary force?
2. How does Alcibiades persuade the voting citizens of Athens to follow his advice?

At the beginning of spring next year the Athenian delegation came back from Sicily. They were accompanied by the Egestaeans, who brought sixty talents of uncoined silver – a month's pay for sixty ships, which was the number they were going to ask the Athenians to send them.

The Athenians held an assembly and listened to what the Egestaeans and their own delegation had to say. The report was encouraging, but untrue, particularly on the question of the money which was said to be available in large quantities in the treasury and in the temples. So they voted in favour of sending sixty ships to Sicily and appointed as commanders with full powers Alcibiades, the son of Clinias, Nicias, the son of Niceratus, and Lamachus, the son of Xenophanes, who were instructed to help the Egestaeans against the Selinuntines, to reestablish Leontini also, if things went well with them in the war, and in general to make the kind of provisions for Sicily which might seem to them most in accordance with Athenian interests.

Five days later another assembly was held to discuss the quickest means of getting the ships ready to sail and to vote any additional supplies that the generals might need for the expedition. Nicias had not wanted to be chosen for the command; his view was that the city was making a mistake and, on a slight pretext which looked reasonable, was in fact aiming at conquering the whole of Sicily – a very considerable undertaking indeed. He therefore came forward to speak in the hope of making the Athenians change their minds. The advice he gave was a follows:

'It is true that this assembly was called to deal with the preparations to be made for sailing to Sicily. Yet I still think that this is a question that requires further thought – is it really a good thing for us to send the ships at all? I think that we ought not to give such hasty consideration to so important a matter and on the credit of foreigners get drawn into a war which does not concern us. So far as I am concerned personally, I gain honour by it and I am less frightened than most people about my own safety – not that I think that a man is any the worse citizen for taking reasonable care of his own safety and his own property; such men are, in fact, particularly anxious, for their own sakes, that the city should prosper. However, just as in the past I have never spoken against my convictions in order to gain honour, so I shall not do it now, but shall tell you what I think is for the best. I know that no speech of mine could be powerful enough to alter your characters, and it would be useless to advise you to safeguard what you have and not to risk what is yours already for doubtful prospects in the future. I shall therefore confine myself to showing you that this is the wrong time for such adventures and that the objects of your ambition are not to be gained easily....'

'Yet these rebels, once crushed, could be kept down; whereas even if we did conquer the Sicilians, there are so many of them and they live so far off that it would be very difficult to govern them. It is senseless to go against people who, even if conquered, could not be controlled, while failure would leave us much worse off than we were before we made the attempt. My opinion is, too, that Sicily, as it is at present, is not a danger to us, and that it would be even less of a danger if it came under the control of Syracuse (the possibility with which the Egestaeans are always trying to frighten you). As things are now it is possible that some Sicilians might come against us independently because of their affection for Sparta; but, supposing them to be all under the control of Syracuse, it is hardly likely that one empire would attack another, because if they were to join the Pelponnesians in destroying our empire, they would probably find that their own empire would be destroyed by the same people and for the same reasons. The best way for us to make ourselves feared by the Hellenes in Sicily is not to go there at all; and the next best thing is to make a demonstration of our power and then, after a short time, go away again. We all know that what is most admired is what is farthest off and least liable to have its reputation put to the test; and if anything went wrong with us, they would immediately look down on us and join our enemies here in attacking us. This is, in fact, Athenians, your own experience with regard to Sparta and her allies. Your successes against them, coming so unexpectedly compared with what you feared at first, have now made you despise them and set your hearts on the conquest of Sicily. But one's enemy's misfortunes are insufficient grounds for self-satisfaction; one can only feel real confidence when one has mastered his designs. And we ought to realize that, as a result of the disgrace they have suffered, the Spartans have only one thought, and that is how they can even now regain their own reputation by overthrowing us – as is natural when one considers that military honour is the be-all and end-all of their existence. So, if we keep our senses, we shall see that what we are fighting for has nothing to do with these Egestaeans in Sicily, who do not even speak our own language: our real problem is to defend ourselves vigorously against the oligarchical machinations of Sparta.

'We should also remember that it is only recently that we have had a little respite from a great plague and from the war, and so are beginning to make good our losses in men and money. The right thing is that we should spend our new gains at home and on ourselves instead of on these exiles who are begging for assistance and whose interest it is to tell lies and make us believe them, who have nothing to contribute themselves except speeches, who leave all the danger to others and, if they are successful, will not be properly grateful, while if they fail in any way they will involve their friends in their own ruin....'

After this speech of Nicias most of the Athenians who came forward to speak were in favour of making the expedition and not going back on the decision which had already been passed, though a few spoke on the other side. The most ardent supporter of the expedition was Alcibiades, the son of Clinias. He wanted to oppose Nicias, with whom he had never seen eye to eye in politics and who had just now made a personal attack on him in his speech. Stronger motives still were his desire to hold the command and his hopes that it would be through him that Sicily and Carthage would be conquered – successes which would at the same time bring him personally both wealth and honour. For he was very much in the public eye, and his enthusiasm for horse-breeding and other extravagances went beyond what his fortune could supply. This, in fact, later on had much to do with the downfall of the city of Athens. For most people became frightened at a quality in him which was beyond the normal and showed itself both in the lawlessness of his private life and habits and in the spirit in which he acted on all occasions. They thought that he was aiming at becoming a dictator, and so they turned against him. Although in a public capacity his conduct of the war was excellent, his way of life made him objectionable to everyone as a person; thus they entrusted their affairs to other hands, and before long ruined the city.

On this occasion Alcibiades came forward and gave the following advice to the Athenians:

'Athenians, since Nicias has made this attack on me, I must begin by saying that I have a better right than others to hold the command and that I think I am quite worthy of the position. As for all the talk there is against me, it is about things which bring honour to my ancestors and myself, and to our country prof-it as well. There was a time when the Hellenes imagined that our city had been ruined by the war, but they came to consider it even greater than it really is, because of the splendid show I made as its representative at the Olympic games, when I entered seven chariots for the chariot race (more than any private indi-vidual has entered before) and took the first, the second, and fourth places, and saw that everything else was arranged in a style worthy of my victory. It is cus-tomary for such things to bring honour, and the fact that they are done at all must also give an impression of power. Again, though it is quite natural for my fellow citizens to envy me for the magnificence with which I have done things in Athens, such as providing choruses and so on, yet to the outside world this also is evidence of our strength. Indeed, this is a very useful kind of folly, when a man spends his own money not only to benefit himself but his city as well. And it is perfectly fair for a man who has a high opinion of himself not to be put on a level with everyone else; certainly when one is badly off one does not find people coming to share in one's misfortunes. And just as no one takes much notice of us if we are failures, so on the same principle one has to put up with it if one is looked down upon by the successful: one cannot demand equal treatment one-self unless one is prepared to treat everyone else as an equal. What I know is that people like this – all, in fact, whose brilliance in any direction has made them prominent – are unpopular in their life-times, especially with their equals and also with others with whom they come into contact; but with posterity you will find people claiming relationship with them, even where none exists, and you will find their countries boasting of them, not as though they were strangers or disreputable characters, but as fellow-countrymen and doers of great deeds. This is what I aim at myself, and because of this my private life comes in for criticism; but the point is whether you have anyone who deals with public affairs better than I do....'

'Do not be put off by Nicias's arguments for non-intervention and his dis-tinctions between the young and the old. Let us instead keep to the old system of our fathers who joined together in counsel, young and old alike, and raised our state to the position it now holds. So now in the same way make it is your endeavour to raise this city to even greater heights, realizing that neither youth nor age can do anything one without the other, but that the greatest strength is developed when one has a combination where all sorts are represented – the inferior types, the ordinary types, and the profoundly calculating types, all together. Remember, too, that the city, like everything else, will wear out of its own accord if it remains at rest, and its skill in everything will grow out of date; but in conflict it will constantly be gaining new experience and growing more used to defend itself not by speeches, but in action. In general, my view is that a city which is active by nature will soon ruin itself if it changes its nature and becomes idle, and that the way that men find their greatest security is in accept-ing the character and the institutions which they actually have, even if they are not perfect, and in living as nearly as possible in accordance with them.'

The Athenians, however, far from losing their appetite for the voyage because of the difficulties in preparing for it, became more enthusiastic about it than ever, and just the opposite of what Nicias had imagined took place. His advice was regarded as excellent, and it was now thought that the expedition was an absolutely safe thing. There was a passion for the enterprise which affected everyone alike. The older men thought that they would either conquer the places against which they were sailing or, in any case, with such a large force, could come to no harm; the young had a longing for the sights and experiences of distant places, and were confident that they would return safely; the general masses and the average soldier himself saw the prospect of getting pay for the time being and of adding to the empire so as to secure permanent paid employment in the future. The result of this excessive enthusiasm of the majority was that the few who actually were opposed to the expedition were afraid of being thought unpatriotic if they voted against it, and therefore kept quiet.

On the Murder of Eratosthenes:
A Husband's Defense
C. 403 BCE

Lysias (c. 459-380 BCE) was one of the most prolific and accomplished legal advocates in antiquity, and he is thought to have composed over 200 speeches to be delivered in court. Most often, drawing on a (more or less selective) reading of the facts in the case, Lysias would compose a compelling speech, designed to help his own cause, or to make the strongest possible case in his client's favor. His was the perfect style of ancient Greek rhetoric: direct and simple phrases coupled with fascinating characterizations, all in the effort to persuade a given group of Athenians. The excerpt below is from one of the most interesting of all Athenian court speeches, the plea of an aggrieved husband attempting to explain why he had murdered his wife's lover. The piece is replete with unique detail about living arrangements, relations between husbands and wives, and interactions between masters and slaves. However, it is also only one side of the story; we do not have the speech for the prosecution....

Source: W.R.M. Lamb, trans., Lysias, (Cambridge: Harvard University Press, 1960), pp. 5-21, 27.

Focus Questions:

1. What does this document suggest about the role of women in Athenian society? How assertive could they be, and under what circumstances?

2. Is Euphiletus (the speaker) telling the truth? What specific elements here might make one doubt his veracity?

... When I, Athenians, decided to marry, and brought a wife into my house, for some time I was disposed neither to vex her nor to leave her too free to do just as she pleased; I kept a watch on her as far as possible, with such observation of her as was reasonable. But when a child was born to me, thence-forward I began to trust her, and placed all my affairs in her hands, presuming that we were now in perfect intimacy. It is true that in the early days, Athenians, she was the most excellent of wives; she was a clever, frugal housekeeper, and kept everything in the nicest order. But as soon as I lost my mother, her death became the cause of all my troubles. For it was in attending her funeral that my wife was seen by this man [Eratosthenes], who in time corrupted her. He looked out for the servant-girl who went to market, and so paid addresses to her mistress by which he wrought her ruin. Now in the first place I must tell you, sirs (for I am obliged to give you these particulars), my dwelling is on two floors, the upper being equal in space to the lower, with the women's quarters above and the men's below. When the child was born to us, its mother suckled it; and in order that, each time that it had to be washed, she might avoid the risk of descending by the stairs, I used to live above, and the women below. By this time it had become such an habitual thing that my wife would often leave me and go down to sleep with the child, so as to be able to give it the breast and stop its crying. Things went on in this way for a long time, and I never suspected, but was simpleminded enough to suppose that my own was the chastest wife in the city. Time went on, sirs; I came home unexpectedly from the country, and after dinner the child started crying in a peevish way, as the servant-girl was annoying it on purpose to make it so behave; for the man was in the house, I learnt it all later. So I bade my wife go and give the child her breast, to stop its howling. At first she refused, as though delighted to see me home again after so long; but when I began to be angry and bade her go, "Yes, so that you," she said, "may have a try here at the little maid. Once before, too, when you were drunk, you pulled her about." At that I laughed, while she got up, went out of the room, and closed the door, feigning to make fun, and she turned the key in the lock. I, without giving a thought to the matter, or having any suspicion, went to sleep in all content after my return from the country.

Towards daytime she came and opened the door. I asked why the doors made a noise in the night; she told me that the child's lamp had gone out, and she had lit it again at our neighbour's. I was silent and believed it was so. But it struck me, sirs, that she had powdered her face, though her brother had died not thirty days before; even so, however, I made no remark on the fact, but left the house in silence.

After this, sirs, an interval occurred in which I was left quite unaware of my own injuries; I was then accosted by a certain old female, who was secretly sent by a woman with whom that man was having an intrigue, as I heard later. This woman was angry with him and felt herself wronged, because he no longer visited her so regularly, and she kept a close watch on him until she discovered what was the cause. So the old creature accosted me where she was on the look-out, near my house, and said, "Euphiletus, do not think it is from any meddlesomeness that I have approached you; for the man who is working both your and your wife's dishonour happens to be our enemy. If, therefore, you take the servant-girl who goes to market and waits on you, and torture her, you will learn all. It is," she said, "Eratosthenes of Oë who is doing this; he has debauched not only your wife, but many others besides; he makes an art of it."

With these words, sirs, she took herself off; I was at once perturbed; all that had happened came into my mind, and I was filled with suspicion, reflecting first how I was shut up in my chamber, and then remembering how on that night the inner and outer doors made a noise, which had never occurred before, and how it struck me that my wife had put on powder. All these things came into my mind, and I was filled with suspicion. Returning home, I bade the servant-girl follow me to the market, and taking her to the house of an intimate friend, I told her I was fully informed of what was going on in my house.

"So it is open to you," I said, "to choose as you please between two things,- either to be whipped and thrown into a mill, never to have any rest from miseries of that sort, or else to speak out the whole truth and, instead of suffering any harm, obtain my pardon for your transgressions. Tell no lies, but speak the whole truth."

The girl at first denied it, and bade me do what I pleased, for she knew nothing; but when I mentioned Eratosthenes to her, and said that he was the man who visited my wife, she was dismayed, supposing that I had exact knowledge of everything. At once she threw herself down at my knees, and having got my pledge that she should suffer no harm, she accused him, first, of approaching her after the funeral, and then told how at last she became his messenger; how my wife in time was persuaded, and by what means she procured his entrances, and how at the Thes-mophoria,[1] while I was in the country, she went off to the temple with his mother. And the girl gave an exact account of everything else that had occurred.

When her tale was all told, I said, "Well now, see that nobody in the world gets knowledge of this; otherwise, nothing in your arrangement with me will hold good. And I require that you show me their guilt in the very act; I want no words, but manifestation of the fact, if it really is so."

She agreed to do this. Then came an interval of four or five days...[2]. But first I wish to relate what took place on the last day. I had an intimate friend named

---

1 A festival in honour of Demeter, celebrated by Athenian matrons in October
2 Some words are missing here in the text.

Sostratus. After sunset I met him as he came from the country. As I knew that, arriving at that hour, he would find none of his circle at home, I invited him to dine with me; we came to my house, mounted to the upper room, and had dinner. When he had made a good meal, he left me and departed; then I went to bed. Eratosthenes, sirs, entered, and the maidservant roused me at once, and told me that he was in the house. Bidding her look after the door, I descended and went out in silence; I called on one friend and another, and found some of them at home, while others were out of town. I took with me as many as I could among those who were there, and so came along. Then we got torches from the nearest shop, and went in; the door was open, as the girl had it in readiness.

We pushed open the door of the bedroom, and the first of us to enter were in time to see him lying down by my wife; those who followed saw him standing naked on the bed. I gave him a blow, sirs, which knocked him down, and pulling round his two hands behind his back, and tying them, I asked him why he had the insolence to enter my house. He admitted his guilt; then he besought and implored me not to kill him, but to exact a sum of money.

To this I replied, "It is not I who am going to kill you, but our city's law, which you have transgressed and regarded as of less account than your pleasures, choosing rather to commit this foul offence against my wife and my children than to obey the laws like a decent person." Thus it was, sirs, that this man incurred the fate that the laws ordain for those who do such things; he had not been dragged in there from the street, nor had he taken refuge at my hearth, as these people say.[3] For how could it be so, when it was in the bedroom that he was struck and fell down then and there, and I pinioned his arms, and so many persons were in the house that he could not escape them, as he had neither steel nor wood nor anything else with which he might have beaten off those who had entered? But, sirs, I think you know as well as I that those whose acts are against justice do not acknowledge that their enemies speak the truth, but lie themselves and use other such devices to foment anger in their hearers against those whose acts are just. So, first read the law. He did not dispute it, sirs: he acknowledged his guilt, and besought and implored that he might not be killed, and was ready to pay compensation in money. But I would not agree to his estimate, as I held that our city's law should have higher authority; and I obtained that satisfaction which you deemed most just when you imposed it on those who adopt such courses. Now, let my witnesses come forward in support of these statements.

* * *

[Witnesses are called and heard supporting his statements.] I therefore, sirs, do not regard this requital as having been exacted in my own private interest, but in that of the whole city. For those who behave in that way, when they see the

---

3 Witnesses for the prosecution. To kill someone on the hearth, the center of the family religion, would be sacrilege.

sort of prizes offered for such transgressions, will be less inclined to trespass against their neighbours, if they see that you also take the same view. Otherwise it were better far to erase our established laws, and ordain others which will inflict the penalties on men who keep watch on their own wives, and will allow full immunity to those who would debauch them. This would be a far juster way than to let the citizens be entrapped by the laws; these may bid a man, on catching an adulterer, to deal with him in whatever way he pleases, but the trials are found to be more dangerous to the wronged parties than to those who, in defiance of the laws, dishonour the wives of others. For I am now risking the loss of life, property and all else that I have, because I obeyed the city's laws.

Socrates' *Apology*, as Reported by Plato
C. 390 BCE

A student of Socrates and the teacher of Aristotle, Plato (c. 427-347 BCE) attempted to defend the memory of his mentor, who had been condemned to death by the majority of a 500-man Athenian jury in 399 BCE. This speech purports to be the one Socrates delivered, to defend himself against the two principal charges against him, i.e. that he had disrespected the state gods and that he had "corrupted the youth" of Athens. The historical context is of great importance in assessing this document. Athens had lost its death-match with Sparta in 404, but the democracy had been restored to the city soon afterward. In this climate, some Athenians were seeking a scapegoat, a figure on whom to fix blame for their defeat, and they naturally turned to Socrates, who had been questioning the behavior, mores, and general purpose in life of his fellow citizens for many decades. Notice, in this excerpt, how Socrates both accepts and refutes the substance of the charges leveled against him.

Source: *Plato: The Collected Dialogues,* Edith Hamilton and Huntington Cairns, eds. (Princeton: University Press, 1961), 5–19.

Focus Questions:

1. What did Socrates see as his mission in Athenian society? How did he arouse the hatred of his fellow citizens, and how might a democracy have considered Socrates its enemy?

Very well, then, I must begin my defense, gentlemen, and I must try, in the short time that I have, to rid your minds of a false impression which is the work of many years. I should like this to be the result, gentlemen, assuming it to be for your advantage and my own; and I should like to be successful in my defense, but I think that it will be difficult, and I am quite aware of the nature of my task. However, let that turn out as God wills. I must obey the law and make my defense.

Let us go back to the beginning and consider what the charge is that has made me so unpopular, and has encouraged Meletus to draw up this indictment. Very well, what did my critics say in attacking my character? I must read out their affidavit, so to speak, as though they were my legal accusers: Socrates is guilty of criminal meddling, in that he inquires into things below the earth and in the sky, and makes the weaker argument defeat the stronger, and teaches others to follow his example. It runs something like that. You have seen it for yourselves in the play by Aristophanes, where Socrates goes whirling round, proclaiming that he is walking on air, and uttering a great deal of other nonsense about things of which I know nothing whatsoever. I mean no disrespect for such knowledge, if anyone really is versed in it—I do not want any more lawsuits brought against me by answer questions for rich and poor alike, and I am equally ready if anyone prefers to listen to me and answer my questions. If any given one of these people becomes a good citizen or a bad one, I cannot fairly be held responsible, since I have never promised or imparted any teaching to anybody, and if anyone asserts that he has ever learned or heard from me privately anything which was not open to everyone else, you may be quite sure that he is not telling the truth. But how is it that some people enjoy spending a great deal of time in my company? You have heard the reason, gentlemen; I told you quite frankly. It is because they enjoy hearing me examine those who think that they are wise when they are not—an experience which has its amusing side. This duty I have accepted, as I said, in obedience to God's commands given in oracles and dreams and in every other way that any other divine dispensation has ever impressed a duty upon man. This is a true statement, gentlemen, and easy to verify. If it is a fact that I am in process of corrupting some of the young, and have succeeded already in corrupting others, and if it were a fact that some of the latter, being now grown up, had discovered that I had ever given them bad advice when they were young, surely they ought now to be coming forward to denounce and punish me. And if they did not like to do it themselves, you would expect some of their families—their fathers and brothers and other near relations—to remember it now, if their own flesh and blood had suffered any harm from me. Certainly a great many of them have found their way into this court, as I can see for myself—first Crito over there, my contemporary and near neighbor, the father of this young man Critobulus, and then Lysanias of Sphettus, the father of Aeschines here, and next Antiphon of Cephisus, over there, the father of Epigenes. Then besides there are all those whose brothers have been members of our circle—Nicostratus, the son of Theozotides, the brother of Theodotus, but Theodotus is dead, so he cannot appeal to his brother, and Paralus here, the son of Demodocus, whose brother was Theages. And here is Adimantus, the son of Ariston, whose brother Plato is over there, and Aeantodorus, whose brother Apollodorus is here on this side. I can name many more besides, some of whom Meletus most certainly ought to have produced as witnesses in the course of his speech. If he forgot to do so then, let him do it now—I am willing to make way for him. Let him state whether he has any such evidence to offer. On the contrary, gentlemen, you will find that they are all prepared to help me—the corrupter and evil genius of their nearest and dearest relatives, as Meletus and Anytus say. The actual victims of my corrupting influence might perhaps be excused for helping me; but as for the uncorrupted, their relations of mature age, what other reason can they have for helping me except the right and proper one, that they know Meletus is lying and I am telling the truth?

CHAPTER 3

Rome: From Republic to Empire

Polybius
"Why Romans and Not Greeks Govern the World"
C. 140 BCE

Polybius (c. 200—110s BCE) was born into a prominent family in Greece and served as a leader in the Third Macedonian War against Rome. After losing to Rome in the Battle of Pydna (168 BCE), he was deported, along with 1000 other Greeks, to and held captive in Italy. Despite his status as an enemy detainee, Polybius became a friend of the family of Scipio Aemilianus, one of Rome's most remarkable and well-connected politicians. In honor of his new home and new associates, Polybius composed a history of Rome's rise to world power in the course of his own lifetime. As an outsider, Polybius may have misinterpreted Rome's imperialistic moves in the Mediterranean, and he may have exaggerated the organizational genius of the Republic and its leaders. However, his famous analysis of Rome's "mixed constitution" has influenced political thinkers for centuries, and it was standard reading in the Age of Enlightenment, when the American Constitution was created. It is important to remember, however, that the Roman Republic, unlike that of the United States, did not have a standard document that could be used as a reference; the word "constitution" in Rome's case was meant in a general, non-textual sense, as the "make-up" or "organization" of Rome's public affairs.

Source: Polybius, *Historiarum reliquiae* (Paris: Didot, 1839), VI, iii–xvii, 338–48, passim; trans. and condensed by Henry A. Myers.

FOCUS QUESTIONS:

1. Despite what Polybius claims here, is there evidence that the Senate was the real center of power in the Roman Republic?
2. What elements of this text remind you of the United States Constitution?

With those Greek states which have often risen to greatness and then experienced a complete change of fortune, it is easy to describe their past and to predict their future. For there is no difficulty in reporting the known facts, and it is not hard to foretell the future by inference from the past. But it is no simple matter to explain the present state of the Roman constitution, nor to predict its future owing to our ignorance of the peculiar features of Roman life in the past. Particular attention and study are therefore required if one wishes to survey clearly the distinctive qualities of Rome's constitution.

Most writers distinguish three kinds of constitutions: kingship, aristocracy, and democracy. One might ask them whether these three are the sole varieties or rather the best. In either case they are wrong. It is evident that the best constitution is one combining all three varieties, since we have had proof of this not only theoretically but by actual experience, Lycurgus having organized the Spartan state under a constitution based upon this principle. Nor can we agree that these three are the only kinds of states. We have witnessed monarchical and tyrannical governments, which differ sharply from true kingship, yet bear a certain resemblance to it. Several oligarchical constitutions also seem to resemble aristocratic ones. The same applies to democracies.

We must not apply the title of kingship to every monarchy, but must reserve it for one voluntarily accepted by willing subjects who are ruled by good judgment and not be terror and violence. Nor can we call every oligarchy an aristocracy, but only one where the government is in the hands of a selected body of the justest and wisest men. Similarly the name of democracy cannot be applied to a state in which the masses are free to do whatever they wish, but only to a community where it is traditional and customary to reverence the gods, honor one's parents, respect one's elders, and obey the laws. Such states, provided the will of the greater number prevails, are to be called democracies.

We should therefore recognize six kinds of governments: the three above mentioned, kingship, aristocracy, and democracy, and the three which are naturally related to them, monarchy, oligarchy, and ochlocracy (mob-rule). The first to arise was monarchy, its growth being natural and unaided: the next is true kingship born from monarchy by planning and reforms. Kingship is transformed into its vicious related form, tyranny; and next, the abolishment of both gives birth to aristocracy. Aristocracy by its very nature degenerates into oligarchy; and when the masses take vengeance on this government for its unjust rule, democracy is born: and in due course the arrogance and lawlessness of this form of government produces mob-rule to complete the cycle. Such is the recurring cycle of constitutions; such is the system devised by nature.

Rome, foreseeing the dangers presented by such a cycle, did not organize her government according to any one type, but rather tried to combine all the good features of the best constitutions. All three kinds of government shared in the control of the Roman state. Such fairness and propriety was shown in the use of these three types in drawing up the constitution, that it was impossible to say with certainty if the whole system was aristocratic, democratic, or monarchical. If one looked at the power of the Consuls, the constitution seemed completely monarchical; if at that of the Senate, it seemed aristocratic; and if at the power of the masses, it seemed clearly to be a democracy.

Roman Consuls exercise authority over all public affairs. All other magistrates except the tribunes are under them and bound to obey them, and they introduce embassies to the Senate. They consult the Senate on matters of urgency, they carry out in detail the provisions of its decrees, they summon assemblies, introduce measures, and preside over the execution of popular decrees. In war their power is almost uncontrolled; for they are empowered to make demands on allies, to appoint military tribunes, and to select soldiers. They also have the right of inflicting punishment on anyone under their command, and spending any sum they decide upon from the public funds. If one looks at this part of the administration alone, one may reasonably pronounce the constitution to be a pure monarchy or kingship.

To pass to the Senate: in the first place it has the control of the treasury, all revenue and expenditure being regulated by it; with the exception of payments made to the consuls, no disbursements are made without a decree of the Senate. Public works, whether constructions or repairs, are under the control of the Senate. Crimes such as treason, conspiracy, poisoning, and assassination, as well as civil disputes, are under the jurisdiction of the Senate. The Senate also sends all embassies to foreign countries to settle differences, impose demands, receive submission, or declare war; and with respect to embassies arriving in Rome it decides what reception and what answer should be given to them. All these matters are in the hands of the Senate, so that in these respects the constitution appears to be entirely aristocratic.

After this we are naturally inclined to ask what part in the constitution is left for the people. The Senate controls all the particular matters I mentioned and manages all finances, and the Consuls have uncontrolled authority as regards armaments and operations in the field. But there is a very important part left for the people. For the people alone have the right to confer honors and inflict punishment, the only bonds by which human society is held together. For where the distinction between rewards and punishment is overlooked, or is observed but badly applied, no affairs can be properly administered. For how can one expect rational administration when good and evil men are held in equal estimation? The people judge cases punishable by a fine, especially when the accused have held high office. In capital cases they are the sole judges. It is the people who bestow office on the deserving, the noblest reward of virtue in a state; the people have the power of approving or rejecting laws, and what is most important of all, they deliberate on questions of war and peace. Further in the case of alliances, terms of peace, and treaties, it is the people who ratify all these. Thus one might plausibly say that the people's share in the government is the greatest, and that the constitution is a democratic one.

Having stated how political power is distributed among the three constitutional forms, I will now explain how each of the three parts is enabled, if they wish, to oppose or cooperate with the other parts. The Consul, when he leaves with his army, appears to have absolute authority in all matters necessary for carrying out his purpose; however, in fact he really requires the support of the people and the Senate. For the legions require constant supplies, and without the consent of the Senate, neither grain, clothing, nor pay can be provided; so that the commander's plans come to nothing, if the Senate chooses to impede them. As for the people it is indispensable for the Consuls to conciliate them, however far away from home they may be; for it is the people who ratify or annul treaties, and what is most important, the Consuls are obliged to account for their actions to the people. So it is not safe for the Consuls to underestimate the importance of the good will of either the Senate or the people.

The Senate, which possess such great power, is obliged to respect the wishes of the people, and it cannot carry out inquiries into the most grave offenses against the state, unless confirmed by the people. The people alone have the power of passing or rejecting any law meant to deprive the Senate of some of its traditional authority. Therefore the Senate is afraid of the masses and must pay due attention to the popular will.

Similarly, the people are dependent on the Senate and must respect its members both in public and in private. Through the whole of Italy a vast number of contracts, which it would not be easy to enumerate, are given out by the Senate for the construction and repair of public buildings, and besides this there are many things which are farmed out, such as navigable rivers, harbors, gardens, mines, lands, in fact everything that forms part of the Roman domains. Now all these matters are undertaken by the people, and everyone is interested in these contracts and the work they involve. Certain people are the actual purchasers of the contracts, others are the partners of these first, others guarantee them, others pledge their own fortunes to the state for this purpose. In all these matters the Senate is supreme. It can grant extension of time; it can relieve the contractor if any accident occurs; and if the work proves to be absolutely impossible to carry out it can liberate him from his contract. There are many ways in which the Senate can either benefit or injure those who manage public property. What is even more important is that the judges in most civil trials are appointed from the Senate. As a result of the fact that all citizens are at the mercy of the Senate, and look forward with alarm to the uncertainty of litigation, they are very shy of obstructing or resisting its decisions. Similarly anyone is reluctant to oppose the projects of the Consuls as all are generally and individually under their authority when in the field.

Such being the power that each part has of hampering the others or cooperating with them, their union is adequate to all emergencies, so that it is impossible to find a better political system than this. Whenever the menace of some common danger from abroad compels them to act in concord and support each other, the strength of the state becomes great, as all are zealously competing in devising means of meeting the need of the hour. Consequently, this peculiar form of constitution posses an irresistible power of attaining every object upon which it is resolved. When they are freed from external menace, and reap the harvest of good fortune and affluence which is the result of their success, and in the enjoyment of this prosperity are corrupted by flattery and idleness and become insolent and overbearing, as indeed happens often enough, it is then especially that we see the state providing itself a remedy for the evil from which it suffers. For when one part having grown out of proportion to the others aims at supremacy and tends to become too predominant, it is evident that none of the three is absolute. The purpose of one can be offset and resisted by the others, and none of them will excessively outgrow the others or treat them with contempt. All parts abide by the traditional constitutional practices because any aggressive impulse is sure to be checked and because they fear from the outset the possibility of being interfered with by the others....

Appian of Alexandria
"War, Slaves, and Land Reform: Tiberius Gracchus"
c. 150 BCE

Living in the triumphant Roman Empire in the 2nd century CE, Appian described the histories and geography of various parts of the Mediterranean, and he also wrote a history of "The Civil Wars" that had brought down the Republic between 133 and 30 BCE. While he was writing about events long after they had occurred and while he often misconstrued the workings of the Roman system, this section of his book is critical for understanding the important events of 133 BCE, a violent and pivotal year for the Republic. Tiberius Sempronius Gracchus was born into one of the most famous and wealthiest families in Rome, and one of his cousins was Scipio Aemilianus, the patron of Polybius (see above). However, his proposal to redistribute a portion of the "ager publicus"—the "public land" that Rome had conquered in Italy—to destitute farmers raised the ire of his fellow elites. As you read, pay particular attention to how this son of the most renowned Roman family labored to ingratiate himself with the humblest of the voting citizens.

Source: *Readings in World Civilizations*, Vol. 1, by Kevin Reilly (New York: St. Martins Press, 1995), 81–87.

FOCUS QUESTIONS:

1. What were Gracchus' motives in making his proposal? How did he appeal to "the people" in pushing it forward?

2. Were the Senators at all justified in resisting Gracchus? What legitimate fears might they have had?

The Romans, as they subdued the Italian nations successively in war, seized a part of their lands and built towns there, or established their own colonies in those already existing, and used them in place of garrisons. Of the land acquired by war they assigned the cultivated part forthwith to settlers, or leased or sold it. Since they had no leisure as yet to allot the part which then lay desolated by war (this was generally the greater part), they made proclamation that in the meantime those who were willing to work it might do so for a share of the yearly crops—a tenth of the grain and a fifth of the fruit. From those who kept flocks was required a share of the animals, both oxen and small cattle. They did these things in order to multiply the Italian race, which they considered the most laborious of peoples, so that they might have plenty of allies at home. But the very opposite thing happened; for the rich, getting possession of the greater part of the undistributed lands, and being emboldened by the lapse of time to believe that they would never be dispossessed, and adding to their holdings the small farms of their poor neighbors, partly by purchase and partly by force, came to cultivate vast tracts instead of single estates, using for this purpose slaves as laborers and herdsmen, lest free laborers should be drawn from agriculture into the army. The ownership of slaves itself brought them great gain from the multitude of their progeny, who increased because they were exempt from military service. Thus the powerful ones became enormously rich and the race of slaves multiplied throughout the country, while the Italian people dwindled in numbers and strength, being oppressed by penury, taxes, and military service. If they had any respite from these evils they passed their time in idleness, because the land was held by the rich, who employed slaves instead of freemen as cultivators.

For these reasons the people became troubled lest they should no longer have sufficient allies of the Italian stock, and lest the government itself should be endangered by such a vast number of slaves. Not perceiving any remedy, as it was not easy, nor exactly just, to deprive men of so many possessions they had held so long, including their own trees, buildings and fixtures, a law was once passed with difficulty at the instance of the tribunes, that nobody should hold more than 500 jugera of this land, or pasture on it more than 100 cattle or 500 sheep. To ensure the observance of this law it was provided also that there should be a certain number of freemen employed on the farms, whose business it should be to watch and report what was going on. Those who held possession of lands under the law were required to take an oath to obey the law, and penalties were fixed for violating it, and it was supposed that the remaining land would soon be divided among the poor in small parcels. But there was not the smallest consideration shown for the law or the oaths. The few who seemed to pay some respect to them conveyed their lands to their relations fraudulently, but the greater part disregarded it altogether.

At length Tiberius Sempronius Gracchus, an illustrious man, eager for glory, a most powerful speaker, and for these reasons well known to all, delivered an eloquent discourse, while serving as tribune, concerning the Italian race, lamenting that a people so valiant in war, and blood relations to the Romans, were declining little by little in the pauperism and paucity of numbers without any hope of remedy. He inveighed against the multitude of slaves as useless in war and never faithful to their masters, and adduced the recent calamity brought upon the masters by their slaves in Sicily, where the demands of agriculture had greatly increased the number of the latter; recalling also the war waged against them by the Romans, which was neither easy nor short, but long-protracted and full of vicissitudes and dangers. After speaking thus he again brought forward the law, providing that nobody should hold more than 500 jugera of the public domain. But he added a provision to the former law, that the sons of the present occupiers might each hold one-half of that amount, and that the remainder should be divided among the poor by triumvirs, who should be charged annually.

This was extremely disturbing to the rich because, on account of the triumvirs, they could no longer disregard the law as they had done before; nor could they buy the allotments of others, because Gracchus had provided against this by forbidding sales. They collected together in groups, and made lamentation, and accused the poor of appropriating the results of their tillage, their vineyards, and their dwellings. Some said that they had paid the price of the land to their neighbors. Were they to lose the money with the land? Others said that the graves of their ancestors were in the ground, which had been allotted to them in the division of their fathers' estates. Others said that their wives' dowries had been expended on the estates, or that the land had been given to their own daughters as dowry. Money-lenders could show loans made on this security. All kinds of wailing and expressions of indignation were heard at once. On the other side were heard the lamentations of the poor—that they had been reduced from competence to extreme penury, and from that to childlessness, because they were unable to rear their offspring. They recounted the military service they had rendered, by which this very land had been acquired, and were angry that they should be robbed of their share of the common property. They reproached the rich for employing slaves, who were always faithless and ill-tempered and for that reason unserviceable in war, instead of freemen, citizens, and soldiers. While these classes were lamenting and indulging in mutual accusations, a great number of others, composed of colonists, or inhabitants of the free towns, or persons otherwise interested in the lands and who were under like apprehensions, flocked in and took sides with their respective factions. Emboldened by numbers and exasperated against each other they attached themselves to turbulent crowds, and waited for the voting on the new law, some trying to prevent its enactment by all means, and others supporting it in every possible way. In addition to personal interest the spirit of rivalry spurred both sides in the preparations they were making against each other for the day of the comitia.

What Gracchus had in his mind in proposing the measure was not wealth, but an increase of efficient population. Inspired greatly by the usefulness of the work, and believing that nothing more advantageous or admirable could ever happen to Italy, he took no account of the difficulties surrounding it. When the time for voting came he advanced many other arguments at considerable length and also asked them whether it was not just to divide among the common people what belonged to them in common; whether a citizen was not worthy of more consideration at all times than a slave; whether a man who served in the army was not more useful than one who did not; and whether one who had a share in the country was not more likely to be devoted to the public interests. He did not dwell long on this comparison between freemen and slaves, which he considered degrading, but proceeded at once to a review of their hopes and fears for the country, saying that the Romans had acquired most of their territory by conquest, and that they had hopes of occupying the rest of the habitable world, but now the question of greatest hazard was, whether they should gain the rest by having plenty of brave men, or whether, through their weakness and mutual jealously, their enemies should take away what they already possessed. After exaggerating the glory and riches on the one side and the danger and fear on the other, he admonished the rich to take heed, and said that for the realization of these hopes they ought to bestow this very land as a free gift, if necessary, on men who would rear children, and not, by contending about small things, overlook larger ones; especially since they were receiving an ample compensation for labor expended in the undisputed title to 500 jugera each of free land, in a high state of cultivation, without cost, and half as much more for each son of those who had sons. After saying much more to the same purport and exciting the poor, as well as others who were moved by reason rather than by the desire for gain, he ordered the scribe to read the proposed law.

Marcus Octavius, another tribune, who had been induced by those in possession of the lands to interpose his veto (for among the Romans the tribune's veto always prevailed), ordered the scribe to keep silence. Thereupon Gracchus reproached him severely and adjourned the comitia to the following day. Then he stationed a sufficient guard, as if to force Octavius against his will, and ordered the scribe with threats to read the proposed law to the multitude. He began to read, but when Octavius again vetoed he stopped. Then the tribunes fell to wrangling with each other, and a considerable tumult arose among the people. The leading citizens besought the tribunes to submit their controversy to the Senate for decision. Gracchus seized on the suggestion, believing that the law was acceptable to all well-disposed persons, and hastened to the senate house. There, as he had only a few followers and was upbraided by the rich, he ran back to the forum and said that he would take the vote at the comitia of the following day, both on the law and on the magistracy of Octavius, to determine whether a tribune who was acting contrary to the people's interest could continue to hold his office. And so he did, for when Octavius, nothing daunted, again interposed, Gracchus distributed the pebbles to take a vote on him first. When the first tribe voted to abrogate the magistracy of Octavius, Gracchus turned to him and begged him to desist from his veto. As he would not yield, the votes of the other tribes were taken. There were thirty-five tribes at that time. The seventeen that voted first angrily sustained this motion. If the eighteenth should do the same it would make a majority. Again did Gracchus, in the sight of the people, urgently importune Octavius in his present extreme danger not to prevent this most pious work, so useful to all Italy, and not to frustrate the wishes so earnestly entertained by the people, whose desires he ought rather to share in his character of tribune, and not to risk the loss of his office by public condemnation. After speaking thus he called the gods to witness that he did not willingly do any despite to his colleague. As Octavius was still unyielding he went on taking the vote. Octavius was forthwith reduced to the rank of a private citizen and slunk away unobserved.

Quintus Mummius was chosen tribune in his place, and the agrarian law was enacted. The first triumvirs appointed to divide the land were Gracchus himself, the prosper of the law, his brother of the same name, and his father-in-law, Appius Claudius, since the people still feared that the law might fail of execution unless Gracchus should be put in the lead with his whole family. Gracchus became immensely popular by reason of the law and was escorted home by the multitude as though he were the founder, not of a single city or race, but of all the nations of Italy. After this the victorious party returned to the fields from which they had come to attend to this business. The defeated ones remained in the city and talked the matter over, feeling bitterly, and saying that as soon as Gracchus should become a private citizen he would be sorry that he had done despite to the sacred and inviolable office of tribune, and had opened such a fountain of discord in Italy.

At the advent of summer the notices for the election of tribunes were given, and as the day for voting approached it was very evident that the rich were earnestly promoting the election of those most inimical to Gracchus. The latter, fearing that evil would befall if he should not be reelected for the following year, summoned his friends from the fields to attend the comitia, but as they were occupied with their harvest he was obliged, when the day fixed for the voting drew near, to have recourse to the plebeians of the city. So he went around asking each one separately to elect him tribune for the ensuing year, on account of the danger he had incurred for them. When the voting took place the first two tribes pronounced for Gracchus. The rich objected that it was not lawful for the same man to hold the office twice in succession. The tribune Rubrius, who had been chosen by lot to preside over the comitia, was in doubt about it, and Mummius, who had been chosen in place of Octavius, urged him to turn over the comitia to his charge. This he did, but the remaining tribunes contended that the presidency should be decided by lot, saying that when Rubrius, who had been chosen in that way, resigned, the casting of lots ought to be done over again for all. As there was much strife over this question, Gracchus, who was getting the worst of it, adjourned the voting to the following day. In utter despair he clothed himself in black, while still in office, and led his son around the forum and introduced him to each man and committed him to their charge, as if he were about to perish at the hands of his enemies.

The poor were moved with deep sorrow, and rightly so, both on their own account (for they believed that they were no longer to live in a free state under equal laws, but were reduced to servitude by the rich), and on account of Gracchus himself, who had incurred such danger and suffering on their behalf. So they all accompanied him with tears to his house in the evening, and bade him be of good courage for the morrow. Gracchus cheered up, assembled his partisans before daybreak, and communicated to them a signal to be displayed in case of a fight. He then took possession of the template on the Capitoline hill, where the voting was to take place, and occupied the middle of the assembly. As he was obstructed by the other tribunes and by the rich, who would not allow the votes to be taken on this question, he gave the signal. There was a sudden shout from those who saw it, and a resort to violence in consequence. Some of the partisans of Gracchus took position around him like bodyguards. Others, having girded themselves, seized the fasces* and staves in the hands of the lictors and broke them in pieces. They drove the rich out of the assembly with such disorder and wounds that the tribunes fled from their places in terror, and the priests closed the doors of the temple. Many ran away pellmell and scattered wild rumors. Some said that Gracchus had deposed all the other tribunes, and this was believed because none of them could be seen. Others said that he had declared himself tribune for the ensuing year without an election.

Under these circumstances the Senate assembled at the temple of Fides. It is astonishing to me that they never thought of appointing a dictator in this emergency, although they had often been protected by the government of a single ruler in such times of peril. Although this resource had been found most useful in former times few people remembered it, either then or later. After reaching the decision that they did reach, they marched up to the Capitol, Cornelius Scipio

Nasica, the pontifex maximus [president of the guild of priests—Ed.], leading the way and calling out with a loud voice, "Let those who would save the country follow me." He wound the border of his toga about his head either to induce a greater number to go with him by the singularity of his appearance, or to make for himself, as it were, a helmet as a sign of battle for those who looked on, or in order to conceal from the gods what he was about to do. When he arrived at the temple and advanced against the partisans of Gracchus they yielded to the reputation of a foremost citizen, for they saw the Senate following with him. The latter wrested clubs out of the hands of the Gracchus themselves, or with fragments of broken benches or other apparatus that had been brought for the use of the assembly, began beating them, and pursued them, and drove them over the precipice. In the tumult many of the Gracchans perished, and Gracchus himself was caught near the temple, and was slain at the door close by the statues of the kings. All the bodies were thrown by night into the Tiber.

So perished on the Capitol, and while still tribune, Gracchus, the son of the Gracchus who was twice consul, and of Cornelia, daughter of that Scipio who subjugated Carthage. He lost his life in consequence of a most excellent design, which, however, he pursued in too violent a manner. This shocking affair, the first that was perpetrated in the public assembly, was seldom without parallels thereafter from time to time. On the subject of the murder of Gracchus the city was divided between sorrow and joy. Some mourned for themselves and for him, and deplored the present condition of things, believing that the commonwealth no longer existed, but had been supplanted by force and violence. Others considered that everything had turned out for them exactly as they wished.

Livy
The Rape of Lucretia and the Origins
of the Republic
C. 10 BCE

Titus Livius (c. 59 BCE—12 CE) wrote a history of Rome, "*ab urbe condita*" ("from the foundation of the city") to his own day, and the original document was composed of 142 books, of which only 35 have survived intact. He wrote in a style called "*annales*", i.e. describing the events that took place, both at home and abroad, in a year-by-year format. As he wrote the majority of this work during the reign of the first Princeps, Augustus, it is generally assumed that his history was designed to appeal to the current regime. Thus, Livy pays particular attention to the virtues that animated the Romans' ancestors, and he celebrates their stern moral codes. In this excerpt, Livy explains how the original form of Roman government, a monarchy, fell to a new "*res publica*", a "public thing" that removed power from the king and placed it, at least theoretically, in the hands of "the people".

Source: *Roman History, by Titus Livius,* translated by John Henry Freese, Alfred John Church, and William Jackson Brodribb (New York: D. Appleton, 1899), pp. 67-69.

FOCUS QUESTIONS:

1. Does this story contain valid information about Roman culture, even if it is not technically true?

2. Building on this story, what might Romans of Livy's generation have thought of the word "*rex*" or "king"?

The young princes also sometimes spent their leisure hours in feasting and mutual entertainments. One day as they were drinking in the tent of Sextus Tarquinius, where Collatinus Tarquinius, the son of Egerius, was also at supper, they fell to talking about their wives. Every one commended his own extravagantly: a dispute thereupon arising, Collatinus said there was no occasion for words, that it might be known in a few hours how far his wife Lucretia excelled all the rest. "If, then," added he, "we have any youthful vigour, why should we not mount our horses and in person examine the behaviour of our wives? let that be the surest proof to every one, which shall meet his eyes on the unexpected arrival of the husband." They were heated with wine. "Come on, then," cried all. They immediately galloped to Rome, where they arrived when darkness was beginning to fall. From thence they proceeded to Collatia, where they found Lucretia, not after the manner of the king's daughters-in-law, whom they had seen spending their time in luxurious banqueting with their companions, but, although the night was far advanced, employed at her wool, sitting in the middle of the house in the midst of her maids who were working around her. The honour of the contest regarding the women rested with Lucretia. Her husband on his arrival, and the Tarquinii, were kindly received; the husband, proud of his victory, gave the young princes a polite invitation. There an evil desire of violating Lucretia by force seized Sextus Tarquinius; both her beauty, and her proved chastity urged him on. Then, after this youthful frolic of the night, they returned to the camp.

After an interval of a few days, Sextus Tarquinius, without the knowledge of Collatinus, came to Collatia with one attendant only: there he was made welcome by them, as they had no suspicion of his design, and, having been conducted after supper into the guest chamber, burning with passion, when all around seemed sufficiently secure, and all fast asleep, he came to the bedside of Lucretia, as she lay asleep, with a drawn sword, and with his left hand pressing down the woman's breast, said: "Be silent, Lucretia; I am Sextus Tarquinius. I have a sword in my hand. You shall die if you utter a word." When the woman, awaking terrified from sleep, saw there was no help, and that impending death was nigh at hand, then Tarquin declared his passion, entreated, mixed threats with entreaties, tried all means to influence the woman's mind. When he saw she was resolved, and uninfluenced even by the fear of death, to the fear of death he added the fear of dishonour, declaring that he would lay a murdered slave naked by her side when dead, so that it should be said that she had been slain in base adultery. When by the terror of this disgrace his lust (as it were victorious) had overcome her inflexible chastity, and Tarquin had departed, exulting in having triumphed over a woman's honour by force, Lucretia, in melancholy distress at so dreadful a misfortune, dispatched one and the same messenger both to her father at Rome, and to her husband at Ardea, bidding them come each with a trusty friend; that they must do so, and use dispatch, for a monstrous deed had been wrought. Spurius Lucretius came accompanied by Publius Valerius, the son of Volesus, Collatinus with Lucius Junius Brutus, in company with whom, as he was returning to Rome, he happened to be met by his wife's messenger. They found Lucretia sitting in her chamber in sorrowful dejection.

On the arrival of the friends the tears burst from her eyes; and on her husband inquiring, whether all was well, "By no means," she replied, "for how can it be well with a woman who has lost her honour? The traces of another man are on your bed, Collatinus. But the body only has been violated, the mind is guiltless; death shall be my witness. But give me your right hands, and your word of honour, that the adulterer shall not come off unpunished. It is Sextus Tarquinius, who, an enemy last night in the guise of a guest, has borne hence by force of arms, a triumph destructive to me, and one that will prove so to himself also, if you be men." All gave their word in succession; they attempted to console her, grieved in the heart as she was, by turning the guilt of the act from her, constrained as she had been by force, upon the perpetrator of the crime, declaring that it is the mind that sins, not the body; and that where there is no intention, there is no guilt. "It is for you to see," said she, "what is due to him. As for me, though I acquit myself of guilt, I do not discharge myself from punishment; nor shall any woman survive her dishonour by pleading the example of Lucretia." She plunged a knife, which she kept concealed beneath her garment, into her heart, and falling forward on the wound, dropped down expiring. Her husband and father shrieked aloud.

While they were overwhelmed with grief, Brutus drew the knife out of the wound, and, holding it up before him reeking with blood, said: "By this blood, most pure before the outrage of a prince, I swear, and I call you, O gods, to witness my oath, that I will henceforth pursue Lucius Tarquinius Superbus, his wicked wife, and all their children, with fire, sword, and all other violent means in my power; nor will I ever suffer them or any other to reign at Rome." Then he gave the knife to Collatinus, and after him to Lucretius and Valerius, who were amazed at such an extraordinary occurrence, and could not understand the newly developed character of Brutus. However, they all took the oath as they were directed, and, their sorrow being completely changed to wrath, followed the lead of Brutus, who from that time ceased not to call upon them to abolish the regal power. They carried forth the body of Lucretia from her house, and conveyed it to the forum, where they caused a number of persons to assemble, as generally happens, by reason of the unheard-of and atrocious nature of an extraordinary occurrence. They complained, each for himself, of the royal villainy and violence. Both the grief of the father affected them, and also Brutus, who reproved their tears and unavailing complaints, and advised them to take up arms, as became men and Romans, against those who dared to treat them like enemies. All the most spirited youths voluntarily presented themselves in arms; the rest of the young men followed also.

Women in Roman Politics:
Manipulators or Manipulated?
C. 100 CE

A prolific man of letters who lived in the Roman Empire in the late 1st and early 2nd centuries CE, Plutarch wrote a series of rhetorical, philosophical, and educational treatises, but he is most famous for his *Parallel Lives*. These were biographies of influential Greek and Roman figures from the past, paired and compared in order to demonstrate their common moral achievements and failings. Twenty-three of these pairs survive (one of the most renowned contrasted Alexander the Great and Julius Caesar, for example), and among these is the *Life of Marc Antony*. A significant portion of this biography, despite its ostensible concern with Antony, details the influence exerted on him by his lover, Queen Cleopatra VII of Egypt (69-30 BCE). Cleopatra is deservedly famous in her own right (and Plutarch's biography was the ultimate source of Shakespeare's play *Antony and Cleopatra*). However, this section of the *Life* also details the role of Antony's legitimate wife Octavia, the sister of Octavian (Caesar), who would become Augustus. Notice that both the Roman matron and the Ptolemaic queen affected Antony's behavior—and the general flow of Roman politics—in this crucial period.

Source: *Plutarch, Parallel Lives*, trans. John Dryden and modernized by A.H. Clough, Vol. V, (New York: Little, Brown and Company, 1909), pp. 189-213.

FOCUS QUESTIONS:

1. How did Cleopatra attempt to manipulate Antony's policies?
2. How did Octavia do the same, and how did her brother use her experiences to his advantage?

Antony first entertained Caesar, this also being a concession on Caesar's part to his sister; and when at length an agreement was made between them, that Caesar should give Antony two of his legions to serve him in the Parthian war, and that Antony should in return leave with him a hundred armed galleys, Octavia further obtained of her husband, besides this, twenty light ships for her brother, and of her brother, a thousand foot for her husband. So, having parted good friends, Caesar went immediately to make war with Pompey to conquer Sicily. And Antony, leaving in Caesar's charge his wife and children, and his children by his former wife Fulvia set sail for Asia.

But the mischief that thus long had lain still, the passion for Cleopatra, which better thoughts had seemed to have lulled and charmed into oblivion, upon his approach to Syria, gathered strength again, and broke out into a flame. And, in fine, like Plato's restive and rebellious horse of the human soul, flinging off all good and wholesome counsel, and breaking fairly loose, he sends Fonteius Capito to bring Cleopatra into Syria. To whom at her arrival he made no small or trifling present, Phoenicia, Coele-Syria, Cyprus, great part of Cilicia, that side of Judaea which produces balm, that part of Arabia where the Nabathaeans extend to the outer sea; profuse gifts, which much displeased the Romans.

... But Octavia, in Rome, being desirous to Antony, asked Caesar's leave to go to him; which he gave her, not so much, say most authors, to gratify his sister, as to obtain a fair pretence to begin the war upon her dishonorable reception. She no sooner arrived at Athens, but by letters from Antony she was informed of his new expedition, and his will that she should await him there. And, though she were much displeased, not being ignorant of the real reason of this usage, yet she wrote to him to know of what place he would be pleased she should send the things she had brought with her for his use; for she had brought clothes for his soldiers, baggage, cattle, money, and presents for his friends and officers, and two thousand chosen soldiers sumptuously armed, to form praetorian cohorts. This message was brought from Octavia to Antony by Niger, one of his friends, who added to it the praises she deserved so well. Cleopatra, feeling her rival already, as it were, at hand, was seized with fear, lest if to her noble life and her high alliance, she once could add the charm of daily habit and affectionate intercourse, she should become irresistible, and be his absolute mistress for ever. So she feigned to be dying for love of Antony, bring her body down by slender diet; when he entered the room, she fixed her eyes upon him in a rapture, and when he left, seemed to languish and half faint away. She took great pains that he should see her in tears, and, as soon as he noticed it, hastily dried them up and turned away, as if it were her wish that he should know nothing of it. All this was acting while he prepared for Media; and Cleopatra's creatures were not

slow to forward the design, upbraiding Antony with his unfeeling, hard-hearted temper, thus letting a woman perish whose soul depended upon him and him alone. Octavia, it was true, was his wife, and had been married to him because it was found convenient for the affairs of her brother that it should be so, and she had the honor of the title; but Cleopatra, the sovereign queen of many nations, had been contented with the name of his mistress, nor did she shun or despise the character whilst she might see him, might live with him, and enjoy him; if she were bereaved of this, she would not survive the loss. In fine, they so melted and unmanned him, that, fully believing she would die if he forsook her, he put off the war and returned to Alexandria, deferring his Median expedition until next summer, though news came of the Parthians being all in confusion with intestine disputes. Nevertheless, he did some time after go into that country, and made an alliance with the king of Media, by marriage of a son of his by Cleopatra to the king's daughter, who was yet very young; and so returned, with his thoughts taken up about the civil war.

When Octavia returned from Athens, Caesar, who considered she had been injuriously treated, commanded her to live in a separate house; but she refused to leave the house of her husband, and entreated him, unless he had already resolved, upon other motives, to make war with Antony, that he would on her account let it alone; it would be intolerable to have it said of the two greatest commanders in the world, that they had involved the Roman people in a civil war, the one out of passion for the other out of resentment about, a woman. And her behavior proved her words to be sincere. She remained in Antony's house as if he were at home in it, and took the noblest and most generous care, not only of his children by her, but of those by Fulvia also. She received all the friends of Antony that came to Rome to seek office or upon any business, and did her utmost to prefer their requests to Caesar; yet this her honorable deportment did but, without her meaning it, damage the reputation of Antony; the wrong he did to such a woman made him hated. Nor was the division he made among his sons at Alexandria less unpopular; it seemed a theatrical piece of insolence and contempt of his country. For, assembling the people in the exercise ground, and causing two golden thrones to be placed on a platform of silver, the one for him and the other for Cleopatra, and at their feet lower thrones for their children, he proclaimed Cleopatra queen of Egypt, Cyprus, Libya, and Coele-Syria, and with her conjointly Caesarion, the reputed son of the former Caesar, who left Cleopatra with child. His own sons by Cleopatra were to have the style of kings of kings; to Alexander he gave Armenia and Media, with Parthia, so soon as it should be overcome; to Ptolemy, Phoenicia, Syria, and Cilicia. Alexander was brought out before the people in the Median costume, the tiara and upright peak, and Ptolemy, in boots and mantle and Macedonian cap done about with the diadem; for this was the habit of the successors of Alexander, as the other was of the Medes and Armenians. And, as soon as they had saluted their parents, the one was received by a guard of Macedonians, the other by one of Armenians. Cleopatra was then, as at other times when she appeared in public, dressed in the habit of the goddess Isis, and gave audience to the people under the name of the New Isis.

Caesar, relating these things in the senate, and often complaining to the people, excited men's minds against Antony. And Antony also sent messages of accusation against Caesar. The principal of his charges were these: first, that he had not made any division with him of Sicily, which was lately taken from Pompey; secondly, that he had retained the ships he had lent him for the war; thirdly, that after deposing Lepidus, their colleague, he had taken for himself the army, governments, and revenues formerly appropriated to him; and, lastly, that he had parcelled out almost all Italy amongst his own soldiers, and left nothing for his. Caesar's answer was as follows: that he had put Lepidus out of government because of his own misconduct; that what he had got in war he would divide with Antony, so soon as Antony gave him a share of Armenia; that Antony's soldiers had no claims in Italy, being in possession of Media and Parthia, the acquisitions which their brave actions under their general had added to the Roman empire.

Antony was in Armenia when this answer came to him, and immediately sent Canidius with sixteen legions towards the sea; but he, in the company of Cleopatra, went to Ephesus, whither ships were coming in from all quarters to form the navy, consisting, vessels of which Cleopatra furnished two hundred, together with twenty thousand talents, and provision for the whole army during the war. Antony, on the advice of Domitius and some others, bade Cleopatra return into Egypt, there to expect the event of the war; but she, dreading some new reconciliation by Octavia's means, prevailed with Canidius, by a large sum of money, to speak in her favor with Antony, pointing out to him that it was not just that one that bore so great a part in the charge of the war should be robbed of her share of glory in the carrying it on; nor would it be politic to disoblige the Egyptians, who were so considerable a part of his naval forces; nor did he see how she was inferior in prudence to any one of the kings that were serving with him; she had long governed a great kingdom by herself alone, and long lived with him, and gained experience in public affairs. These arguments (so the fate that destined all to Caesar would have it), prevailed; and when all their forces had met, they sailed together to Samos, and held high festivities....

This over, he gave Priene to his players for a habitation, and set sail for Athens, where fresh sports and playacting employed him. Cleopatra, jealous of the honors Octavia had received at Athens (for Octavia was much beloved by the Athenians), courted the favor of the people with all sorts of attentions. The Athenians, in requital, having decreed her public honors, deputed several of the citizens to wait upon her at her house; amongst whom went Antony as one, he being an Athenian citizen, and he it was that made the speech. He sent orders to Rome to have Octavia removed out of his house. She left it, we are told, accompanied by all his children, except the eldest by Fulvia, who was then with his father, weeping and grieving that she must be looked upon as one of the causes of the war. But the Romans pitied, not so much her, as Antony himself, and more particularly those who had seen Cleopatra, whom they could report to have no way the advantage of Octavia either in youth or in beauty.

The speed and extent of Antony's preparations alarmed Caesar, who feared he might be forced to fight the decisive battle that summer. For he wanted many necessaries, and the people grudged very much to pay the taxes; freemen being called upon to pay a fourth part of their incomes, and freed slaves an eighth of their property, so that there were loud outcries against him, and disturbances throughout all Italy. And this is looked upon as one of the greatest of Antony's oversights, that he did not then press the war. For he allowed time at once for Caesar to make his preparations, and for the commotions to pass over. For while people were having their money called for, they were mutinous and violent; but, having paid it, they held their peace. Titius and Plancus, men of consular dignity and friends to Antony, having been ill used by Cleopatra, whom they had most resisted in her design of being present in the war came over to Caesar, and gave information of the contents of Antony's will, with which they were acquainted. It was deposited in the hands of the vestal virgins, who refused to deliver it up, and sent Caesar word, if he pleased, he should come and seize it himself, which he did. And, reading it over to himself, he noted those places that were most for his purpose, and, having summoned the senate, read them publicly. Many were scandalized at the proceeding, thinking it out of reason and equity to call a man to account for what was not to be until after his death. Caesar specially pressed what Antony said in his will about his burial; for he had ordered that even if he died in the city of Rome, his body, after being carried in state through the forum, should be sent to Cleopatra at Alexandria. Calvisius, a dependent of Caesar's, urged other charges in connection with Cleopatra against Antony; that he had given her the library of Pergamus, containing two hundred thousand distinct volumes; that at a great banquet, in the presence of many guests, he had risen up and rubbed her feet, to fulfil some wager or promise; that he had suffered the Ephesians to salute her as their queen; that he had frequently at the public audience of kings and princes received amorous messages written in tablets made of onyx and crystal, and read them openly on the tribunal; that when Furnius, a man of great authority and eloquence among the Romans, was pleading, Cleopatra happening to pass by in her chair, Antony started up and left them in the middle of their cause, to follow at her side and attend her home.

Calvisius, however, was looking upon as the inventor of most of these stories. Antony's friends went up and down the city to gain him credit, and sent one of themselves, Geminius, to him, to beg him to take heed and not allow himself to be deprived by yote of his authority, and proclaimed a public enemy to the Roman state. But Geminius no sooner arrived in Greece but he was looked upon as one of Octavia's spies; at their suppers he was made a continual butt for mockery, and was put to sit in the least honorable places; all which he bore very well, seeking only an occasion of speaking with Antony. So, at supper, being told to say what business he came about, he answered he would keep the rest for a soberer hour, but one thing he had to say, whether full or fasting, that all would go well if Cleopatra would return to Egypt. And on Antony showing his anger at it, "You have done well, Geminius," said Cleopatra, "to tell your secret without being put to the rack." So Geminius, after a few days, took occasion to make his escape and go to Rome. Many more of Antony's friends were drive from him by the insolent usage they had from Cleopatra's flatterers, amongst whom were Marcus Silanus and Dellius the historian. And Dellius says he was afraid of his life, and that Glaucus, the physician, informed him of Cleopatra's design against him. She was angry with him for having said that Antony's friends were served with sour wine, while at Rome Sarmentus, Caesar's little page (his *delicia*, as the Romans call it), drank Falernian.

As soon as Caesar had completed his preparations, he had a decree made, declaring war on Cleopatra, and depriving Antony of the authority which he had let a woman exercise in his place. Caesar added that he had drunk potions that had bereaved him of his senses, and that the generals they would have to fight with would be Mardion the eunuch, Pothinus, Iras, Cleopatra's hairdressing girl, and Charmion, who were Antony's chief state-councillors.

CHAPTER 4

Imperial Rome and Early Christianity

Gnostic Teachings on Jesus, According to Irenaeus
C. 170 CE

It is important to note, however, that "Christianity" was a diverse, inchoate force in the first three centuries of its history, and it might be more accurately described as competing "Christianities". Various people, with widely divergent beliefs, claimed to be Christians, and many of the earliest Christian documents detail the controversies that arose between these communities of faith. Irenaeus (c. 130-202) was the Bishop of Lyons in Gaul, and a defender of what he considered Christian "orthodoxy", or "correct belief". He set out his views in a document entitled *Adversus haereses* (*Against the Heresies*), challenging views that are called, by present-day religious historians, "Gnostic". Gnostics believed that they were privy to special "knowledge" ("*gnosis*" in Greek) about divine matters, and they formed communities in pockets of the Empire. These elements of Christianity would later be suppressed by the dominant Church structure, and, aside from fortuitous discoveries like the Nag Hammadi Library, Gnostic beliefs can only be determined from the words of their opponents. Speaking against their notions, Irenaeus characterized— though he may also have misrepresented—the teachings of Basileides, especially concerning the divinity of Jesus.

Source: *A New Eusebius: Documents illustrating the history of the Church to AD 337*, edited by J. Stevenson (Cambridge, UK: SPCK, 1987), pp. 76-77.

FOCUS QUESTIONS:

1. Why might some "Christians" have disbelieved in the literal and physical death of Jesus?

2. Why, in Irenaeus' opinion, do Basileides and others of his type promote such beliefs?

Basileides again, that he may appear to have discovered something more sublime and plausible, (i.e. than Satorninus, who has just been mentioned) gives an immense development to his doctrines. He sets forth that Mind was first born of the unborn Father, that from him, again, was born Logos, from Logos Prudence, from Prudence Wisdom and Power, and from Power and Wisdom the powers, and princes and angels, whom he also calls the *first*; and that by them the first heaven was made. Then other powers, being formed by emanation from these, created another heaven similar to the first; and in like manner, when others, again, had been formed by emanation from them, corresponding exactly to those above them, these, too, framed another third heaven; and then from this third, in downward order, there was a fourth succession of descendants; and so on, after the same fashion, they declare that more and more princes and angels were formed, and three hundred and sixty-five heavens. Wherefore the year contains the same number of days in conformity with the number of the heavens.

Those angels who occupy the lowest heaven, that, namely, which is visible to us, formed all the things which are in the world, and made allotments among themselves of the earth and of those nations which are upon it. The chief of them is he who is thought to be the God of the Jews; and inasmuch as he desired to render the other nations subject to his own people, that is, the Jews, all the other princes resisted and opposed him. Wherefore all other nations rushed upon his nation. But the Father without birth and without name, perceiving that they would be destroyed, sent his own first-begotten Mind (he it is who is called Christ) to bestow deliverance on them that believe in him, from the power of those who made the world. He appeared, then, on earth as a man, to the nations of these powers, and wrought miracles. Wherefore he did not himself suffer death, but a certain Simon of Cyrene, being compelled, bore the cross in his stead; Simon was transfigured by him, that he might be thought to be Jesus, and was crucified, through ignorance and error, while Jesus himself received the form of Simon, and, standing by, laughed at them. For since he was an incorporeal power, and the mind of the unborn Father, he transfigured himself as he pleased, and thus ascended to him who had sent him, deriding them, inasmuch as he could not be laid hold of, and was invisible to all. Those, then, who know these things have been freed from the princes who formed the world; so that one must not confess him who was crucified, and was called Jesus, and was sent by the Father, that by this dispensation he might destroy the works of the makers of the world. If any one, therefore, he declares, confesses the crucified, that man is still a slave, and under the power of those who formed our bodies; but he who denies him has been freed from these beings, and is acquainted with the dispensation of the unborn Father.

Salvation belongs to the soul alone, for the body is by nature subject to corruption. He declares, too, that the prophecies were derived from those princes who were the makers of the world, but the law was specially given by their chief, who led the people out of the land of Egypt. He attaches no importance to meats offered to idols, thinks them of no consequence, and makes use of them without any hesitation; he holds also the practice of other religious rites (?), and of every kind of lust, a matter of perfect indifference.

[Irenaeus then goes on to comment on their use of magic, and of mysterious names for the heavenly powers, including Caulacau, the name under which the Saviour went.

They practice secrecy, and do not disclose membership of the sect.] 'Do thou,' they say, 'know all, but let nobody know thee.' For this reason, persons of such a persuasion are also ready to recant, or rather it is impossible that they should suffer on account of a mere name, since they are like to all. The multitude, however, cannot understand these matters, but only one out of a thousand, or two out of ten thousand. They declare that they are no longer Jews, and that they are not yet Christians; and that it is not at all fitting to speak openly of their mysteries, but right to keep them secret by preserving silence.

Tertullian
"What Has Jerusalem to do with Athens?"
C. 200 CE

Tertullian (c. 160-240 CE) was a native of Carthage, a convert to Christianity around 195, and a passionate admirer of martyrs like Perpetua. Trained in philosophy, law, and rhetoric, Tertullian turned his considerable skills to defending Christianity against those who rejected its intellectual and ethical merit. He also attacked, in the On the Prescription of the Heretics, those Christians who were attempting to conflate ancient philosophy and Christian doctrine. In this segment of the work, Tertullian poses his famous question, asking whether Christians have the duty, or even the right, to study "pagan" works. It is significant to note that Tertullian was, himself, aware of all of these philosophical and literary movements, even though he wished to proscribe them from other Christians.

Source: *Sources of the Western Tradition: Volume I: From Ancient Times to the Enlightenment* ,ed. Marvin Perry, Joseph R. Peden, and Theodore H. Von Laue, (Boston: Houghton Mifflin Co., 1995), p. 182. Reprinted from Early Latin Theology, translated and edited by S.I. Greenslade, Vol. V: The Library of Christian Classics, (Philadelphia: Westminster Press).

FOCUS QUESTIONS:

1. Why did Tertullian condemn Greco-Roman philosophy and literature as dangerous for Christians?

2. Compare Tertullian's words here with Paul's speech to the Athenians in Acts. Are these opinions consistent?

... Worldly wisdom culminates in philosophy with its rash interpretation of God's nature and purpose. It is philosophy that supplies the heresies with their equipment.... The idea of a mortal soul was picked up from the Epicureans, and the denial of the restitution of the flesh was taken from the common tradition of the philosophical schools.... Heretics and philosophers [ponder] the same themes and are caught up in the same discussions. What is the origin of evil and why? The origin of man, and how?... A plague on Aristotle, who taught them dialectic [logical argumentation], the art which destroys as much as it builds, which changes its opinions like a coat, forces its conjectures, is stubborn in argument, works hard at being contentious and is a burden even to itself. For it reconsiders every point to make sure it never finishes a discussion.

From philosophy come those fables and... fruitless questionings, those "words that creep like as doth a canker." To hold us back from such things, the Apostle [Paul] testifies expressly in his letter to the Colossians [Colossians 2:8] that we should beware of philosophy. "Take heed lest any man [beguile] you through philosophy or vain deceit, after the tradition of men," against the providence of the Holy Ghost. He had been at Athens where he had come to grips with the human wisdom which attacks and perverts truth, being itself divided up into its own swarm of heresies by the variety of its mutually antagonistic sects. What has Jerusalem to do with Athens, the Church with [Plato's] Academy, the Christian with the heretic? Our principles come from the Porch of Solomon, who had himself taught that the Lord is to be sought in simplicity of heart. I have no use for Stoic or a Platonic or a dialectic Christianity. After Jesus Christ we have no need of speculation, after the Gospel no need of research. When we come to believe, we have no desire to believe anything else; for we begin by believing that there is nothing else which we have to believe.

Eusebius of Caesarea,
Selections from *The Life of Constantine*
c. 330 CE

The bishop of Caesarea in Palestine, Eusebius (260-341 CE) wrote volumes on church doctrine and church history. His most famous work is the *History of the Church*, which remains critical for our understanding of early Christianity. As a contemporary of the emperor Constantine, Eusebius was wit-ness to the great events around Constantine's accession to control of the empire and his historic action in granting tolerance to Christianity.

Source: Medieval Source Book: Eusebius of Caesarea, *The Life of the Blessed Emperor Constantine*

FOCUS QUESTIONS:

1. What is the nature of Constantine's conversion?
2. What is his relationship with God?
3. What is the fate of pagans, including Maxentius?

CHAPTER XXVII: That after reflecting on the Dawn fall [sic] of those who had worshiped Idols, he made Choice of Christianity.

Being convinced, however, that he needed some more powerful aid than his military forces could afford him, on account of the wicked and magical enchantments which were so diligently practiced by the tyrant, (1) he sought Divine assistance, deeming the possession of arms and a numerous soldiery of secondary importance, but believing the co-operating power of Deity invincible and not to be shaken. He considered, therefore, on what God he might rely for protection and assistance. While engaged in this enquiry, the thought occurred to him, that, of the many emperors who had preceded him, those who had rested their hopes in a multitude of gods, and served them with sacrifices and offerings, had in the first place been deceived by flattering predictions, and oracles which promised them all prosperity, and at last had met with an unhappy end, while not one of their gods had stood by to warn them of the impending wrath of heaven; while one alone who had pursued an entirely opposite course, who had condemned their error, and honored the one Supreme God during his whole life, had found him to be the Saviour and Protector of his empire, and the Giver of every good thing. Reflecting on this, and well weighing the fact that they who had trusted in many gods had also fallen by manifold forms of death, without leaving behind them either family or offspring, stock, name, or memorial among men: while the God of his father had given to him, on the other hand, manifestations of his power and very many tokens: and considering farther that those who had already taken arms against the tyrant, and had marched to the battle-field under the protection of a multitude of gods, had met with a dishonorable end (for one of them (2) had shamefully retreated from the contest without a blow, and the other, (3) being slain in the midst of his own troops, became, as it were, the mere sport of death (4)); reviewing, I say, all these considerations, he judged it to be folly indeed to join in the idle worship of those who were no gods, and, after such convincing evidence, to err from the truth; and therefore felt it incumbent on him to honor his father's God alone.

CHAPTER XXVIII: How, while he was praying, God sent him a Vision of a Cross of Light in the Heavens at Mid-day, with an Inscription admonishing him to conquer by that.

Accordingly he called on him with earnest prayer and supplications that he would reveal to him who he was, and stretch forth his right hand to help him in his present difficulties. And while he was thus praying with fervent entreaty, a most marvelous sign appeared to him from heaven, the account of which it might have been hard to believe had it been related by any other person. But since the victorious emperor himself long afterwards declared it to the writer of this history, (1) when he was honored with his acquaintance and society, and confirmed his statement by an oath, who could hesitate to accredit the relation, especially since the testimony of after-time has established its truth? He said that about noon, when the day was already beginning to decline, he saw with his own eyes the trophy of a cross of light in the heavens, above the sun, and bearing the inscription, CONQUER BY THIS. At this sight he himself was struck with amazement, and his whole army also, which followed him on this expedition, and witnessed the miracle. (2)

CHAPTER XXIX: How the Christ of God appeared to him in his Sleep, and commanded him to use in his Wars a Standard made in the Form of the Cross.

He said, moreover, that he doubted within himself what the import of this apparition could be. And while he continued to ponder and reason on its meaning, night suddenly came on; then in his sleep the Christ of God appeared to him with the same sign which he had seen in the heavens, and commanded him to make a likeness of that sign which he had seen in the heavens, and to use it as a safeguard in all engagements with his enemies.

CHAPTER XXXVII: Defeat of Maxentius's Armies in Italy.

Constantine, however, filled with compassion on account of all these miseries, began to arm himself with all warlike preparation against the tyranny. Assuming therefore the Supreme God as his patron, and invoking His Christ to be his preserver and aid, and setting the victorious trophy, the salutary symbol, in front of his soldiers and body-guard, he marched with his whole forces, trying to obtain again for the Romans the freedom they had inherited from their ancestors.

And whereas, Maxentius, trusting more in his magic arts than in the affection of his subjects, dared not even advance outside the city gates, (1) but had guarded every place and district and city subject to his tyranny, with large bodies of soldiers, (2) the emperor, confiding in the help of God, advanced against the first and second and third divisions of the tyrant's forces, defeated them all with ease at the first assault, (3) and made his way into the very interior of Italy.

The Conversion of Georgia,
from The Life of Saint Nino
337 CE

The country of Georgia is one of the oldest Christian countries in the world. Tradition accords the conversion of the country to St. Nino, who traveled to Georgia from her home in Cappadocia (present-day Turkey) and converted first Queen Nana and then her husband King Mirian around 330 CE, who formerly adhered to a local variant of Zorastrianism. The extract below is from *The Conversion of Kartli* composed early in the seventh century at a time when Georgian Christianity began to take a more nationalistic character. At this time, Georgia was divided into two distinct regions, with Kartli being the eastern half of the country. In the passage below, King Mirian, who unlike his wife, Nana, at first resisted Nino's prosletyzing, is dramatically converted to the Christian faith.

Source: *Rewriting Caucasian History: The Medieval Armenian Adaptation of the Georgian Chronicles*, trans. by Robert W. Thompson (Oxford: Clarendon Press, 1996), pp.118-120.

Focus Questions:

1. How is the pre-Christian religion of King Mirian portrayed in this account?

2. What other Christian conversion stories does this account resemble? What is the significance of the reference to Christianity as "the religion of the Romans?"

It happened one summer's day, a Saturday, that the king (Mirian) went out to hum in the vicinity of Muxnari. That secret enemy, the devil, approached and infused his heart with love for the idols and fire. He decided to serve them totally and to kill with the sword all Christians. The king said to his four counselors: "We are worth to be badly treated by our gods, because we have neglected to serve them and we have allowed the bewitched Christians to preach their religion in our land. For by sorcery they reform their miracles. Now this is my decision, that we put to a cruel end all those Who trust in the crucified one, and that we pursue more zealously the service of our gods who are the masters of Kartli (Georgia). We shall compel Nana, my wife, to recant and abandon the religion of the crucified one. And if she does not obey, I shall forget my love for her and destroy her along with the others."

The counselors confirmed his decision because they were fervent for this undertaking, which they had desired from the beginning but had not dared to indicate openly. The king crossed the whole district of Muxnari, and went up the high mountain of T'xot'i in order to look towards Kaspi and Uplis-Cixe. He reached the summit of the mountain, when at mid-day the sun grew dark over the mountain and it became like the dark night (of) eternity. The gloom covered the region in all directions, and they were scattered from each other in distress and anxiety. The king remained alone; he wandered through the mountains and forests, terrified and shaking in fear. He stood at a certain spot and abandoned hope of salvation. But when he recovered his sense, he reasoned thus in his heart. "Behold, I have called on my gods, yet I found no relief. Now I could not be rescued from this distress through hope in the cross and crucified one which Nino preaches and through which she works cures? For I am alive in hell, and I do not know if this perdition has occurred for the whole land or if it was only for me. Now if this ordeal is merely for me, O God of Nino, turn this darkness into light for me and show me my dwelling. Then I shall confess your name and shall set up the wood of the cross and worship it. I shall also build a house for my prayers and become obedient to the religion of the Romans."

Traditional Roman Religious Practices
C. 382 CE

Roman "religion" (the word probably derives from "re-ligio", a "mutual binding" between gods and men) rarely depended on the personal beliefs and ethical behavior of the devotee. More often, it was a matter of form and ritual, as the worshipper was enjoined to perform the ritual in the correct way, in order to gain the god's favor. However, it is important to note that various individuals in antiquity were clearly as attached to their gods as some of their counterparts are today. Christianity did not arise in a vacuum of empty and meaningless rituals; even when it began to be associated with the Emperors, in the 4th century CE, many "pagans" refused to abandon their accustomed deities and practices. While Christianity became the official state religion in the late 4th century, the visible signs of previous religions were still maintained in many parts of official life. In 382, however, the Altar of Victory, which had been erected in the Senate house by Augustus, was ordered removed, as being out-of-keeping with Christian principles. Nevertheless the non-Christian Symmachus (c. 340-402 CE), as quoted in the final excerpt here, attempted to persuade the Emperor (unsuccessfully) that traditional religion ought to be respected.

Source: *As the Romans Did: A Sourcebook in Roman Social History,*ed. Jo-Ann Shelton, (New York: Oxford University Press, 1998), 366, 371–74, 379–80, 390–91.

FOCUS QUESTIONS:

1. In what ways could Roman religious practice be considered "scientific" in its performance?

2. What argument does Symmachus use to support his position on the Altar of Victory? Would it have been convincing to 4th-century Christians?

A HYMN TO DIANA, BY CATULLUS, *POEMS*

Diana, we are in your care, we chaste girls and boys. Come, chaste boys and girls, let us sing in praise of Diana.

O daughter of Leto, mighty offspring of mightiest Jupiter, you who were born beside the Delian olive tree, queen of the mountains and the green forests and the trackless glens and the murmuring streams.

You are called Juno Lucina by women in the agony of childbirth. You are called powerful Trivia. You are called Luna, with your borrowed light.

You, goddess, measuring out the year's progress by your monthly phases, do fill the farmer's humble storerooms with fine produce.

Hallowed be thy name, whatever name it is that you prefer. And, as in years past you have been accustomed to do, so now, too, protect and preserve the race of Romulus with your kindly favor.

PLINY THE ELDER, *NATURAL HISTORY*

It apparently does no good to offer a sacrifice or to consult the gods with due ceremony unless you also speak words of prayer. In addition, some words are appropriate for seeking favorable omens, others for warding off evil, and still others for securing help. We notice, for example, that our highest magistrates make appeals to the gods with specific and set prayers. And in order that no word be omitted or spoken out of turn, one attendant reads the prayer from a book, another is assigned to check it closely, a third is appointed to enforce silence. In addition, a flutist plays to block out any extraneous sounds. There are recorded remarkable cases where either ill-omened noises have interrupted and ruined the ritual or an error has been made in the strict wording of the prayer.

CATO THE ELDER, *ON AGRICULTURE*

Before you harvest your crops, you should offer a sow as a preliminary sacrifice in the following manner. Offer a sow to Ceres before you store up the following crops: spelt, wheat, barley, beans, and rape seed. Before you slaughter the sow, invoke Janus,[1] Jupiter, and Juno, offering incense and wine.

Offer sacrificial crackers to Janus with the following words: "Father Janus, in offering to you these sacrificial crackers I humbly pray that you may be benevolent and well disposed toward me and my children and my home and my family."

---

1 Janus was the god of all beginnings (January) and thus appropriately invoked at the beginning of the harvest. He was also the god of doorways and was frequently represented as having two faces, each looking in the opposite direction, even as a door has two faces.

Offer an oblation cracker to Jupiter and honor him with the following words: "Jupiter, in offering to you this oblation cracker I humbly pray that you may be benevolent and well disposed toward me and my children and my home and my family, being honored by this oblation cracker."

Afterward offer wine to Janus with the following words: "Father Janus, just as I humbly prayed when I offered to you the sacrificial crackers, so now for the same purpose be honored with sacrificial wine,"

And afterward offer wine to Jupiter with the following words: "Jupiter, be honored by the oblation cracker, be honored by the sacrificial wine."

And then slaughter the sow as a preliminary sacrifice. When the internal organs have been cut out,[2] offer sacrificial crackers to Janus and honor him in the same terms as when you earlier offered him crackers. Offer an oblation cracker to Jupiter and honor him in the same terms as before. Likewise, offer wine to Janus and offer wine to Jupiter in the same terms as it was offered when you earlier offered the sacrificial crackers and the oblation crackers. Afterward offer the internal organs and wine to Ceres.

CATO THE ELDER, *ON AGRICULTURE 141*

It is necessary to purify your farmland in the following way. Have a pig-sheep-bull procession led around the land, while the following words are spoken: "With the benevolence of the gods, and hoping that everything may turn out well, I entrust to you the responsibility of having the pig-sheep-bull procession led around my farm, field, and land, wherever you decide the animals ought to be led or carried."

Invoke Janus and Jupiter with an offering of wine; then speak these words: 'Father Mars, I pray and entreat you to be benevolent and well disposed toward me and my home and my family. And for this reason I have ordered a pig-sheep-bull procession to be led around my field, land, and farm, so that you will hinder, ward off, and turn away diseases seen and unseen, barrenness and crop losses, disasters and storms; and so that you will allow the vegetable crops, the grain crops, the vineyards, and the orchards to grow and achieve a productive maturity; and so that you will protect the shepherds and the flocks and bestow safety and good health upon me and my home and my family. For these reasons, therefore, and because of the purifying of my farm, land, and field, and the offering of a sacrifice for purification, even as I have prayed, be honored by the sacrifice of the suckling pigsheep-bull. For this reason, therefore, Father Mars, be honored by this suckling pig-sheep-bull sacrifice."

Slaughter the sacrificial animals with a knife. Bring forward sacrificial crack-

---

2 The internal organs were first inspected carefully to ascertain the will of the gods [taking an augury] and then burned on the altar. The rest of the pig was eaten by the people who witnessed the sacrifice.

ers, and an oblation cracker, and offer them. When you slaughter the pig, lamb, and calf, you must use these words:

"For this reason, therefore, be honored by the sacrifice of the pig-sheep-bull."... If all the sacrificial victims are not perfect, speak these words: "Father Mars, if somehow the suckling pig-sheep-bull sacrifice was not satisfactory to you, I offer this new pig-sheep-bull sacrifice as atonement." If there is doubt about only one or two of the animals, speak these words:"Father Mars, since that pig was not satisfactory to you, I offer this pig as atonement."

SYMMACHUS, *DISPATCHES TO THE EMPEROR*

Every man has his own customs and his own religious practices. Similarly, the divine mind has given to different cities different religious rites which protect them. And, just as each man receives at birth his own soul, so, too, does each nation receive a genius[3] which guides its destiny. We should also take into account the bestowal of favors, which, more than anything else, proves to man the existence of gods. For, since no human reasoning can illuminate this matter, from where else can knowledge of the gods come, and come more correctly, than from the recollection and evidences of prosperity? If the long passage of time gives validity to religious rites, we must keep faith with so many centuries and we must follow our fathers, who followed their fathers and therefore prospered.

Let us imagine that Rome herself is standing before us now and addressing these words to you:

"Best of emperors, fathers of the fatherland, respect my age! The dutiful performance of religious rites has carried me through many years. Let me enjoy the ancient ceremonies, for I do not regret them. Let me live in my own way, for I am free. This is the religion which made the whole world obedient to my laws. These are the rites which drove back Hannibal from my walls and the Senones from my Capitol. Have I been preserved only for this-to be rebuked in my old age? I will consider the changes which people think must be instituted, but modification, in old age, is humiliating and too late."

And so we are asking for amnesty for the gods of our fathers, the gods of our homeland. It is reasonable to assume that whatever each of us worships can be considered one and the same. We look up at the same stars, the same sky is above us all, the same universe encompasses us. What difference does it make which system each of us uses to find the truth? It is not by just one route that man can arrive at so great a mystery.

---

3 Guardian Spirit.

PART 2

The Middle Ages
(500 C.E. – 1500 C.E.)

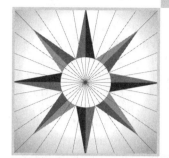

CHAPTER 5

Islam, Byzantium, and the Making of Europe

Priscus Panites at the Court of Attila the Hun
c. 450

A politician and historian based at the court of the Eastern Roman Emperors in Constantinople, Priscus was part of an embassy sent to Attila the Hun in 449. His account is, thus, a first-hand view of one of the most famous "barbarian" invaders of the 5th century. A perceptive observer of court customs, in both the "civilized" and the "barbarian" worlds, Priscus described the people he met on this trip, including a defector from the Roman Empire who had found a comfortable home with the barbarian.

Source: *Readings in European History*, edited by James Harvey Robinson (Boston: Ginn and Company, 1904), 30-33.

Focus Questions:

1. Why did this man leave the protection of the Empire?
2. What lessons might Priscus have drawn from this encounter?
3. Were the "barbarians" more "civilized" than the Romans, in some respects?

A man whom, from his Scythian dress, I took for a barbarian, came up and addressed me in Greek, with the word "Hail!" I was surprised at a Scythian speaking Greek. For the subjects of the Huns, swept together from various lands, speak, beside their own barbarous tongue, either Hunnic or Gothic, or – as many as have commercial dealings with the western Romans -Latin; but none of them speak Greek readily, except captives from the Thracian or Illyrian seacoast; and these last are easily known to any stranger by their torn garments and the squalor of their head, as men who have met with a reverse. This man, on the contrary, resembled a well-to-do Scythian, being well dressed, and having his hair cut in a circle after Scythian fashion.

Having returned his salutation, I asked him who he was and whence he had come into a foreign land and adopted Scythian life. When he asked me why I wanted to know, I told him that his Hellenic speech had prompted my curiosity. Then he smiled and said that he was born a Greek and had gone as a merchant to Viminacium, on the Danube, where he had stayed a long time, and married a very rich wife. But the city fell a prey to the barbarians, and he was stripped of his prosperity, and on account of his riches was allotted to Onegesius [a Hunnish leader] in the division of the spoil, as it was the custom among the Scythians for the chiefs to reserve for themselves the rich prisoners. Having fought bravely against the Romans and the Acatiri, he had paid the spoils he won to his master, and so obtained freedom. He then married a barbarian wife and had children, and had the privilege of partaking at the table of Onegesius.

He considered his new life among the Scythians better than his old life among the Romans, and the reasons he urged were as follows: "After war the Scythians live at leisure, enjoying what they have got, and not at all, or very little, disturbed. The Romans, on the other hand, are in the first place very liable to be killed, if there are any hostilities, since they have to rest their hopes of protection on others, and are not allowed, by their tyrants, to use arms. And those who do use them are injured by the cowardice of their generals, who cannot properly conduct war.

"But the condition of Roman subjects in time of peace is far more grievous than the evils of war, for the exaction of the taxes is very severe, and unprincipled men inflict injuries on others because the laws are practically not valid against all classes. A transgressor who belongs to the wealthy classes is not punished for his injustice, while a poor man, who does not understand business, undergoes the legal penalty, -that is, if he does not depart this life before the trial, so long is the course of lawsuits protracted, and so much money is expended on them. The climax of misery is to have to pay in order to obtain justice. For no one will give a hearing to the injured man except he pay a sum of money to the judge and the judge's clerks."

In reply to this attack on the empire, I asked him to be good enough to listen with patience to the other side of the question. "The creators of the Roman Republic," I said, "who were wise and good men, in order to prevent things from being done at haphazard, made one class of men guardians of the laws, and appointed another class to the profession of arms, who were to have no other object than to be always ready for battle, and to go forth to war without dread, as though to their ordinary exercise, having by practice exhausted all their fear beforehand. Others again were assigned to attend to the cultivation of the ground, to support themselves and those who fight in their defense by contributing the military corn supply....To those who protect the interests of the litigants a sum of money is paid by the latter, just as a payment is made by the farmers to the soldiers. Is it not fair to support him who assists and requite him with kindness?...

"Those who spend money on a suit and lose it in the end cannot fairly put it down to anything but the injustice of their case. And as to the long time spent on lawsuits, that is due to anxiety for justice, that judges may not fail in passing accurate judgments by having to give sentence offhand; it is better that they should reflect, and conclude the case more tardily, than that by judging in a hurry they should both injure man and transgress against the Deity, the institutor of justice...

"The Romans treat their slaves better than the king of the Scythians treats his subjects. They deal with them as fathers or teachers, admonishing them to abstain from evil and follow the lines of conduct which they have esteemed honorable; they reprove them for their errors like their own children. They are not allowed, like the Scythians, to inflict death on their slaves. They have numerous ways of conferring freedom; they can manumit not only during life, but also by their wills, and the testamentary wishes of a Roman in regard to his property are law."

My interlocutor shed tears, and confessed that the laws and constitution of the Romans were fair, but deplored that the officials, not possessing the spirit of former generations, were ruining the state.

The Confession of Saint Patrick
c. 450

Patricius (c. 389-461), the son of a Christian family in the Roman province of Britannia, was seized in a raid by Irish pagans and brought back to their island as a slave. Managing to escape, he entered a monastery on the continent and was ordained a missionary to Ireland in 432. Although there were some Christians in the south of Ireland before Patrick's mission, establishment of Christianity in this area was largely the result of Patrick's thirty years of missionary activity. Soon before his death, Patrick composed a *Confession* that includes a brief account of his life, his personal struggles, and his mission to his adopted country.

Source: *The Book of Letters of Saint Patrick the Bishop,ed.* and trans. D.R. Howlett, (Dublin: Four Courts Press, 1994), 53, 57-65, 67-69, 93.

FOCUS QUESTIONS:

1. How did Patrick maintain his faith under difficult conditions?
2. How did he draw on these experiences in his later career?

PART I

    I, Patrick, a sinner, very rustic, and the least of all the faithful, and very contemptible in the estimation of most men, had as father a certain man called Calpornius, a deacon, son of Potitus, a presbyter, who was in the town Bannaventa Berniae, for he had a little villa nearby, where I conceded capture. In years I was then almost sixteen. For I was ignorant of the true God, and I was led to Ireland in captivity with so many thousands of men according to our deserts, because we withdrew from God, and we did not keep watch over His precepts, and we were not obedient to our priests, who kept admonishing our salvation, and the Lord led down over us the wrath of His anger and dispersed us among many gentiles even as far as the furthest part of land, where now my insignificance is seen to be among members of a strange race. And there the Lord opened the consciousness of my unbelief so that, perhaps, late, I might remember my delicts, and that I might turn with a whole heart to the Lord my God, Who turned His gaze round on my lowliness and took pity on my adolescence and ignorance and kept watch over me before I knew Him and before I was wise or distinguished between good and bad, and He fortified me and consoled me as a father [consoles] a son.

* * *

    As an adolescent, more precisely, as an almost wordless boy, I conceded capture before I knew what I ought to seek or what to avoid. Whence therefore today I blush for shame and vehemently thoroughly fear to strip naked my unlearnedness, because I cannot unfold in speech to those learned in conciseness as, however, my spirit and mind longs, and the emotion of my consciousness suggests. But if, consequently, it had been given to me just as also to others, even so I would not be silent on account of what should be handed back [from me to God]. And if by chance it seems to certain men that I put myself forward in this, with my lack of knowledge and my rather slow tongue, but even so it is, however, written, "Stammering tongues will swiftly learn to speak peace." How much more ought we to seek, we who are, he affirms, The letter of Christ for salvation as far as the furthest part of land, and if not learned, yet valid and very vigorous, written in your hearts not with ink but by the Spirit of the living God, and again the Spirit testifies even rustic work created by the Most High. Whence I, the extreme rustic, a refugee, untaught, doubtless, who do not know how to look forward into the future, but that I do know most certainly, that indeed before I was humbled. I was like a stone that lies in deep mud, and He Who is powerful came and in His pity He raised me up and assuredly to be sure lifted me upward and placed me on the highest wall and therefore I ought forcefully to shout out for something that should be handed back to the Lord also for His benefits so great here and for eternity, which [benefits] the mind of men cannot estimate. Whence, moreover, be astonished, consequently, you great and small who fear God, and you, sirs [lords], clever rhetoricians hear therefore and examine who roused me up, a fool, from the midst of those who seem to be wise and learned by experience in law and powerful in speech and in everything and inspired me, assuredly, beyond the others of this execrable world..., in order even after my death to leave behind a legacy to my brothers and Sons whom I have baptized in the Lord, so many thousands of men....

PART II

But after I had come to Ireland, I was consequently pasturing domestic animals daily, and often in the day I was praying. More and more the love of God and fear of Him was approaching, and faith was being increased, and the Spirit was being stirred up, so that in a single day up to a hundred prayers, and in a night nearly the same, even as I was staying in forests and on the mountain, and before dawn I was roused up to prayer, through snow, through frost, through rain, and I was feeling nothing bad, nor was there any sloth in me, as I see now, because the Spirit was being fervent in me then, and there, to be sure, on a certain night in a dream I heard a voice saying to me, "It is well that you are fasting, bound soon to go to your fatherland." And again after a very little time I heard the answer saying to me, "Look, your ship is ready." And it was not near, but perhaps two hundred miles and I had never been there, nor did I have any single acquaintance among men there, and then later I turned to flight, and I abandoned the man with whom I had been for six years, and I came in the power of God, Who was directing my way toward the good, and I was fearing nothing until I came through to that ship, and on that day on which I came through the ship set out from its own place, and I spoke as I had the wherewithal to ship with them, and the captain, it displeased him, and he responded sharply with indignation, "By no means will you seek to go with us."

And when I heard these things I separated myself from them, so that I would come to the little hut where I was staying, and on the journey I began to pray, and before I could bring the prayer to the highest perfection I heard one of them, and he was shouting out vigorously after me, "Come soon, because these men are calling you", and immediately I returned to them, and they began to say to me, "Come, because we are receiving you on faith, make friendship with us in whatever way you will have wished" and on that day, to be sure, I refused to suck their nipples on account of the fear of God, but nevertheless I hoped to come by them to the faith of Jesus Christ, as they were gentiles, and because of this I got my way with them, and we shipped at once.

And after a three-day period we reached land, and for twenty-eight days we made a journey through the desert, and food was not forthcoming for them, and hunger prevailed over them, and on the next day the captain began to say to me,

"What is it, Christian? You say your God is great and all-powerful. Why therefore can you not pray for us, because we are imperilled by hunger, for it is not likely that we may ever see any man."

But I said confidently to them, "Be turned in faith with a whole heart to the Lord my God, because nothing is impossible to Him, so that today He may dispatch food to you until you should be satisfied on your way, as there was abundance everywhere for Him." And with God helping it was made so.

Look, a flock of pigs appeared in the way before our eyes, and they killed many of them, and there they remained two nights and were well fed, and they were refilled with their flesh, because many of them fainted away, and were left behind half-alive along the way, and after this they gave the highest thanks to God, and I was made honourable in their eyes, and from this day they had food abundantly; they even discovered [lit.'came upon'] forest honey, and they offered a part to me, and one of them said, "It is a [pagan] sacrifice." Thanks be to God, I tasted nothing from it.

* * *

And again after a few years in the Britains I was with my parents, who received me as a son, and in faith requested me whether now I, after such great tribulations which I bore, I should not ever depart from them. And there to be sure I saw in a vision of the night a man coming as if from Ireland, whose name [was] Victoricius, with innumerable epistles, and he gave me one of them, and I read the beginning of the epistle containing 'the Voice of the Irish', and while I was reciting the beginning of the epistle I kept imagining hearing at that very moment the voice of those very men who were beside the Forest of Foclut, which is near the Western Sea [lit.'the sea of the setting (sc. of the sun)'], and thus they shouted out as if from one mouth, "We request you, holy boy, that you come and walk farther among us." And I was especially stabbed at heart, and I could not read further. And thus I have learned by experience, thanks be to God, that after very many years the Lord has supplied them according to their clamour.

PART V

Look, again and again briefly I will set out the words of my Confession.

I bear testimony in truth and in exultation of heart before God and His holy angels that I have never had any occasion besides the Gospel and His promises that I should ever go back to that gentile people whence earlier I had barely escaped.

But I beseech those believing and fearing God, whoever will have deigned to look on or receive this writing, which Patrick, a sinner, untaught, to be sure, wrote down in Ireland, that no man should ever say that by my ignorance, if I have accomplished or demonstrated any small thing according to the acceptable purpose of God, but that you judge and it must be most truly believed that it was the gift of God, and this is my Confession before I die.

Prologue of the *Corpus Juris Civilis*
c. 530

By the 6th century CE, the Roman legal system was in dire need of reform. Legal officials had, for many centuries, relied upon an unwieldy body of materials, many of which were contradictory, in order to make judgments in the cases that came before them. Roman law was based on statutes (laws passed by assemblies of the people, resolutions passed by the Senate, and pronouncements by the Emperors), edicts issued by "Praetors" in the Roman system, and the opinions of legal scholars. Soon after his accession to the throne at Constantinople in 527, the Emperor Justinian launched the project that would eventually be known as the *Digest* of Roman law, an edited selection of the most important of these sources of law that could be used as a handy reference by a judge facing a difficult case. This document represented one of the greatest compilation efforts of the early medieval world, but it also resulted in the discarding of heaps of legal books and other materials that historians would dearly love to have today.

Source: From The Digest of Justinian,C. H. Monro, ed. (Cambridge, MA: Cambridge University Press, 1904).

FOCUS QUESTIONS:

1. How did the compilers of the Digest justify their attention to this material, much of which was composed in a pre-Christian context?
2. What materials might have been lost in this process?

THE DIGEST PROLOGUE

The Emperor Caesar, Flavius, Justinianus, Pious, Fortunate, Renowned, Conqueror, and Triumpher, Ever Augustus, to Tribonianus His Quaestor.,

Greeting:

With the aid of God governing Our Empire which was delivered to Us by His Celestial Majesty, We carry on war successfully. We adorn peace and maintain the Constitution of the State, and have such confidence in the protection of Almighty God that We do not depend upon Our arms, or upon Our soldiers, or upon those who conduct Our Wars, or upon Our own genius, but We solely, place

Our reliance upon the providence of the Holy Trinity, from which are derived the elements of the entire world and their disposition throughout the globe.

Therefore, since there is nothing to be found in all things as worthy of attention as the authority of the law, which properly regulates all affairs both divine and human, and expels all injustice; We have found the entire arrangement of the law which has come down to us from the foundation of the City of Rome and the times of Romulus, to be so confused that it is extended to an infinite length and is not within the grasp of human capacity; and hence We were first induced to begin by examining what had been enacted by former most venerated princes, to correct their constitutions, and make them more easily understood; to the end that being included in a single Code, and having had removed all that is superfluous in resemblance and all iniquitous discord, they may afford to all men the ready assistance of true meaning.

After having concluded this work and collected it all in a single volume under Our illustrious name, raising Ourself above small and comparatively insignificant matters, We have hastened to attempt the most complete and thorough amendment of the entire law, to collect and revise the whole body of Roman jurisprudence, and to assemble in one book the scattered treatises of so many authors which no one else has herebefore ventured to hope for or to expect and it has indeed been considered by Ourselves a most difficult undertaking, nay, one that was almost impossible; but with Our hands raised to heaven and having invoked the Divine aid, We have kept this object in Our mind, confiding in God who can grant the accomplishment of things which are almost desperate, and can Himself carry them into effect by virtue of the greatness of His power.

We desire you to be careful with regard to the following: if you find in the old books anything that is not suitably arranged, superfluous, or incomplete, you must remove all superfluities, supply what is lacking, and present the entire work in regular form, and with as excellent an appearance as possible.

You must also observe the following, namely: if you find anything which the ancients have inserted in their old laws or constitutions that is incorrectly worded, you must correct this, and place it in its proper order, so that it may appear to be true, expressed in the best language, and written in this way in the first place; so that by comparing it with the original text, no one can venture to call in question as defective what you have selected and arranged.

Since by an ancient law, which is styled the Lex Regia, all the rights and power of the Roman people were transferred to the Emperor, We do not derive Our authority from that of other different compilations, but wish that it shall all be entirely Ours, for how can antiquity abrogate our laws?

The Book of Emperors and Kings: Charlemagne and Pope Leo III
c. 1150

This is an excerpt from a German epic poem of the 12th century that traced the history of the Germanic kings and emperors up to the crusade of Conrad III in 1147. The writer is evidently a partisan of the "Emperors" who claimed the title given by Pope Leo III to Charlemagne in Rome on Christmas Day, 800. The document is thus both a product of its own era, when Popes and Emperors came into conflict, and an attempt to glorify Charlemagne's role in European history. While the account is not to be trusted on all counts, it illustrates the struggle between religious and political authorities, and it also draws attention to the role of religious belief in military encounters in the period.

Source: *The Book of Emperors and Kings* (Der Keiser und der Kunige buoch). Trans. Henry A. Myers from text published as Die Kaiserchronik eines Regensburger Geistlichen, ed. Eduward Schröder, in Monumenta Germaniae Historica, Deutsche Chroniken(Hannover: Hahn, 1892), vol. 1, 339–53, passim.

FOCUS QUESTIONS:

1. How powerful was Pope Leo relative to Charlemagne, at least as described here?
2. How does the Pope solidify his position by associating himself with Charlemagne?
3. In what ways was Charlemagne's military policy motivated by religion?

The Empire remained without a head. The lords of Rome set the crown on Saint Peter's Altar. Meeting all together, they swore before the people that never again would they choose a king—nor judge, nor anyone else to rule them—from the kin of the preceding house, which had proven unable to maintain faith and honor with them. They wanted kings from other lands....

According to a custom of those days, young princes from all over the Empire were raised and instructed with great care at the court in Rome. The Romans gave them the sword of knighthood when the time came..., sending the young heirs back to their homelands. This helped keep all the dominions mindful of serving Rome.

It came to pass that Pippin, a mighty king of Karlingen,[1] had two fine sons. One of them named Leo came to hold Saint Peter's throne after being raised in Rome, while Charles, the other, stayed home.

One night when Charles fell asleep, a voice called out to him three times: "Arise, beloved Charles, and hurry to Rome! Your brother Leo needs you!" And quickly Charles made ready, saying nothing to anyone about what he intended to do until he asked leave of the King to go....

When the young Prince asked for leave, his father granted it to him gladly and bestowed gifts upon his son in a manner worthy of a mighty king....

Charles really undertook his journey more for [the chance to pray at the tombs of] the divine Apostles than for his brother's sake. Early and late in the day his thoughts, which he revealed to no one, were filled with love of God....

When Charles arrived in Rome, he was given a fine reception by old and young.... Pope Leo sang a mass then in honor of the Holy Ghost and to strengthen the Prince's spirit. Then he received God's Body. All who were there praised God, finding Charles so worthy and to their liking that the law should make him their ruler.

Charles did not listen to what was being said: He had made his journey for the sake of prayer, and he let no commotion distract him. He entered churches barefoot and, imploring God's mercy, he prayed for his soul. This steadfast devotion brought him every worldly honor, too....

Thus he spent four weeks so wrapped in prayer and meditation that no one could approach him to speak, until once his brother, Pope Leo, and all the people fell at his feet. Charles pointed out to God in Heaven that if he were to prove unworthy he never should have made his journey. Then he received the royal emblems, and they set a magnificent crown on his head. All those there in Rome rejoiced that day, and all said, "Amen."

Then the King sat in judgment, and the Pope made complaint before him that church properties and the collection of tithes, entrusted to him by his predecessors for his use in the saving of souls, were being granted away from his jurisdiction, and that his benefices had been taken from him. His complaint angered a number of the nobles.

Then Charles spoke these true ruler's words: "Never in this world, I feel sure, did anyone make a gift to honor God in order that another might take it. That would clearly be robbery.... Whoever would take anything away from gifts bestowed on God's houses, through which God's work is furthered, would be despised of God and could not remain a good Christian. . . ." Then those nobles departed, full of resentment. Charles also had no desire to remain there any longer.

---

1 "Karlingen," the name given by several medieval German writers to the domain of Charlemagne and his ancestors, is probably a derivation by analogy on the assumption that the name of the great Charles (Karl) was given to his whole family domain. Similarly, his grandson Lothar's name was applied to Lorraine (Lotharingen).

Charles returned to Ripuaria.[2] The Romans realized very well that he was their rightful judge, but stupid men among them ridiculed the others for ever having proclaimed him ruler.... In Saint Peter's Cathedral they caught the Pope and pushed his eyes out of their sockets..., and sent him blind to the King in Ripuaria.

Nothing remained for the Pope to do but set out on the journey in his hapless condition. He rode on a donkey and took with him two of his chaplains, desiring no other escort....

The Pope arrived in Ingelheim with his two chaplains and rode into the King's courtyard. When the King saw him coming, he said to one of his men: "Someone has attacked this pilgrim, and we shall do justice in his cause if we can. He seems badly injured. Someone must have robbed him...."

The King strode quickly across the courtyard . . . and said: "Good pilgrim, if you wish to stay here with me, I will gladly take you in. Tell me if your misfortune is such that I can help you with it. Why don't you dismount?"

The noble Pope wanted to draw closer to the King. His head hung at a strange angle, and his eyes stared askew. "That God should have granted me your presence!" he began.. . ."It has not been long since I sang a mass for you at Rome, when I could still see." As he spoke these words, the noble King recognized him and was so shocked that he could neither see nor hear.... His body went limp and he could not speak....

When the Emperor had recovered, the Pope told him sorrowfully: "I have come here that you may take pity on me. It was because of you that I lost my eyes: they blinded me to get even with you. Still, Brother, you must pull yourself together, and weep no more...."

The Emperor himself lifted him down and carried him across the courtyard into his private chamber. There they sat together, and Charles told his men to go outside. "Brother," he said, "how did this happen to you? Let me hear your complaint, and then my forces of justice will right the wrong."

Pope Leo answered the King: "Brother, after you left Rome, the Romans very soon betrayed their loyalty to me in a conspiracy. They caught me in the Cathedral and committed this terrible crime upon me. Brother, we must bear this patiently: I seek vengeance only in Heaven, and you must not injure any of them for this."

"It would be doing God a dishonor to spare those murderers!" the noble King replied. "Ah! How sorely that would injure Christendom. I am called 'Judge' and 'Ruler': and this means I have the duty of judging over the peoples.. . . I must

---

2 Territorial home of one historic group of the Franks on the Rhine River; for the author, this location is sometimes synonymous with "Karlingen," sometimes one of its provinces.

defend Christendom with the sword. You will have them sorely regret their crime against you. I will avenge your eyes, or I will renounce my sword."

Then he dispatched messengers to King Pippin to tell him of his great need and let the nobles of Karlingen know that if they ever wanted to render God a loving service they should hurry to him. And there were none in Karlingen but who proclaimed all with one voice: "Woe to the fatal hour that Rome was ever founded!"...

The messengers galloped ceaselessly from land to land and from lord to vassal: all men were willing to come to the cause of Charles. Farmers and merchants, too—no one could hold them back. They left all their belongings and set out to join Charles. The mourning and grief over the news traveled through Christendom from people to people, and the streams of warriors converged like clouds over the Great Saint Bernard Pass.. . . The book does not give a number for the total army, but it was the greatest military expedition that ever descended on Rome.

When the army had advanced to within sight of the Aventine Hill in Rome, the worthy King asked three days and nights for himself. This annoyed his great lords, who went to him to say that it ill became his office to pause there, now that they had come so close that they could see the city which had aggrieved them.

"First we must pray to God, for we must gain His leave to carry through," answered the King. "Then we shall fight with ease...."

Early one morning the voice of God spoke to him: "God in Heaven commands you, King, to remain here no longer. Ride on to Rome: God has rendered judgment, and just vengeance shall overtake them."

And so the King's banner was raised, and Charles let word pass through his whole army that when the knights were prepared for battle they should keep their eyes upon the banner and ride in close formation hearts swelling with high spirits, Charles's men swarmed over the hill....

Owî, what an army this was that besieged Rome and the Lateran for seven days and seven nights, so menacingly that no one would fight against it! On the eighth day—this is the truth I am telling you—the Romans ordered the city gates opened and offered to let the King enter with this condition: that any man who could prove himself innocent of committing, aiding, or advising the crime would remain in the King's favor, while the King would deal with the guilty ones after deciding on a just sentence....

As the Emperor sat in judgment and the document naming the guilty men was read, the accused all fervently denied their guilt when they were called forward. The King ordered them to submit to trial by combat for their unwillingness to confess. But then the Romans objected that this was not according to their law, and that no Emperor had ever forced such treatment on them before; instead, they should prove their innocence by swearing with their two fingers.

Then King Charles spoke:"I doubt that any crime so great was ever committed before. Don't be overhasty now: I imagine my brother saw at the time who did it." Still, when so very many of the accused offered their oaths in the Cathedral, the King said: I will not deprive you of recourse to your own law any longer; however, I know of a youth here named Pancras. If you are willing to swear an oath at his grave and if he tolerates it, then I will be willing to believe you."

Icy fear seized the Romans at the mention of this test. As they came to the place sacred to Saint Pancras and were supposed to hold up their fingers and to keep asserting their innocence under oath, one man was overcome, and panic gripped all the rest. They retreated in fear and fled back over the bridge although a fair number went back to Saint Peter's Cathedral.

Charles hesitated no longer but rode after them angrily. For three days, he and his men struck them down, and for three days they carried them out. Then they washed down the floor stones.. . . Charles fell on his knees before Saint Peter's tomb and made his plea to Christ:"Lord God in Heaven, how can I be any good to You as King when You let such shame befall me? Sinner that I may be, I do make every attempt to judge the people in a manner worthy of You. The Romans swore allegiance to a Pope, and You granted him a portion of Your power that he might loose the people from their sins and bind them. I [ask]... that you give the evil people of Rome something to recognize Your hidden power by: then they will know for certain that You are a true God. Grant me this, Holy Christ!"

A second time Charles, the noble King, fell to the ground and said: "Hail noble Saint Peter! You are really a divine stalwart of God, a watchman of Christendom. Think now, my lord, what I am going through! You are a summoner of the Kingdom of Heaven. Just look at your Pope! I left him sound of body in your care. Blinded was how I found him, and if you do not heal the blind man today I shall destroy your Cathedral and ruin the buildings and grounds donated to you, and then I shall leave him for you blind as he is, and go back again to Ripuaria."

Quickly the noble Pope Leo made himself ready and said his confession. As he spoke the last word, he saw a heavenly light with both his eyes. Great are hidden powers of God.

The Pope turned around and spoke to the multitude: "My dearest children gathered from afar, be glad of heart, for the Kingdom of God is drawing near to you. God has heard you and because of your holy prayer has turned His face toward you. Here, at this very place, you are called to be public witnesses that a great miracle has happened.. . . I can see with both eyes better than I ever saw in this world."...

The Pope consecrated him as Emperor and granted absolution to all his comrades in arms. Owî, what joy there was in Rome then! The whole people rejoiced then and sang: "Gloria in excelsis Deo."

Then Charles laid down the Imperial Law, as an angel recited the true words of God to him.... And so the mighty Emperor left us many good laws, which God caused to be spoken before him....

The very first laws the Emperor established dealt with what seemed to him to be the most exalted matters, those concerning bishops and priests, for the Imperial Law of Constantine had been sadly neglected. At the same time, he established laws governing tithes and gifts of property to the Church....

Now I shall tell you about what the peasant is to wear according to the Imperial Law: his clothes may be black or gray, and he is allowed no other.... He is to have shoes of cow leather only and seven yards of towcloth for his shirt and breeches. He is to spend six days at the plow and doing plenty of other work; on Sunday he is to go to Church, carrying his animal goad openly in his hand. If a sword is found on a peasant, he is to be led bound to the churchyard fence, where he is to be tied and his skin and hair are to be flayed. If he is threatened by enemies, however, let him defend himself with a pitchfork. This law King Charles established for his peasants....

Emperor Charles besieged a walled city called Arles [France], which actually took him more than seven years. The inhabitants had considered him unworthy of his office. By way of an underground canal, wine was conveyed to them in plentiful supply, but finally Charles's cunning succeeded in cutting off their source. When

the inhabitants could not hold out any longer, they threw open the city gates and fought fiercely, offering no terms at all. So many were slain on both sides that there is no man who can tell another how many of either the Christians or the heathens were lying there dead after the battle. No one could tell the dead apart until the Emperor solved the problem with God's help: He found the Christians lying separately in well adorned coffins. Now that is a wonder really worth telling about....

The Emperor and his men turned toward Galicia [in Spain], where the king of the heathens inflicted great losses upon them. The Christian soldiers were all slain, and Charles barely escaped from the battle. Today the stone stays wet on which Charles sat afterwards, weeping passionately as he lamented his sins, saying: "Hail to You, God sublime! Grant me mercy for my poor soul. Take me out of this world, so that my people will no longer be punished because of me. I can never be consoled again."

Then an angel comforted him, saying: "Charles, beloved of God, your joy will come to you quickly. Bid your messengers make haste to summon virgin women—leave the married ones at home—for God will reveal His power through them. If you will fear and love God, the maidens will win your honor back again for you."

The messengers made haste and thoroughly searched through all the lands. They gathered together the maidens and brought them together... where the Emperor was waiting for them. Many a young maid came to join the host, fifty-three thousand—I am telling you this as a fact—and sixty-six more....

When all the maidens arrived in a valley since named for Charles, they readied themselves for battle in formations just like men....

Each heathen sentry was struck by wonder as to who this people could be, for it all seemed very strange to them. They hurried back, and one of them said to their king: "Sire, even though we slew the old ones, we must tell you for a fact that the young ones have followed them here. I have the feeling they want to slake their thirst for vengeance. They are big around the chest. Sire, if you fight with them, it will not come to any good end. Their hair is long, and their gait is very graceful: They are fine knights indeed. They are a terrifying lot.... No force could ever be assembled on this earth to defeat them...."

At the advice of his experienced counsellors, their king turned over hostages to the Emperor. The king then had himself baptized—how well he suddenly believed in God!—and all his people with him.. . . Thus God made Charles victorious without the thrust of a spear or the blow of a sword, and the maidens well realized that God in Heaven was with them.

Charles and his heroines returned to their own homes back in the Empire. On the way, the worthy maidens came to a green meadow. Tired from the expedition, the heroines stuck their spearshafts into the ground and stretched out their arms in the form of a cross, sleeping on the ground after praising God for the goodness which He had shown them. They stayed there overnight, and a great miracle occurred. Their spearshafts had turned green and had sent forth leaves and blossoms. That is why the place is called "Woods of the Spearshafts"; it can be seen to this day.

Charles, the rich and powerful, built a mighty and beautiful church for the praise of Holy Christ, the honor of Saint Mary and all God's maidens, and the solace of Christendom. Since through chastity and spiritual purity the maids achieved[3] their victory, the church is called Domini Sanctitas.

---

3 This church is the Emperor's Chapel, the main and oldest part of the Aachen Cathedral, also called Saint Mary's.

Science and Mathematics: Al-Ghazzali, "On the Separation of Mathematics and Religion" 1058-1111

The Islamic community during the Middle Ages and beyond was not simply concerned with matters of faith and obedience to doctrine. As Muslim armies covered North Africa and the Middle East, even venturing into Europe, they carried with them some of the great advancements of Islamic civilization. Muslim learning was embraced in such academic centers as Córdoba, Spain, where Jewish scholars were central in establishing a conduit of knowledge to the West by translating Arabic science and medical texts into Spanish and Latin. Many of these ideas in astronomy, medicine, advanced mathematics, law, literature, poetry, philosophy, and history fell on deaf ears in the West because of the fear of doctrinal contamination. Indeed, for Western Christians, the followers of Allah were the "Infidel," to be feared and opposed through Crusades to recapture the Holy Land for the glory of a Christian God.

The sources below are from Abu Hamid al-Ghazzali (1058–1111), one of the greatest Muslim jurists, theologians, and mystics, and Abu Bakr Muhammad ibn Zakariya al-Razi (865–925), a noted Persian physician, philosopher, and scholar.

Source[s]: Claud Field, trans., "On the Separation of Mathematics and Religion" from Al-Ghazzali, The Confession of Al-Ghazzali (London: John Murray Publishers Ltd., 1908), pp. 33–34. William A. Greenhill, trans., "On the Causes of Small-Pox" from Abu Bekr Muhammad Ibn Zacariya Al-Razi, A Treatise on Small-Pox and Measles (London, 1848), pp. 28–31.

FOCUS QUESTIONS:

1. What do the selections on mathematics and the scientific description of smallpox tell you about Islamic values?
1. According to Al-Ghazzali, should mathematics and religion be separated? Why or why not?

Mathematics comprises the knowledge of calculation, geometry, and cosmography: it has no connection with the religious sciences, and proves nothing for or against religion; it rests on a foundation of proofs which, once known and understood, cannot be refuted. Mathematics tend, however, to produce two bad results.

The first is this: Whoever studies this science admires the subtlety and clearness of its proofs. His confidence in philosophy increases, and he thinks that all its departments are capable of the same clearness and solidity of proof as mathematics. But when he hears people speak on the unbelief and impiety of mathematicians, of their professed disregard for the Divine Law, which is notorious, it is true that, out of regard for authority, he echoes these accusations, but he says to himself at the same time that, if there was truth in religion, it would not have escaped those who have displayed so much keenness of intellect in the study of mathematics.

Next, when he becomes aware of the unbelief and rejection of religion on the part of these learned men, he concludes that to reject religion is reasonable. How many of such men gone astray I have met whose sole argument was that just mentioned...

It is therefore a great injury to religion to suppose that the defence of Islam involves the condemnation of the exact sciences. The religious law contains nothing which approves them or condemns them, and in their turn they make no attack on religion. The words of the Prophet, "The sun and the moon are two signs of the power of God; they are not eclipsed for the birth or the death of any one; when you see these signs take refuge in prayer and invoke the name of God"—these words, I say, do not in any way condemn the astronomical calculations which define the orbits of these two bodies, their conjunction and opposition according to particular laws.

AL-RAZI, ON THE CAUSES OF SMALL-POX

Although [scholars] have certainly made some mention of the treatment of the Small-Pox (but without much accuracy and distinctness), yet there is not one of them who has mentioned the cause of the existence of the disease, and how it comes to pass that hardly any one escapes it, or who has disposed the modes of treatment in their right places. And for this reason I...have mentioned whatever is necessary for the treatment of this disease, and have arranged and carefully disposed everything in its right place, by god's permission...

I say then that every man, from the time of his birth until he arrives at old age, is continually tending to dryness; and for this reason the blood of children and infants is much moister than the blood of young men, and still more so than that of old men...Now the Small-Pox arises when the blood putrefies and ferments, so that the superfluous vapors are thrown out of it, and it is changed from the blood of infants, which is like must, into the blood of young men, which is like wine perfectly ripened: and the Small-Pox itself may be compared to the fermentation and the hissing noise which takes place in must at that time. And this is the reason why children, especially males, rarely escape being seized with this disease, because it is impossible to prevent the blood's changing from this state into its second state...

As to young men, whereas their blood is already passed into the second state, its maturation is established, and the superfluous particles of moisture which necessarily cause putrefaction are now exhaled; hence it follows that this disease only happens to a few individuals among them, that is, to those whose vascular system abounds with too much moisture, or is corrupt in quality with a violent inflammation...

And as for old men, the Small-Pox seldom happens to them, except in pestilential, putrid, and malignant constitutions of the air, in which this disease is chiefly prevalent. For a putrid air, which has an undue proportion of heat and moisture, and also an inflamed air, promotes the eruption of this disease.

CHAPTER 6

The Consolidation and Interaction of States and Ideas

Letter of Pope Gregory VII to the Bishop of Metz, 1081

Pope between 1073 and 1085, Gregory VII was one of the great power-brokers in Medieval Europe. An advocate both of reform and of a strengthened papacy, Gregory came into conflict with many of Europe's secular rulers, chief among them the Holy Roman Emperor Henry IV (1050-1106). The major confrontation between them was the "Investiture Conflict", a struggle over the right of secular rulers to "invest" Church officials with the symbols of their authority. In 1077, Gregory forced Henry to come to him as a simple penitent at Canossa in Italy and to beg for his forgiveness. Reflecting on this episode, and his ongoing disputes with other European kings, Gregory argued, in this letter to a Church subordinate, for the primacy of the Pope over all secular authorities.

Source: *Documents of the Christian Church*, ed. Henry Bettenson (New York: Oxford University Press, 1970), 104–110.

FOCUS QUESTIONS:

1. What does Gregory believe is the ultimate basis of the power he holds?
2. What point is he attempting to make by bringing up historical examples?
3. How might Henry IV (still seething after Canossa) have responded to these claims?

Bishop Gregory, servant of the servants of God, to his beloved brother in Christ, Hermann bishop of Metz, greeting and apostolic benediction. It is doubtless owing to a dispensation of God that, as we learn, thou art ready to endure trials and dangers in defence of the truth. For such is His ineffable grace and wonderful mercy that He never allows His chosen ones completely to go astray— never permits them utterly to fall or to be cast down. For, after they have been afflicted by a period of persecution—a useful term of probation as it were,—He makes them, even if they have been for a time fainthearted, stronger than before. Since, moreover, manly courage impels one strong man to act more bravely than another and to press forward more boldly—even as among cowards fear induces one to flee more disgracefully than another,—we wish, beloved, with the voice of exhortation, to impress this upon thee: thou shouldst the more delight to stand in the army of the Christian faith among the first, the more thou art convinced that the conquerors are the most worthy and the nearest to God. Thy request, indeed, to be aided, as it were, by our writings and fortified against the madness of those who babble forth with impious tongue that the authority of the holy and apostolic see had no authority to excommunicate Henry—a man who despises the Christian law; a destroyer of the churches and of the empire; a patron and companion of heretics—or to absolve any one from the oath of fealty to him, seems to us to be hardly necessary when so many and such absolutely decisive warrants are to be found in the pages of Holy Scripture. Nor do we believe, indeed, that those who (heaping up for themselves damnation) impudently detract from the truth and contradict it have added these assertions to the audacity of their defence so much from ignorance as from a certain madness.

For, to cite a few passages from among many, who does not know the words of our Lord and Saviour Jesus Christ who says in the gospel: 'Thou art Peter and upon this rock will I build my church, and the gates of hell shall not prevail against it; and I will give unto thee the keys of the kingdom of Heaven; and whatsoever thou shalt bind upon earth shall be bound also in Heaven, and whatsoever thou shalt loose upon earth shall be loosed also in Heaven'? [Matthew xvi. 18, 19.] Are kings excepted here? Or are they not included among the sheep which the Son of God committed to St Peter? Who, I ask, in view of this universal concession of the power of binding and loosing, can think that he is withdrawn from the authority of St Peter, unless, perhaps, that unhappy man who is unwilling to bear the yoke of the Lord and subjects himself to the burden of the devil, refusing to be among the number of Christ's sheep? It will help him little to his wretched liberty that he shake from his proud neck the divinely granted power of Peter. For the more any one, through pride, refuses to bear it, the more heavily shall it press upon him unto damnation at the judgement.

The holy fathers, as well in general councils as in their writings and doings, have called the Holy Roman Church the universal mother, accepting and serving with great veneration this institution founded by the divine will, this pledge of a dispensation to the church, this privilege entrusted in the beginning and confirmed to St Peter the chief of the apostles. And even as they accepted its statements in confirmation of their faith and of the doctrines of holy religion, so also they received its judgements—consenting in this, and agreeing as it were with one spirit and one voice: that all greater matters and exceptional cases, and judgements over all churches, ought to be referred to it as to a mother and a head; that from it there was no appeal; that no one should or could retract or reverse its decisions....

. . . Shall not an authority founded by laymen—even by those who do not know God,—be subject to that authority which the providence of God Almighty has for His own honour established and in his mercy given to the world? For His Son, even as He is undoubtingly believed to be God and man, so is He considered the highest priest, the head of all priests, sitting on the right hand of the Father and always interceding for us. Yet He despised a secular kingdom, which makes the sons of this world swell with pride, and came of His own will to the priesthood of the cross. Who does not know that kings and leaders are sprung from men who were ignorant of God, who by pride, robbery, perfidy, murders—in a word, by almost every crime at the prompting of the devil, who is the prince of this world—have striven with blind cupidity and intolerable presumption to dominate over their equals, that is, over mankind? To whom, indeed, can we better compare them, when they seek to make the priests of God bend to their feet, than to him who is head over all the sons of pride[1] and who, tempting the Highest Pontiff Himself, the Head of priests, the Son of the Most High, and promising to Him all the kingdoms of the world, said: 'All these I will give unto Thee if Thou wilt fall down and worship me'?[2] who can doubt but that the priests of Christ are to be considered the fathers and masters of kings and princes and of all the faithful? Is it not clearly pitiful madness for a son to attempt to subject to himself his father, a pupil his master; and for one to bring into his power and bind with iniquitous bonds him by whom he believes that he himself can be bound and loosed not only on earth but also in Heaven? This the emperor Constantine the Great, lord of all the kings and princes of nearly the whole world, plainly understood—as the blessed Gregory reminds us in a letter to the emperor Maurice, when, sitting last after all the bishops, in the holy council of Nicaea, he presumed to give no sentence of judgement over them, but addressed them as gods and decreed that they should not be subject to his judgement but that he should be dependent upon their will....

. . . Many pontiffs have excommunicated kings or emperors. For, if particular examples of such princes is needed, the blessed pope Innocent excommunicated the emperor Arcadius for consenting that St John Chrysostom should be expelled from his see. Likewise another Roman pontiff, Zachary, deposed a king of the Franks, not so much for his iniquities as because he was not fitted to exercise so great power. And in his stead he set up Pepin, father of the emperor Charles the Great, in his place—releasing all the Franks from the oath of fealty which they had sworn him. As, indeed, the holy church frequently does by its authority when it absolves servitors from the fetters of an oath sworn to such bishops as, by apostolic sentence, are deposed from their pontifical rank. And the

---

1 Job xli. 34.
2 Matt. iv. 9.

blessed Ambrose—who, although a saint, was still not bishop over the whole church—excommunicated and excluded from the church the emperor Theodosius the Great for a fault[3] which, by other priests, was not regarded as very grave. He shows, too, in his writings that gold does not so much excel lead in value as the priestly dignity transcends the royal power; speaking thus towards the beginning of his pastoral letter: 'The honour and sublimity of bishops, brethren, is beyond all comparison. If one should compare them to resplendent kings and diademed princes it would be far less worthy than if one compared the base metal lead to gleaming gold. For, indeed, one can see how the necks of kings and princes are bowed before the knees of priests; and how, having kissed their right hands, they believe themselves strengthened by their prayers.' And a little later: 'Ye should know, brethren, that we have mentioned all this to show that nothing can be found in this world more lofty than priests or more sublime than bishops.'

Furthermore every Christian king, when he comes to die, seeks as a pitiful suppliant the aid of a priest, that he may escape hell's prison, may pass from the darkness into the light, and at the judgement of God may appear absolved from the bondage of his sins. Who, in his last hour (what layman, not to speak of priests), has ever implored the aid of an earthly king for the salvation of his soul? And what king or emperor is able, by reason of the office he holds, to rescue a Christian from the power of the devil through holy baptism, to number him among the sons of God, and to fortify him with the divine unction? Who of them can by his own words make the body and blood of our Lord,—the greatest act in the Christian religion? Or who of them possesses the power of binding and loosing in heaven and on earth? From all of these considerations it is clear how greatly the priestly office excels in power.

Who of them can ordain a single clerk in the holy Church, much less depose him for any fault? For in the orders of the Church a greater power is needed to depose than to ordain. Bishops may ordain other bishops, but can by no means depose them without the authority of the apostolic see. Who, therefore, of even moderate understanding, can hesitate to give priests the precedence over kings? Then, if kings are to be judged by priests for their sins, by whom can they be judged with better right than by the Roman pontiff?

In short, any good Christians may far more properly be considered kings than may bad princes. For the former, seeking the glory of God, strictly govern themselves, whereas the latter, seeking the things which are their own and not the things of God, are enemies to themselves and tyrannical oppressors of others. Faithful Christians are the body of the true king, Christ; evil rulers, that of the devil. The former rule themselves in the hope that they will eternally reign with the Supreme Emperor, but the sway of the latter ends in their destruction and

---

3 A savage massacre in Thessalonica, 390, as a reprisal for a riot.

eternal damnation with the prince of darkness, who is king over all the sons of pride.

It is certainly not strange that wicked bishops are of one mind with a bad king, whom they love and fear for the honours which they have wrongfully obtained from him. Such men simoniacally ordain whom they please and sell God even for a paltry sum. As even the elect are indissolubly united with their Head, so also the wicked are inescapably leagued with him who is the head of evil, their chief purpose being to resist the good. But surely we ought not so much to denounce them as to mourn for them with tears and lamentations, beseeching God Almighty to snatch them from the snares of Satan in which they are held captive, and after their peril to bring them at last to a knowledge of the truth.

We refer to those kings and emperors who, too much puffed up by worldly glory, rule not for God but for themselves. Now, since it belongs to our office to admonish and encourage every one according to the rank or dignity which he enjoys, we endeavour, by God's grace, to arm emperors and kings and other princes with the weapon of humility, that they may be able to allay the waves of the sea and the floods of pride. For we know that earthly glory and the cares of this world usually tempt men to pride, especially those in authority. So that they neglect humility and seek their own glory, desiring to lord it over their brethren. Therefore it is of especial advantage for emperors and kings, when their minds tend to be puffed up and to delight in their own glory, to discover a way of humbling themselves, and to realize that what causes their complacency is the thing which should be feared above all else. Let them, therefore, diligently consider how perilous and how much to be feared is the royal or imperial dignity. For very few are saved of those who enjoy it; and those who, through the mercy of God, do come to salvation are not so glorified in the Holy Church by the judgement of the Holy Spirit as are many poor people. For, from the beginning of the world until our own times, in the whole of authentic history we do not find seven emperors or kings whose lives were as distinguished for religion and so adorned by miracles of power as those of an innumerable multitude who despised the world—although we believe many of them to have found mercy in the presence of God Almighty. For what emperor or king was ever so distinguished by miracles as were St Martin, St Antony and St Benedict—not to mention the apostles and martyrs? And what emperor or king raised the dead, cleansed lepers, or healed the blind? See how the Holy Church praises and venerates the Emperor Constantine of blessed memory, Theodosius and Honorius, Charles and Louis as lovers of justice, promoters of the Christian religion, defenders of the churches: it does not, however, declare them to have been resplendent with such glorious miracles. Moreover, to how many kings or emperors has the holy church ordered chapels or altars to be dedicated, or masses to be celebrated in their honour? Let kings and other princes fear lest the more they rejoice at being placed over other men in this life, the more they will be subjected to eternal fires. For of them it is written: 'The powerful shall powerfully suffer torments.' And they are about to render account to God for as many men as they have had subjects under their dominion. But if it be no little task for any private religious man to guard his own soul: how much labour will there be for those who are rulers over many thousands of souls? Moreover, if the judgement of the Holy Church severely punishes a sinner for the slaying of one man, what will become of those who, for the sake of worldly glory, hand over many thousands to death? And such persons, although after having slain many they often say with their lips 'I have sinned,' nevertheless rejoice in their hearts at the extension of their (so-called) fame. They do not regret what they have done. Nor are they grieved at having sent their brethren down to Tartarus. As long as they do not repent with their whole heart, nor agree to give up what they have acquired or kept through bloodshed, their repentance remains without the true fruit of penitence before God.

Therefore they should greatly fear and often call to mind what we have said above, that out of the innumerable host of kings in all countries from the beginning of the world, very few are found to have been holy; whereas in one single see—the Roman—of the successive bishops from the time of blessed Peter the Apostle, nearly one hundred are counted amongst the most holy. And why is this, unless because kings and princes, enticed by vain glory, prefer, as has been said, their own things to things spiritual, whereas the bishops of the Church, despising vain glory, prefer God's will to earthly things? The former are quick to punish offences against themselves, but lightly tolerate those who sin against God. The latter readily pardon those who sin against themselves, but do not readily forgive offenders against God. The former, too bent on earthly achievements, think little of spiritual ones; the latter, earnestly meditating on heavenly, things, despise the things of earth....

Anna Comnena, from *The Alexaid* 1083–1153

Scholars have recently shed much light on the important role of Byzantine empresses in shaping the affairs of the state. Princess Anna Comnena (1083–1153) is considered one of the first female historians. The extract below is from *The Alexiad*, a fifteen-volume which work that she composed when she was fifty-five years old and living in a monastery. It sheds invaluable light on her royal family, the Comneni, and especially the reign of her father, Alexios I.

Source: Comnena, Anna. *The Alexiad* (London 1928), Volume I: 123–25.

FOCUS QUESTIONS:

1. How does Anna Comnena portray her grandmother?

2. Anna Comnena felt that was born to rule, though she never did. How much of her description is an expression of frustrated ambition?

One might be amazed that my father accorded his mother such high honor in these matters and that he deferred to her in all respects, as if her were turning over the reins of the empire to her and running alongside her while she drove the imperial chariot, contenting himself simply with the title of emperor. Indeed, he had already passed beyond the period of boyhood, an age especially when lust for power grows in men of such nature [as Alexius]. He took upon himself the wars against the barbarians and whatever battles and combats pertained to them, while he entrusted to his mother the complete management of [civil] affairs: the selection of civil magistrates, the collection of incoming revenues and the expenses of the government. A person who has reached this point in my text may blame my father for entrusting management of the empire to the gynaiconites [women's section of the palace]. But if he had known this woman's spirit, how great she was in virtue and intellect and how extremely vigorous, he would cease his reproach and his criticism would be changed into admiration. For my grandmother was so dextrous in handling affairs of state and so highly skilled in controlling and running the government, that she was not only able to manage the Roman empire but could have handled every empire under the sun. She had a vast amount of experience and understood the internal workings of many things: she knew how each affair began and to what result it might lead, which actions were destructive and which rather were beneficial. She was exceedingly acute in discerning whatever course of action was necessary and in carrying it out safely. She was not only acute in her thought, but was no less proficient in her manner of speech. Indeed, she was a persuasive orator, neither verbose nor stretching her phrases out at great length; nor did she quickly lose the sense of her argument. What she began felicitously she would finish even more so...

But, as I was saying, my father, after he had assumed power, managed by himself the strains and labors of war, while making his mother a spectator to these actions, but in other affairs he set her up as ruler, and as if he were her servant he used to say and do whatever she ordered. The emperor loved her deeply and was dependent upon her advice (so much affection had he for his mother), and he made his right hand the executor of her orders, his ear paid heed to her words, and everything which she accepted or rejected the emperor likewise accepted or rejected. In a word, the situation was thus: Alexius possessed the external formalities of imperial power, but she held the power itself. She used to promulgate laws, to manage and administer everything while he confirmed her arrangements, both written and unwritten, either through his signature or by oral commands, so that he seemed the instrument of her imperial authority and not himself the emperor. Everything which she decided or ordered he found satisfactory. Not only was he very obedient to her as is fitting for a son to his mother, but even more he submitted his spirit to her as to a master in the science [episteme] of ruling. For he felt that she had attained perfection in everything and far surpassed all men of that time in prudence and in comprehension of affairs.

Benjamin of Tudela,
Selection from *Book of Travels*
1127–1174

Benjamin of Tudela (1127–1174 CE) was a Rabbi from Spain who made an extended journey to Jerusalem (1160–1172). On his journey he traveled via Byzantium, Syria, Persia, Mesopotamia, and Palestine before returning home twelve years later. Back home, Benjamin wrote a very descriptive travelogue that provides an excellent source on the condition of medieval Jewish communities and the local Christian or Islamic cultures.

Source: Adler, Marcus Nathan, trans., *The Itinerary of Benjamin of Tudela* (New York: Philipp Feldheim, Inc., 1907).

FOCUS QUESTIONS:

1. How do Benjamin's descriptions compare with those of Liutprand?
2. Trace the origins of people and goods to find the reach of Constantinople.
3. Why are the Jews treated badly by the Greeks?

A three days' voyage brings one to Abydos, which is upon an arm of the sea which flows between the mountains, and after a five days' journey the great town of Constantinople is reached. It is the capital of the whole land of Javan, which is called Greece. Here is the residence of the King Emanuel the Emperor. Twelve ministers

12 BENJAMIN OF TUDELA

are under him, each of whom has a palace in Constantinople and possesses castles and cities; they rule all the land. At their head is the King Hipparchus, the second in command is the Megas (p. 20) Domesticus, the third Dominus, and the fourth is Megas Ducas, and the fifth is Oeconomus Megalus; the others bear names like these. The circumference of the city of Constantinople is eighteen miles; half of it is surrounded by the sea, and half by land, and it is situated upon two arms of the sea, one coming from the sea of Russia, and one from the sea of Sepharad.

All sorts of merchants come here from the land of Babylon, from the land of Shinar, from Persia, Media, and all the sovereignty of the land of Egypt, from the land of Canaan, and the empire of Russia, from Hungaria, Patzinakia, Khazaria, and the land of Lombardy and Sepharad. It is a busy city, and merchants come to it from every country by sea or land, and there is none like it in the world except Bagdad, the great city of Islam. In Constantinople is the church of Santa Sophia, and the seat of the Pope of the Greeks, since the Greeks do not obey the Pope of Rome. There are also churches according to the num-ber of the days of the year. A quantity of wealth beyond telling is brought hither year by year as tribute from the two islands and the castles and villages which are there.

(p. 21) And the like of this wealth is not to be found in any other church in the world. And in this church there are pillars of gold and silver, and lamps of silver and gold more than a man can count. Close to the walls of the palace is also a place of amusement belonging to the king, which is called the Hippodrome, and every year on the anniversary of the birth of Jesus the king gives a great entertainment there. And in that place men from all the races of the world come before the king and queen with jugglery and without jugglery,

13 CONSTANTINOPLE

and they introduce lions, leopards, bears, and wild asses, and they engage them in combat with one another; and the same thing is done with birds. No entertainment like this is to be found in any other land.

This King Emanuel built a great palace for the seat of his government upon the sea-coast, in addition to the palaces which his fathers built, and he called its name Blachernae. He overlaid its columns and walls with gold and silver, and engraved thereon representations of the battles before his day and of his own combats. He also set up a throne of gold and of precious stones, (p. 22) and a golden crown was suspended by a gold chain over the throne, so arranged that he might sit thereunder. It was inlaid with jewels of priceless value, and at night time no lights were required, for every one could see by the light which the stones gave forth. Countless other buildings are to be met with in the city. From every part of the empire of Greece tribute is brought here every year, and they fill strongholds with garments of silk, purple, and gold. Like unto these storehouses and this wealth, there is nothing in the whole world to be found. It is said that the tribute of the city amounts every year to 20,000 gold pieces, derived both from the rents of shops and markets, and from the tribute of merchants who enter by sea or land.

The Greek inhabitants are very rich in gold and precious stones, and they go clothed in garments of silk with gold embroidery, and they ride horses, and look like princes. Indeed, the land is very rich (p. 23) in all cloth stuffs, and in bread, meat, and wine.

Wealth like that of Constantinople is not to be found in the whole world. Here also are men learned in all the books of the Greeks, and they eat and drink every man under his vine and his fig tree.

They hire from amongst all nations warriors called Loazim (Barbarians) to fight with the Sultan Masud, King of the Togarmim (Seljuks), who are called Turks; for the natives are not warlike, but are as women who have no strength to fight.

14 BENJAMIN OF TUDELA

No Jews live in the city, for they have been placed behind an inlet of the sea. An arm of the sea of Marmora shuts them in on the one side, and they are unable to go out except by way of the sea, when they want to do business with the inhabitants. In the Jewish quarter are about 2,000 Rabbanite Jews and about 500 Karaites, and a fence divides them. Amongst the scholars are several wise men, at their head being the chief rabbi R. Abtalion, R. Obadiah, R. Aaron Bechor Shoro, R. Joseph Shir-Guru, and R. Eliakim, the warden. And amongst them there are artificers in silk and many rich merchants. No Jew (p. 24) there is allowed to ride on horseback. The one exception is R. Solomon Hamitari, who is the king's physician, and through whom the Jews enjoy considerable alleviation of their oppression. For their condition is very low, and there is much hatred against them, which is fostered by the tanners, who throw out their dirty water in the streets before the doors of the Jewish houses and defile the Jews' quarter (the Ghetto). So the Greeks hate the Jews, good and bad alike, and subject them to great oppression, and beat them in the streets, and in every way treat them with rigour. Yet the Jews are rich and good, kindly and charitable, and bear their lot with cheerfulness. The district inhabited by the Jews is called Pera.

From Constantinople it is two days' voyage to Rhaedestus, with a community of Israelites of about 400, at their head being R. Moses, R. Abijah, and R. Jacob. From there it is two days to Callipolis (Gallipoli), where there are about 200 Jews, at their bead being R. Elijah Kapur, R. Shabbattai Zutro, and R. Isaac Megas, which (p. 25) means "great" in Greek. And from here it is two days to Kales. Here there are about fifty Jews, at their head being R. Jacob and R. Judah. From here it is two days' journey to the island of Mytilene, and there are Jewish congregations in ten localities on the island. Thence it is three days' voyage to the island of Chios, where there are about 400 Jews, including R. Elijah Heman and R. Shabtha. Here grow the trees from which mastic is obtained. Two days' voyage takes one to the island of Samos, where there are 300 Jews, at their head being R. Shemaria, R. Obadiah, and R. Joel. The islands have many congregations of Jews. From Samos it is three days to Rhodes, where there are about 400 Jews, at their head being R. Abba, R. Hannanel, and R. Elijah. It is four days' voyage from here to Cyprus, where there are Rabbanite Jews and Karaites; there

15 THE GREEK ISLANDS—ANTIOCH

are also some heretical Jews called Epikursin, whom the Israelites have excommunicated in all places. They profane the eve of the sabbath, and observe the first night of the week, which is the termination of the Sabbath.

Christian Armies Besiege Lisbon, 1147

On their way to join the Second Crusade, knights from England, Germany, Flanders, and Normandy interrupted their voyage to assist King Alfonso of Portugal as he was besieging Lisbon. This city had been held by Muslim rulers since the eighth century, and Christian leaders had been engaged in the effort of *"Reconquista"* ("Reconquest") to put Iberia back in Christian hands. In return for their help, the King promised that this multinational force could plunder and pillage the city when it fell. Lisbon went on to become the capital of the Kingdom of Portugal in 1255. The source here is an anonymous chronicler, but one who seems to have been present at the siege and to have written his account soon afterward.

Source: *Medieval Iberia: Readings from Christian, Muslim and Jewish Sources,*ed. Olivia Remie Constable, (Philadelphia: University of Pennsylvania Press, 1997), 135-36.

Focus Questions:

1. In what ways did both the besieged and the besiegers suffer in this encounter?

2. How were the city's Muslim defenders treated by these Christian knights?

Then our men, attending more strictly to the siege, began to dig a subterranean mine between the tower and the Porta do Ferro in order that they might bring down the wall. When this had been discovered, for it was quite accessible to the enemy, it proved greatly to our detriment after the investment of the city, for many days were consumed in its vain defense. Besides, two Balearic mangonels were set up by our forces-one on the river bank which was operated by seamen, the other in front of the Porta do Ferro, which was operated by the knights and their table companions. All these men having been divided into groups of one hundred, on a given signal the first hundred retired and another took their places, so that within the space of ten hours five thousand stones were hurled. And the enemy were greatly harassed by this action. Again the Normans and the English and those who were with them began the erection of a movable tower eighty-three feet in height. Once more, with a view to bringing down the wall, the men of Cologne and the Flemings began to dig a mine beneath the wall of the stronghold higher up-a mine which, marvelous to relate, had five entrances and extended inside to a depth of forty cubits from the front; and they completed it within a month.

Meanwhile, hunger and the stench of corpses greatly tormented the enemy, for there was no burial space within the city. And for food they collected the refuse which was thrown out from our ships and borne up by the waves beneath their walls. A ridiculous incident occurred as a result of their hunger when some of the Flemings, while keeping guard among the ruins of houses, were eating figs and, having had enough, left some lying about unconsumed. When this was discovered by four of the Moors, they came up stealthily and cautiously like birds approaching food. And when the Flemings observed this, they frequently scattered refuse of this sort about in order that they might lure them on with bait. And, finally, having set snares in the accustomed places, they caught three of the Moors in them and thereby caused enormous merriment among us.

When the wall had been undermined and inflammable material had been placed within the mine and lighted, the same night at cockcrow about thirty cubits of the wall crumbled to the ground. Then the Moors who were guarding the wall were heard to cry out in their anguish that they might now make an end of their long labors and that this very day would be their last and that it would have to be divided with death, and that this would be their greatest consolation for death, if, without fearing it, they might exchange their lives for ours. For it was necessary to go yonder whence there was no need of returning; and, if a life were well ended, it would nowhere be said to have been cut short. For what mattered was not how long but how well a life had been lived; and a life would have lasted as long as it should, even though not as long as it naturally could, provided it closed in a fitting end. And so the Moors gathered from all sides for the defense of the breach in the wall, placing against it a barrier of beams. Accordingly, when the men of Cologne and the Flemings went out to attempt an entrance, they were repulsed. For, although the wall had collapsed, the nature of the situation [on the steep hillside] prevented an entry merely by the heap [of ruins]. But when they failed to overcome the defenders in a hand-to-hand encounter, they attacked them furiously from a distance with arrows, so that they looked like hedgehogs as, bristling with bolts, they stood immovably at the defense and endured as if unharmed. Thus the defense was maintained against the onslaught of the attackers until the first hour of the day, when the latter retired to camp. The Normans and the English came under arms to take up the struggle in place of their associates, supposing that an entrance would be easy now that the enemy were wounded and exhausted. But they were prevented by the leaders of the Flemings and the men of Cologne, who assailed them with insults and demanded that we attempt an entrance in any way it might be accomplished with our own engines; for they said that they had prepared the breach which now stood open for themselves, not for us. And so for several days they were altogether repulsed from the breach.

Philip II Augustus
Expels the Jews from France
1182

This is an excerpt from the "Deeds of Philip Augustus", composed by a physician, monk, and historian named Rigord (c. 1145-1209). An admirer of the French King, and an eyewitness of many of the events he chronicles, Rigord offered this account to Philip Augustus during his reign and it is thus by no means an objective account. This is particularly important in this section of the text, which details the expulsion of the Jews from Philip's kingdom in 1182. Jews had lived in France for hundreds of years, and their money-lenders had been of particular importance to the King when he desperately needed money. Because of Christian prejudice and antagonism, Jews were forbidden to own land in most parts of Europe, and they were forced, if lucky enough, to make their living by borrowing money at interest, a practice permitted in Judaism but forbidden, by strict interpretation, in Christianity. However, Philip's dependence did not prevent him for treating Jews brutally, holding them for ransom, canceling the terms of their loans, and taking a percentage of their earnings at his own whim. Even this expulsion was not permanent; the Jews were recalled in 1198, but Philip tightened his control (and exploitation) of their businesses. Notice that the author of this document does not explore all sides of the story, preferring instead to stress the supposed outrages of the Jews themselves.

Source: *Readings in Western History,* Robinson, 426-428.

Focus Questions:

1. What charges does Rigord bring against the Jews, and in what terms does he justify their treatment?
2. How is King Philip depicted in this document?

[Philip Augustus had often heard] that the Jews who dwelt in Paris were wont every year on Easter day, or during the sacred week of our Lord's Passion, to go down secretly into underground vaults and kill a Christian as a sort of sacrifice in contempt of the Christian religion. For a long time they had persisted in this wickedness, inspired by the devil, and in Philip's father's time many of them had been seized and burned with fire. St. Richard, whose body rests in the church of the Holy Innocents-in-the-Fields in Paris, was thus put to death and crucified by the Jews, and through martyrdom went in blessedness to God. Wherefore many miracles have been wrought by the hand of God through the prayers and intercessions of St. Richard, to the glory of God, as we have heard.

And because the most Christian King Philip inquired diligently, and came to know full well these and many other iniquities of the Jews in his forefathers' days, therefore he burned with zeal, and in the same year in which he was invested at Rheims with the holy governance of the kingdom of the French, upon a Sabbath, the first of March, by his command, the Jews throughout all France were seized in their synagogues and then despoiled of their gold and silver and garments, as the Jews themselves had spoiled the Egyptians at their exodus from Egypt. This was a harbinger of their expulsion, which by God's will soon followed....

At this time a great multitude of Jews had been dwelling in France for a long time past, for they had flocked thither from divers parts of the world, because peace abode among the French, and liberality; for the Jews had heard how the kings of the French were prompt to act against their enemies, and were very merciful toward their subjects. And therefore their elders and men wise in the law of Moses, who were called by the Jews *didascali*, made resolve to come to Paris.

When they had made a long sojourn there, they grew so rich that they claimed as their own almost half of the whole city, and had Christians in their houses as menservants and maidservants, who were open backsliders from the faith of Jesus Christ, and *judaized* with the Jews. And this was contrary to the decree of God and the law of the Church. And whereas the Lord had said by the mouth of Moses in Deuteronomy (xxiii. 19,20), "Thou shalt not lend upon usury to thy brother," but "to a stranger," the Jews in their wickedness understood by "stranger" every Christian, and they took from the Christians their money at usury. And so heavily burdened in this wise were citizens and soldiers and peasants in the suburbs, and in the various towns and villages, that many of them were constrained to part with their possessions. Others were bound under oath in houses of the Jews in Paris, held as if captives in prison.

The most Christian King Philip heard of these things, and compassion was stirred within him. He took counsel with a certain hermit, Bernard by name, a holy and religious man, who at that time dwelt in the forest of Vincennes, and asked him what he should do. By his advice the king released all Christians of his kingdom from their debts to the Jews, and kept a fifth part of the whole amount for himself.

Finally came the culmination of their wickedness. Certain ecclesiastical vessels consecrated to God – the chalices and crosses of gold and silver bearing the image of our Lord Jesus Christ crucified – had been pledged to the Jews by way of security when the need of the churches was pressing. These they used so vilely, in their impiety and scorn of the Christian religion, that from the cups in which the body and blood of our Lord Jesus Christ was consecrated they gave their children cakes soaked in wine....

In the year of our Lord's Incarnation 1182, in the month of April, which is called by the Jews Nisan, an edict went forth from the most serene king, Philip

Augustus, that all the Jews of his kingdom should be prepared to go forth by the coming feast of St. John the Baptist. And then the king gave them leave to sell each his movable goods before the time fixed, that is, the feast of St. John the Baptist. But their real estate, that is, houses, fields, vineyards, barns, winepresses, and such like, he reserved for himself and his successors, the kings of the French.

When the faithless Jews heard this edict some of them were born again of water and the Holy Spirit and converted to the Lord, remaining steadfast in the faith of our Lord Jesus Christ. To them the king, out of regard for the Christian religion, restored all their possessions in their entirety, and gave them perpetual liberty.

Others were blinded by their ancient error and persisted in their perfidy; and they sought to win with gifts and golden promises the great of the land, -counts, barons, archbishops, bishops, -that through their influence and advice, and through the promise of infinite wealth, they might turn the king's mind from his firm intention. But the merciful and compassionate God, who does not forsake those who put their hope in him and who doth humble those who glory in their strength,...so fortified the illustrious king that he could not be moved by prayers nor promises of temporal things....

The infidel Jews, perceiving that the great of the land, through whom they had been accustomed easily to bend the king's predecessors to their will, had suffered repulse, and astonished and stupefied by the strength of mind of Philip the king and his constancy in the Lord, exclaimed, "Scema Israhel!" and prepared to sell all their household goods. The time was now at hand when the king had ordered them to leave France altogether, and it could not be in any way prolonged. Then did the Jews sell all their movable possessions in great haste, while their landed property reverted to the crown. Thus the Jews, having sold their goods and taken the price for the expenses of their journey, departed with their wives and children and all their households in the aforesaid year of the Lord 1182.

Behâ ed-Din
Richard I Massacres Prisoners after Taking Acre
c. 1195

The recapture of Jerusalem by the Muslim leader Salah ed-Din (Saladin) in 1187 triggered a Third Crusade from Western Europe. At the key point in the campaign, King Richard I of England and King Philip II Augustus of France led a successful siege of the Muslim stronghold at Acre, on the Palestinian coast. Both armies suffered outbreaks of disease, a critical shortage of water, and complex negotiations that often broke down. As part of the terms of surrender in August 1191, the Crusaders held 2700 Muslims, men, women, and children, as hostages against Saladin's completion of the remainder of the terms. When Saladin failed, at least in Richard's estimation, to fulfill his part of the bargain, Richard ordered the execution of the hostages. Behâ ed-Din, a member of Saladin's court, was a witness to the massacre, and he describes it in vivid detail.

Source: T. A. Archer, ed., *The Crusade of Richard I* (New York: G. P. Putnams, 1885), pp. 127–31.

FOCUS QUESTIONS:

1. How did religion motivate the behavior of the combatants on both sides?
2. Does this document suggest that Richard I, famed for "chivalry," did not deserve that reputation?

BEHÂ ED-DIN

The same day Hossâm ad-Din Ibn Barîc…brought news that the king of France had set out for Tyre, and that they had come to talk over the matter of the prisoners and to see the true cross of the Crucifixion if it were still in the Muslim camp, or to ascertain if it really had been sent to Bagdad. It was shewn to them, and on beholding it they shewed the profoundest reverence, throwing themselves on the ground till they were covered with dust, and humbling themselves in token of devotion. These envoys told us that the French princes had accepted the Sultan's proposition, viz., to deliver all that was specified in the treaty by three installments at intervals of a month. The Sultan then sent an envoy to Tyre with rich presents, quantities of perfumes, and fine raiment—all of which were for the king of the French.

…Ibn Bar"c and his comrades returned to the king of England while the Sultan went off with his bodyguard and his closest friends to the hill that abuts on Shefa'Amr…Envoys did not cease to pass from one side to the other in the hope of laying the foundation of a firm peace. These negotiations continued till our men had procured the money and the tale of the prisoners that they were to deliver to the French at the end of the first period in accordance with the treaty. The first installment was to consist of the Holy Cross, 100,000 dinars and 1,600 prisoners. Trustworthy men sent by the Franks [French, or Europeans] to conduct the examination found it all complete saving only the prisoners who had been demanded by name, all of whom had not yet been gathered together. And thus the negotiations continued to drag on till the end of the first term…

This proposition the Sultan rejected, knowing full well that if he were to deliver the money, the cross, and the prisoners, while our men were still kept captive by the Franks, he would have no security against treachery on the part of the enemy, and this would be a great disaster to Islam.

Then the king of England, seeing all the delays interposed by the Sultan to the execution of the treaty, acted perfidiously as regards his Muslims prisoners. On their yielding the town he had engaged to grant them life, adding that if the Sultan carried out the bargain he would give them freedom and suffer them to carry off their children and wives; if the Sultan did not fulfil his engagements they were to be made slaves. Now the king broke his promises to them and made open display of what he had till now kept hidden in his heart, by carrying out what he had intended to do after he had received the money and the Frank prisoners. It is thus that people of his nation ultimately admitted.

In the afternoon of Tuesday…about four o'clock, he came out on horseback with all the Frankish army; knights, footmen, Turcoples, and advanced to the pits at the foot of the hill of Al 'Ayâdîyeh to which place he had already sent on his tents. The Franks, on reaching the middle of the plain that stretches between this hill and that of Keisân, close to which place the sultan's advanced guard had drawn back, ordered all the Muslims prisoners, whose martyrdom God had decreed for this day, to be brought before him. They numbered more than three thousand and were all bound with ropes. The Franks then flung themselves upon them all at once and massacred them with sword and lance in cold blood. Our advanced guard had already told the Sultan of the enemy's movements and he sent it some reinforcements, but only after the massacre. The Muslims, seeing what was being done to the prisoners, rushed against the Franks and in the combat, which lasted till nightfall, several were slain and wounded on either side. On the morrow morning our people gathered at the spot and found the Muslims stretched out upon the ground as martyrs for the faith. They even recognised some of the dead, and the sight was a great affliction to them. The enemy had only spared the prisoners of note and such as were strong enough to work.

The motives of this massacre are differently told; according to some, the captives were slain by way of reprisal for the death of those Christians whom the Muslims had slain. Others again say that the king of England, on deciding to attempt the conquest of Ascalon, thought it unwise to leave so many prisoners in the town after his departure. God alone knows what the real reason was.

Unam Sanctam:
Pope Boniface VIII on the Two Swords
1302

Gregory's aggressive stance did not insure the permanent authority of the popes over the kings and emperors of Europe. Two centuries later, Pope Boniface VIII (1294-1303) tried to limit the perennial conflicts between the kings of France and England, and he attempted, through a "papal bull" (an official pronouncement) in 1296, to prohibit monarchs from taxing church officials without papal permission. King Philip IV the Fair of France and King Edward I of England rejected the bull and retaliated against this assertive clergyman. After a series of encounters, the Pope issued another bull, called *"Unam Sanctam"* ("The One Holy (Church)", in Latin), portions of which are listed below. Philip responded by having the Pope arrested (and, according to some sources, handled roughly), and Boniface died a few weeks later. Shortly after this, a French Pope, Clement V (1305-1314) was escorted by the King to Avignon, France, beginning the so-called "Babylonian Captivity" of the papacy.

Source: "The Bull Unam Sanctam of Boniface VIII," in Translations and Reprints from the *Original Sources of European History*, vol. III, no. 6, (Philadelphia: The Department of History of the University of Pennsylvania, 1912), 20–23; reprinted in ed. John L. Beatty and Oliver A. Johnson, *Heritage of Western Civilization*, vol. 1, 7th edition, (Englewood Cliffs, NJ: Prentice Hall, 1991), 319–21.

Focus Questions:

1. What are the "two swords", and what did Boniface see as the proper relationship between them?
2. Compare this document with the letter of Gregory VII. Would a secular ruler have been impressed with either?

That there is one Holy Catholic and Apostolic Church we are impelled by our faith to believe and to hold—this we do firmly believe and openly confess—and outside of this there is neither salvation or remission of sins, as the bridegroom proclaims in Canticles, "My dove, my undefiled is but one; she is the only one of her mother; she is the choice one of her that bare her." The Church represents one mystic body and of this body Christ is the head; of Christ, indeed. God is the head. In it is one Lord, and one faith, and one baptism. In the time of the flood, there was one ark of Noah, prefiguring the one Church, finished in one cubit, having one Noah as steersman and commander. Outside of this, all things upon the face of the earth were, as we read, destroyed. This Church we venerate and this alone, the Lord saying through his prophets, "Deliver my soul, O God, from the sword; my darling from the power of the dog." He prays thus for his soul, that is for Himself, as head, and also for the body, which He calls one, namely, the Church on account of the unity of the bridegroom, of the faith, of the sacraments, and of the charity of the Church. It is that seamless coat of the Lord, which was not rent, but fell by lot. Therefore, in this one and only Church, there is one body and one head—not two heads as if it were a monster—namely, Christ and Christ's Vicar. Peter and Peter's successor, for the Lord said to Peter himself, "Feed my sheep": my sheep, he said, using a general term and not designating these or those sheep, so that we must believe that all the sheep were committed to him. If, then, the Greeks or others, shall say that they were not entrusted to Peter and his successors, they must perforce admit that they are not of Christ's sheep, as the Lord says in John, "there is one fold, and one shepherd."

In this Church and in its power are two swords, to wit, a spiritual and a temporal, and this we are taught by the words of the Gospel, for when the Apostles said, "Behold, here are two swords" (in the Church, namely, since the Apostles were speaking), the Lord did not reply that it was too many, but enough. And surely he who claims that the temporal sword is not in the power of Peter has but ill understood the word of our Lord when he said, "Put up the sword in its scabbard." Both, therefore, the spiritual and material swords, are in the power of the Church, the latter indeed to be used for the Church, the former by the Church, the one by the priest, the other by the hand of kings and soldiers, but by the will and sufferance of the priest. It is fitting, moreover, that one sword should be under the other, and the temporal authority subject to the spiritual power. For when the Apostle said "there is no power but of God and the powers that are of God are ordained," they would not be ordained unless one sword were under the other, and one, as inferior, was brought back by the other to the highest place. For, according to the Holy Dionysius, the law of divinity is to lead the lowest through the intermediate to the highest. Therefore, according to the law of the universe, things are not reduced to order directly, and upon the same footing, but the lowest through the intermediate and the inferior through the superior. It behooves us, therefore, the more freely to confess that the spiritual power excels in dignity and nobility any form whatsoever of earthly power, as spiritual interests exceed the temporal in importance. All this we see fairly from the giving of tithes, from the benediction and sanctification, from the recognition of this power and the control of the same things. For the truth bearing witness, it is for the spiritual power to establish the earthly power and judge it, if it be not good. Thus, in the case of the Church and the power of the Church, the prophecy of Jeremiah is fulfilled: "See, I have this day set thee over the nations and over the kingdoms"—and so forth. Therefore, if the earthly power shall err, it shall be judged by the spiritual power: if the lesser spiritual power err, it shall be judged by the higher. But if the supreme power err, it can be judged by God alone and not by man, the apostles bearing witness saying, the spiritual man judges all things but he himself is judged by no one. Hence this power, although given to man and exercised by man, is not human, but rather divine power, given by the divine lips to Peter, and founded on a rock for Him and his successors in Him whom he confessed, the Lord saying to Peter himself, "Whatsoever thou shalt bind," etc. Whoever, therefore, shall resist this power, ordained by God, resists the ordination of God, unless there should be two beginnings, as the Manichaean imagines. But this we judge to be false and heretical, since, by the testimony of Moses, not in the beginnings, but in the beginning, God created the heaven and the earth. We, moreover, proclaim, declare, and pronounce that it is altogether necessary to salvation for every human being to be subject to the Roman Pontiff.

Given at the Lateran the twelfth day before the Kalends of December, in our eighth year, as a perpetual memorial of this matter.

The Penitentials
c. 1575

The proper "administration" of the fourth sacrament often required further explanation. Accordingly, "penitentials" were issued to help priests learn and understand their duties as confessors for the faithful. Confession with penance had been imposed on parishioners at least once per year by the Fourth Lateran Council in 1215. The following is attributed to Cardinal St. Charles Borromeo (1543-1584), who advocated Church reform and discipline during the Counter-Reformation. This excerpt includes the introduction to the document, which outlines the purpose of the penitential and a selection of penances required for various sins listed under each commandment (in the Ten Commandments).

Source:"The Milan Penitential of Cardinal Borromeo (ca. 1565–82)"; reprinted in *Medieval Handbooks of Penance: A Translation of the principal libri poenitentialesand selections from related documents*, ed. John T. McNeill and Helena M. Gamer, (NewYork: Octagon Books, Inc., 1965) 364–68.

Focus Questions:

1. What was the duty of the priest in applying the penances correctly?
2. With what kinds of sins was this penitential concerned, and which were considered the worst?

Penitential Canons, Knowledge of Which Is Necessary for Parish Priests and Confessors, Set Forth according to the Plan and Order of the Decalog

The fathers taught how very necessary for priests who are engaged in hearing the confessions of penitents is aknowledge of the penitential canons. And indeed if all things that pertain to the method of penance are to beadministered not only with prudence and piety but also with justice, assuredly the pattern of this ought to betaken from the penitential canons. For there are, so to speak, two rules by which priests and confessors are so directed as both to discern the gravity of an offense committed and in relation to this to impose a true penance:that they severally accurately investigate both the things that pertain to the greatness of the sin and those thatpertain to the status, condition, and age of the penitent and the inmost sorrow of the contrite heart—and then,that they temper the penance with their own justice and prudence. And indeed the method explained by thefathers so disposed these things and everything else that is complicated of this necessary knowledge, that, aswas said above in its proper place, the penitential canons set forth according to the plan of the Decalog are held over to the last part of the book, whence some knowledge of them can be drawn by the confessor-priests themselves....

The chief penitential canons collected according to the order of the Decalog from various councils and penitentiary books in the Instruction of St. Charles B[orromeo]

On the First Commandment of the Decalog

1. He who falls away from the faith shall do penance for ten years.

2. He who observes auguries and divinations [and] he who makes diabolical incantations, seven years. One whobeholds things to come in an astrolabe, two years.

3. If anyone makes knots or enchantments, two years.

4. He who consults magicians, five years.

On the Second Commandment

1. Whoever knowingly commits perjury, shall do penance for forty days on bread and water, and seven succeeding years; and he shall never be without penance. And he shall never be accepted as a witness; and after these things he shall take communion.

2. He who commits perjury in a church, ten years.

3. If anyone publicly blasphemes God or the Blessed Virgin or any saint, he shall stand in the open in front ofthe doors of the church on seven Sundays, while the solemnities of the masses are performed, and on the last ofthese days, without robe and shoes, with a cord tied about his neck; and on the seven preceding Fridays he shall fast on bread and water; and he shall then by no means enter the church. Moreover, on each of these seven Sundays he shall feed three or two or one, if he is able. Otherwise he shall do another penance; if he refuses, heshall be forbidden to enter the church; in [case of] his death he shall be denied ecclesiastical burial.

4. He who violates a simple vow shall do penance for three years.

On the Third Commandment

1. He who does any servile work on the Lord's day or on a feast day shall do penance for seven days on bread and water.

2. If anyone violates fasts set by Holy Church, he shall do penance for forty days on bread and water.

3. He who violates the fast in Lent shall do a seven-day penance for one day.

4. He who without unavoidable necessity eats flesh in Lent shall not take communion at Easter and shall thereafter abstain from flesh.

On the Fourth Commandment

1. He who reviles his parents shall be a penitent for forty days on bread and water.

2. He who does an injury to his parents, three years.

3. He who beats [them], seven years.

4. If anyone rises up against his bishop, his pastor and father, he shall do penance in a monastery all the days ofhis life.

5. If anyone despises or derides the command of his bishop, or of the bishop's servants, or of his parish priest, he shall do penance for forty days on bread and water.

On the Fifth Commandment

1. He who kills a presbyter shall do penance for twelve years.

2. If anyone kills his mother, father, or sister, he shall not take the Lord's body throughout his whole life, exceptat his departure; he shall abstain from flesh and wine, while he lives; he shall fast on Monday, Wednesday, and Friday.

3. If anyone kills a man he shall always be at the door of the church, and at death he shall receive communion.[Sections 4–10 omitted.]

On the Sixth Commandment [Sections 1–6 omitted.]

1. If any woman paints herself with ceruse or other pigment in order to please men, she shall do penance forthree years.

2. If a priest is intimate with his own spiritual daughter, that is, one whom he has baptized or who has confessed to him, he ought to do penance for twelve years; and if the offense is publicly known, he ought to be deposed and do penance for twelve years on pilgrimage, and thereafter enter a monastery to remain there throughout hislife. For adultery penances of seven, and of ten, years, are imposed; for unchaste kissing or embracing apenance of thirty days is commanded.

On the Seventh Commandment

1. If anyone commits a theft of a thing of small value he shall do penance for a year.

2. He who steals anything from the furniture of a church or from the treasury, or ecclesiastical property, orofferings made to the church shall be a penitent for seven years.

3. He who retains to himself his tithe or neglects to pay it, shall restore fourfold and do penance for twenty days on bread and water.

4. He who takes usury commits robbery; he shall do penance for three years on bread and water.

On the Eighth Commandment

1. He who conspires in falsification of evidence shall be a penitent for five years.

2. A forger shall do penance on bread and water as long as he lives.

3. If anyone slanders his neighbor, he shall be a penitent for seven days on bread and water.

On the Ninth and Tenth Commandments

1. He who basely covets another's goods and is avaricious shall be a penitent for three years.

2. If anyone desires to commit fornication, if a bishop, he shall be a penitent for seven years; if a presbyter, five;if a deacon or monk three; if a cleric or layman, two years.

CHAPTER 7

Society and Culture in the High Middle Ages

Sports in the City of London
1180

This document was designed as an introduction to a biography of St. Thomas à Becket, the Archbishop of Canterbury who was murdered on the orders of King Henry II of England in 1170. The author, William FitzStephen, was an assistant to Becket and claimed to have special knowledge of the slain man, creating a biography in his honor about 10 years after his death. However, FitzStephen begins this account with a scene of life in London during the reign of Henry II. It is remarkable evidence that not all aspects of life in the Middle Ages were precarious and dreary.

Source: William FitzStephen, *A Description of London*, prefixed to his Life of Thomas a Becket, trans. H. E. Butler, (Historical Association, 1934) reprinted in *Everyone a Witness: The Plantagenet Age*, ed. Arthur S. Finlay, (New York: Thomas Y. Crowell, 1976), 112–14.

FOCUS QUESTIONS:

1. What sorts of sports were particularly popular in London durinf this period?
2. How violent were these activities, in which the citizens took such pleasure?

London in place of shows in the theatre and stage-plays has holier plays, wherein are shown forth the miracles wrought by Holy Confessors or the sufferings which glorified the constancy of Martyrs.

Moreover, each year upon the day called Carnival—to begin with the sports of boys (for we were all boys once)— boys from the schools bring fighting-cocks to their master, and the whole forenoon is given up to boyish sport; for they have a holiday in the schools that they may watch their cocks do battle. After dinner all the youth of the City goes out into the fields in a much-frequented game of ball. The scholars of each school have their own ball, and almost all the workers of each trade have theirs also in their hands. Elder men and fathers and rich citizens come on horseback to watch the contests of their juniors and after their fashion are young again with the young; and it seems that the motion of their natural heat is kindled by the contemplation of such violent motion and by their partaking in the joys of untrammelled youth.

Every Sunday in Lent after dinner a 'fresh swarm of young gentles' goes forth on war-horses, 'steeds skilled in the contest, of which each is 'apt and schooled to wheel in circles round'. From the gates burst forth in throngs the lay sons of citizens, armed with lance and shield, the younger with shafts forked at the end, but with steel point removed. 'They wake war's semblance' and in mimic contest exercise their skill at arms. Many courtiers come too, when the King is in residence; and from the households of Earls and Barons come young men not yet invested with the belt of knighthood, that they may there contend together. Each one of them is on fire with hope of victory. The fierce horses neigh, 'their limbs tremble; they champ the bit; impatient of delay they cannot stand still'. When at length 'the hoof of trampling steeds careers along', the youthful riders divide their hosts; some pursue those that fly before, and cannot overtake them; others unhorse their comrades and speed by.

At the feast of Easter they make sport with naval tourneys, as it were. For a shield being strongly bound to a stout pole in mid-stream, a small vessel, swiftly driven on by many an oar and by the river's flow, carries a youth standing at the prow, who is to strike the shield with his lance. If he break the lance by striking the shield and keep his feet unshaken, he has achieved his purpose and fulfilled his desire. If, however, he strike it strongly without splintering his lance, he is thrown into the rushing river, and the boat of its own speed passes him by. But there are on each side of the shield two vessels moored, and in them are many youths to snatch up the striker who has been sucked down by the stream, as soon as he emerges into sight or 'once more bubbles on the topmost wave'. On the bridge and the galleries above the river are spectators of the sport 'ready to laugh their fill'.

On feast-days throughout the summer the youths exercise themselves in leaping, archery and wrestling, putting the stone, and throwing the thonged javelin beyond a mark, and fighting with sword and buckler. 'Cytherea leads the dance of maidens and the earth is smitten with free foot at moonrise.'

In winter on almost every feast-day before dinner either foaming boars and hogs, armed with 'tusks lightning-swift', themselves soon to be bacon, fight for their lives, or fat bulls with butting horns, or huge bears, do combat to the death against hounds let loose upon them.

When the great marsh that washes the northern walls of the City is frozen, dense throngs of youths go forth to disport themselves upon the ice. Some gathering speed by a run, glide sidelong, with feet set well apart, over a vast space of ice. Others make themselves seats of ice like millstones and are dragged along by a number who run before them holding hands. Sometimes they slip owing to the greatness of their speed and fall, every one of them, upon their faces. Others there are, more skilled to sport upon the ice, who fit to their feet the shin-bones of beasts, lashing them beneath their ankles, and with ironshod poles in their hands they strike ever and anon against the ice and are borne along swift as a bird in flight or a bolt shot from a mangonel. But sometimes two by agreement run one against the other from a great distance and, raising their poles, strike one another. One or both fall, not without bodily hurt, since on falling they are borne a long way in opposite directions.

Many of the citizens delight in taking their sport with birds of the air, merlins and falcons and the like, and with dogs that wage warfare in the woods. The citizens have the special privilege of hunting in Middlesex, Hertfordshire and all Chiltern, and in Kent as far as the river Cray.

Excerpts *from The History of the Life and Travels of Rabban Bar Sawma*

Bar Rabban Sawma (1260–1313 CE) was a Christian monk from northern China. He was a member of a group of Turks who, like a number of steppe peoples, had been converted to Nestorian Christianity by missionaries from the Middle East. Rabban Sawma traveled with a companion, Markus, on pilgrimage to Jerusalem but was sidetracked on a diplomatic mission for the Mongol khan. He went to Byzantium and Western Europe seeking allies for a combined attack intended to push the Mamluk Egyptians out of Jerusalem. Rabban Sawma died after returning to Baghdad, having never reached Jerusalem.

Source: Sir E. A. Wallis Budge, trans., The Monks of Kublai Kahn Emperor of China. (London: The Religious Tract Society, 1928)

FOCUS QUESTIONS:

1. Why was Rabban Sawma's theology questioned so closely in Rome?

2. How did the Nestorians and Europeans react to one another?

3. Compare Sawma'a experiences with those of European travelers going east.

THE MONKS OF KUBLAI KAHN EMPEROR OF CHINA
CHAPTER VII.
(47) ON THE DEPARTURE OF RABBAN SAWMA TO THE COUNTRY

OF THE ROMANS IN THE NAME OF KING ARGHON AND OF THE CATHOLICUS MAR YAHBH-ALLAHA.

Now MAR YAHBH-ALLAHA, the Catholicus, increased in power, and his honour before the King and Queens grew greater daily. He pulled down the church of MAR SHALITA which was in MARAGHAH, and he rebuilt it at very great expense. And instead of using [the old] beams [and making a single roof] he made [the new church] with two naves (*haikili*); and by the side of it he built a cell in which to live. For his affection for the house of King ARGHON was very warm, because ARGHON loved the Christians with his whole heart. And ARGHON intended to go into the countries of Palestine and Syria and to subjugate them and take possession of them, but he said to himself, "If the Western Kings, who are Christians, will not help me I shall not be able to fulfill my desire." Thereupon he asked the Catholicus to give him a wise man (48), "one who is suitable and is capable of undertaking an embassy, that we may send him to those kings." And when the Catholicus saw that there was no man who knew (166) the language except Rabban Sawma, and knowing that he was fully capable of this, he commanded him to go [on the embassy].

THE JOURNEY OF RABBAN SAWMA; TO THE COUNTRY OF THE ROMANS IN THE NAME OF KING ARGHON AND OF THE CATHOLICUS MAR YAHBHALLAHA.

Then RABBAN SAWMA said, "I desire this embassy greatly, and I long to go." Then straightway King ARGHON wrote for him "Authorities" (*pukdana*) to the king of the Greeks, and the king of the PER-OGAYE (Franks?) that is to say Romans, and Yarlike [i.e. the "Ordinances" of the Mongolian kings], and letters, and gave him gifts for each of the kings [addressed by him]. And to RABBAN SAWMA he gave two thousand mathkale (£1,000?) of gold, and thirty good riding animals, and a Paiza (see above, pp. 62, 63). And RABBAN SAWMA came to the cell of the Catholicus to obtain letter from MAR YAHBH-ALLAHA, and to say farewell to him. The Catholicus gave his permission to depart (49), but when the time for his departure arrived, it did not please the Catholicus to permit him to go. For he said [unto Rabban Sawma], "How can this possibly take place? Thou hast been the governor of my cell, and thou knowest that through thy departure my affairs will fall into a state of utter confusion." And having said such words as (167) these they said farewell to each other, weeping as they did so. And the Catholicus sent with him letters, and gifts which were suitable for presentation to Mar Papa (the Pope), and gifts [i.e. offerings] according to his ability.

RABBAN SAWMA IN ITALY AND IN GREAT ROME.

And he departed from Constantinople and went down to the sea. And he saw on the sea-shore a monastery of the Romans, and there were laid up in its treasure-house two funerary coffers of silver; in the one was the head of MAR

JOHN CHRYSOSTOM, and in the other that of MAR PAPA who baptized CON-STANTINE. And he went down to the sea [i.e. embarked on a ship] and came to the middle thereof, where he saw a mountain from which smoke ascended all the day long and in the night time fire showed itself on it. And no man is able to approach the neighbourhood of it because of the stench of sulphur [proceeding therefrom]. Some people say that there is a great serpent there. This sea is called the "Sea of Italy." Now it is a terrible sea, and very many thousands of (54) people have perished therein. And after two months of toil, and weariness, and exhaustion, RABBAN SAWMA (171) arrived at the sea-shore, and he landed at the name of which was NAPOLI (Naples); the name of its king was IRID SHARDALO [= IL RE SHARL DU or, the King Charles II?]. And he went to the king and showed him the reason why they had come; and the king welcomed him and paid him honour. Now it happened that there was war between him and another king, whose name was IRID ARKON [= the King of Aragon, JAMES II?]. And the troops of the one had come in many ships, and the troops of the other were ready, and they began to fight each other, and the King of ARAGON (?) conquered King CHARLES II, and slew twelve thousand [of] his men, and sunk their ships in the sea. [According to Chabot this naval engagement took place in the Bay of Sorrento on St. John's Day, June 24, 1287, and the great eruption of Mount Etna on June 18.] Meanwhile RABBAN SAWMA and his companions sat upon the roof the mansion in which they lived, and they admired the way in which the Franks waged war for they attacked none of the people except those who were actually combatants (55). And from that place they travelled inland on horses, and they passed through towns and villages and marvelled because they found no land which was destitute of buildings. On the road they heard that MAR PAPA [Honorius IV who died in 1287] was dead. (172) And the Cardinals said unto him, "For the present rest thyself, and we will discuss the matter together later"; and they assigned to him a mansion and caused him to be taken down thereto.

Three days later the Cardinals sent and summoned RABBAN SAWMA to their presence. And when he went to them they began to ask him questions, saying, "What is thy quarter of the world, and why hast thou come?" And he replied in the selfsame words he had already spoken to them (57). And they said unto him, "Where doth the Catholicus live? And the Cardinals. And thus they did, and [their act] was pleasing to those Cardinals. And when RABBAN SAWMA went into their presence no man stood up before him, for by reason of the honourable nature of the Throne, the twelve Cardinals were not in the habit of doing this. And they made RABBAN SAWMA sit down with them, and one of them asked him, "How art thou after all the fatigue of the road?" And he made answer to him, "Through you prayers I am well and rested." And the Cardinal said unto him, "For what purpose hast thou (173) come hither?" And RABBAN SAWMA said unto him, "The Mongols and the Catholicus of the East have sent me to Mar Papa concerning the matter of Jerusalem; and they have sent letters with me." And the

Cardinals said unto him, "For the present rest thyself, and we will discuss the matter together later"; and they assigned to him a mansion and caused him to be taken down thereto.

Three days later the Cardinals sent and summoned RABBAN SAWMA to their presence. And when he went to them they began to ask him questions, saying, "What is thy quarter of the world, and why has thou come?" And he replied in the selfsame words he had already spoden to them (57). And they said unto him, "Where doth the Catholicus live? And which of the Apostles taught the Gospel in thy quar-ter of the world?" And he answered them, saying, "MAR THOMAS, and MAR ADDAI, and MAR MARI taught the Gospel in our quarter of the world, and we hold at the present time the canons [or statutes] which they delivered unto us." The Cardinals said unto him, "Where is the Throne of the Catholicus?" He said to them, "In BAGHDAD." They answered, What position hast thou there?" And he replied, "I am a deacon in the Cell of the Catholicus, and the director of the disciples, and the Visitor-General." The Cardinals said, "It is a marvellous thing (174) that thou who art a Christian, and a dea-con of the Throne of the Patriarch of the East has come upon an embassy from the king of the Mongols." And RABBAN SAWMA said unto them, "Know ye, O our Fathers, that many of our Fathers

have gone into the countries of the Mongols, and Turks, and Chinese and have taught them the Gospel, and at the present time there are many Mongols who are Christians. For many of the sons of the Mongol kings and queens (58) have been baptized and confess Christ. And they have established churches in their military camps, and they pay honour to the Christians, and there are among them many who are believers. Now the king [of the Mongols], who is joined in the bond of friendship with the Catholicus, hath the desire to take PALESTINE, and the countries of SYRIA, and he demandeth from you help in order to take JERUSALEM. He hath chosen me and hath sent me to you because, being a Christian, my word will be believed by you." And the Cardinals said unto him, "What is thy confession of faith? To what 'way' art thou attached? Is it that which Mar Papa holdeth today or some other one?" RABBAN SAWMA replied, "No man hath come to us Orientals from the Pope. The holy Apostle whose names I have mentioned taught us the Gospel, and to what they delivered unto us we have clung to the present day." The Cardinals (175) said unto him, "How dost thou believe? Recite thy belief, article by article." RABBAN SAWMA replied to them, saying:

THE BELIEF OF RABBAN SAWMA, WHICH THE CARDINALS DEMANDED FROM HIM.

"I believe in One God, hidden, everlasting, without beginning and without (59) end, Father, and Son, and Holy Spirit: Three Persons, coequal and indivisible; among Whom there is none who is first, or last, or young, or old: in Nature they are One, in Persons they are three: the Father is the Begetter, the Son is the Begotten, the Spirit proceedeth.

"In the last time one of the Persons of the Royal Trinity, namely the Son, put on the perfect man, Jesus Christ, from MARY the holy virgin; and was united to Him Personally (*parsopaith*), and in him saved (or redeemed) the world. In His Divinity He is eternally of the Father; in His humanity He was born [a Being] in time of MARY; the union is inseparable and indivisible for ever; the union is without mingling, and without mixture, and without compaction. The Son of this union is perfect God (60) and perfect man, two Natures (*keyanin*), and two Persons (*kenomin*)—one parsopa (…)

The Cardinals said unto him, "Doth the Holy Spirit proceed from the Father or from the Son, or is it separate?" RABBAN SAWMA replied, (176) "Are the Father, and the Son, and the Spirit associated in the things which appertain to the Nature (*keyana*) or separate?" The Cardinals answered, "They are associated in the things which concern the Nature (*keyana*) but are separate in respect of individual qualities." RABBAN SAWMA said, "What are their individual qualities?" The Cardinals replied, "Of the Father, the act of begetting: of the Son the being begotten: of the Spirit the going forth (proceeding)." RABBAN SAWMA said, "Which of Them is the cause of that Other?" And the Cardinals replied, "The Father is the cause of the Son, and the Son is the cause of the Spirit." RABBAN SAWMA said, "If they are coequal in Nature (*keyana*), and in operation, and in power, and in authority (or dominion), and the Three Persons (*kenome*) are One, how is it possible for one of Them to be the cause of the Other? For of necessity (61) the Spirit also must be the cause of some other thing; but the discussion is extraneous to the Confession of faith of wise men. We cannot find a demonstration resembling this statement of yours.

"For behold, the soul is the cause both of the reasoning power and the act of living, but the reasoning power is not the cause of the act of living. The sphere of the sun is the cause of light and heat, and heat is not the cause of light. Thus we think that which is correct, (177) namely, that the Father is the cause of the Son and the Spirit, and that both the Son and the Spirit are causation of His. Adam begot Seth, and made Eve to proceed [from him], and they are three; because in respect there is absolutely no difference between begetting and making to go forth (or proceed)."

Then the Cardinals said unto him, "We confess that the Spirit proceedeth from the Father and the Son, but not as we said, for we were only putting thy modesty [or, religious belief?] to the test." And RAB-BAN SAWMA said, "It is not right that to something which is one, two, three, or four causes should be [assigned]; on the contrary I do not think that this resembleth our Confession of Faith." Now though the Cardinals restrained (62) his speech by means of very many demonstrations, they held him in high esteem because of his power of argument.

Then RABBAN SAWMA said unto them, "I have come from remote countries neither to discuss, nor to instruct [men] in matter of the Faith, but I came that I might receive a blessing from MAR PAPA, and from the shrines of the saints and to make known the words of King [ARGHON] and the Catholicus. If it be pleasing in your eyes, let us set aside discussion, and do ye give attention and direct someone to show us the churches here and the shrines of the saints; [if ye will (178) do this] ye will confer a very great favour on your servant and disciple."

Then the Cardinals summoned the Amir of the city and certain monks and commanded them to show him the churches and the holy places that were there; and they went forth straightway and saw the places which we will now mention. First of all they went into the church of PETER and PAUL. Beneath the Throne is a naos, and in this is laid (63) the body of SAINT PETER, and above the throne is an altar. The altar which is in the middle of that are [sic], temple has four doorways, and in each of these two folding doors worked with designs in fro [sic]; MAR PAPA celebrates the Mass at this altar, and no per-son besides himself may stand on the bench of that altar. Afterwards they saw the Throne of MAR PETER whereon they make MAR PAPA to sit when they appoint him. And the also saw the strip of fine [or thin] linen on which our Lord impressed His image and sent to King ABHGAR of URHAI (Edessa). Now the extent of that temple and its splendour cannot be described; it stands on one hundred and eight pillars. In it is another altar at which the King of their Kings receives the laying on of hands [i.e. is consecrated and crowned], and is proclaimed "Ampror (Emperor) King of Kings," by the Pope. And they say that after the prayer Mar Papa takes up the Crown with his feet (179) and clothes the Emperor with it (64), that is to say, places it upon his own head [to show], as they say, that priesthood reigneth over sovereignty[or kingship].

And when they had seen all the churches and monasteries that were in Great Rome, they went outside the city to the church of MAR PAUL the Apostle, where under the altar is his tomb. And there, too, is the chain wherewith Paul was bound when he was dragged to that place. And in that altar there are also a reliquary of gold herein is the head of MAR STEPHEN the Martyr, and the hand of MAR KHANANYA (ANANIAS) who baptized PAUL. And the staff of PAUL the Apostle is also there. And from that place they went to the spot where PAUL the Apostle, was crowned [with martyrdom]. They say that when his head was cut off it leaped up thrice into the air, and at each time cried out CHRIST! CHRIST! And that from each of the three places on which his head fell there came forth waters which were useful for healing purposes, and for giving help to all those who were afflicted. And in that place there is a great shrine (65) wherein are the bones of martyrs and famous Fathers, and they were blessed by them.

And they went also to the Church of my Lady MARYAM, and of MAR JOHN the Baptist, and saw therein the seamless tunic of our Lord. And there is also in that church the tablet [or (180) slab] on which our Lord consecrated the Offering and gave it to His disciples. And each year Mar Papa consecrates on that tablet the Paschal Mysteries. There are in that church four pillars of copper [or brass], each of which is six cubits in thickness; these, they say, the kings brought from Jerusalem. They saw also there the vessel in which CONSTANTINE, the victorious king, was baptized; it is made of black stone [basalt?] polished. Now that church is very large and broad, and there are in the nave (*haikla*) one hundred and forty white marble pillars. They saw also the place where SIMON KIPA [i.e. Simon the Rock] disputed with SIMON [Magus], and where the latter fell down and his bones were broken.

From that place they went into the church of MART MARYAM, and [the priests] brought out for them reliquaries made of beryl (crystal?), wherein was (66) the apparel of MART MARYAM, and a piece of wood on which our Lord had lain when a child. They saw also the head of MATTHEH the Apostle, in a reliquary of silver. And they saw the foot of PHILIP, the Apostle, and the arm of JAMES, the son of ZABHDA!

(ZEBEDEE), in the Church of the Apostles, which was there. And after these [sights] they saw buildings which it is impossible to describe in words, and as the histories of those buildings would make any description of them very long I abandon [the attempt]. (181) After this RABBAN SAWMA and his companions returned to the Cardinals, and thanked them for having held him to be worthy to see these shrines and to receive blessings from them. And RABBAN SAWMA asked from them permission to go to the king who dwelleth in Rome; and they permitted him to go, and said, "We cannot give thee an answer until the [new] Pope is elected."

And they went from that place to the country of TUSZKAN (TUSCANY), and were honourably entreated, and thence they (67) went to GINOH (GENOA). Now the latter country has no king, but the people thereof set up to rule over it some great man with whom they are pleased.

And when the people of GENOA heard that an ambassador of King ARGHON had arrived, their Chief went forth with a great crowd of people, and they brought him into the city.

And there was there a great church with the name of SAINT SINALORNIA (SAN LORENZO), in which was the holy body of MAR JOHN the Baptist, in a coffer of pure silver. And RABBAN SAWMA and his companions saw also a six-sided paten, made of emerald, and the people there told them that it was off this paten from which our Lord ate the Passover with His disciples, and that it was brought there when Jerusalem was captured. And from that place they went to the country of ONBAR, [according to Bedjan, Lombardy] and they saw that the people there (182) did not fast during the first Sabbath of Lent. And when they asked them, "Wherefore do ye do thus, and separate yourselves from all [other]

Christians" (68), they replied, "This is our custom. When we were first taught the Gospel our fathers in the Faith were weakly and were unable to fast. Those who taught them the Gospel commanded them to fast forty days only."

College Life:
Letters between Students and their Fathers
c. 1200

The "university" was one of the longest-lasting products of the zenith of High Medieval culture. It developed from cathedral schools, in which masters instructed adolescent boys in the seven "liberal arts" that were the standard curriculum of the era. The first charter granted to a *"universitas"* specifically, was at Bologna in 1158. Its purpose was to protect the students against the incursions of the town, and it also allowed them to appoint or dismiss professors at will. This "union" bound together the members of a "guild", and from these guild markers derive most of the regalia we still use in academic settings in the modern university. However, then as now, the university was not merely a setting for instruction in the *trivium* and *quadrivium*. One must remember that these were young men, often living far from home and on their own, and the masters could not be everywhere at once....

Source: *Sources of the Western Tradition: Volume I: From Ancient Times to the Enlightenment,* ed. Marvin Perry, Joseph R. Peden, and Theodore H. Von Laue, (Boston: Houghton Mifflin Co., 1995), 182. Used with permission from G.G. Coulton, Life in the Middle Ages, Vol. 3, (Cambridge: Cambridge University Press, 1928/29).

FOCUS QUESTIONS:

1. What temptations awaited a student at a medieval university?
2. What entanglements and difficulties could arise between constituents of the "town" and the "gown"?

FATHERS TO SONS
I

I have recently discovered that you live dissolutely and slothfully, preferring license to restraint and play to work and strumming a guitar while the others are at their studies, whence it happens that you have read but one volume of law while your more industrious companions have read several. Wherefore I have decided to exhort you herewith to repent utterly of your dissolute and careless ways, that you may no longer be called a waster and your shame may be turned to good repute.

II

I have learned—not from your master, although he ought not to hide such things from me, but from a certain trustworthy source—that you do not study in your room or act in the schools as a good student should, but play and wander about, disobedient to your master and indulging in sport and in certain other dishonorable practices which I do not now care to explain by letter.

SONS TO FATHERS
I

"Well-beloved father, I have not a penny, nor can I get any save through you, for all things at the University are so dear: nor can I study in my Code or my Digest, for they are all tattered. Moreover, I owe ten crowns in dues to the Provost, and can find no man to lend them to me; I send you word of greetings and of money.

The Student hath need of many things if he will profit here; his father and his kin must needs supply him freely, that he be not compelled to pawn his books, but have ready money in his purse, with gowns and furs and decent clothing, or he will be damned for a beggar; wherefore, that men may not take me for a beast, I send you word of greetings and of money.

Wines are dear, and hostels, and other good things; I owe in every street, and am hard bested to free myself from such snares. Dear father, design to help me! I fear to be excommunicated; already have I been cited, and there is not even a dry bone in my larder. If I find not the money before this feast of Easter, the church door will be shut in my face: wherefore grant my supplication, for I send you word of greetings and of money.

L'envoy

Well-beloved father, to ease my debts contracted at the tavern, at the baker's, with the doctor and the bedells [a minor college official], and to pay my subscriptions to the laundress and the barber, I send you word of greetings and of money."

II

Sing unto the Lord a new song, praise him with stringed instruments and organs, rejoice upon the high-sounding cymbals, for your son has held a glorious disputation, which was attended by a great number of teachers and scholars. He answered all questions without a mistake, and no one could get the better of him or prevail against his arguments. Moreover he celebrated a famous banquet, at which both rich and poor were honoured as never before, and he has duly begun to give lectures which are already so popular that others' classrooms are deserted and his own are filled.

Manorial Court Records
1246–1247

The lord of the manor held a regular court for his tenants, both free and unfree, regulating rights in land and settling disputes according to local custom. For the unfree serfs, this was their only court for legal redress. In England, the manorial courts sometimes absorbed the local "hundred courts" over which the county sheriff theoretically presided. As a result, the jurisdiction of the manorial court varied according to the petitioners and the cases involved. Below are some 13th-century records of manorial courts held by the Abbey of Bec in England.

Source: Maitland, F. W., ed. *Select Pleas in Manorial and Other Seignorial Courts* (Publications of the Selden Society: London, 1889), 6–9, 11–13.

FOCUS QUESTIONS:

1. How was the lord's power demonstrated in this court?
2. What evidence is there for independence of thought and action among those who live on the lord's land?

PLEAS OF THE MANORS IN ENGLAND OF THE ABBEY OF BEC FOR THE HOKEDAY TERM, 1246

Bledlow [Buckinghamshire]. Saturday before Ascension Day.

1 The court has presented that Simon Combe has set up a fence on the lord's land. Therefore let it be abated.[1]

2 Simone Combe gives 18 d[2]. for leave to compromise with Simon Besmere. Pledges, John Sperling and John Harding.

3 A day is given to Alice of Standen at the next court to produce her charter and her heir.

4 John Sperling complains that Richard of Newmere on the Sunday next before S. Bartholomew's day last past with his cattle, horses and pigs wrongfully destroyed the corn on his [John's] land to his damage to the extent of one thrave of wheat, and to his dishonour to the extent of two shillings; and of this

---

1 Removed.
2 The abbreviations for coins were: d. = pence, s. = shilling, and l = pound. Twelve pence = 1 shilling and 20 shillings = 1 pound. The amount 6s.8d. was equal to 1 mark which was not a coin, but an amount of money. (For example: The old expression "2 bits" equals a quarter coin, but there was never coin minted that equaled one "bit") Three marks = 1 pound.

he produces suit. And Richard comes and defends all of it. Therefore let him go to the law six-handed.[3] His pledges, Simon Combe and Hugh Frith.

Swincombe [Oxfordshire]. Sunday before Ascension Day.

5 Richard Rastold [essoins himself][4] of the general summons by William Henry's son.

6 Hugh Pike and Robert his son are in mercy for wood of the lord thievishly carried away. The fine for each, 6s. 8 d. Pledges, Richard Mile and William Shepherd.

7 Peter Alexander's son in mercy for the same. Fine, 2 s. Pledge, Alexander his father.

8 Henry Mile in mercy for waste of the lord's corn. Pledges, Richard Mile and William Shepherd.

9 John Smith in mercy for not producing what he was pledge to produce. Pledges, Richard Etys and Hugh Wood. Fine, 12 d.

10 Roger Abovewood and William Shepherd in mercy for not producing what they were pledges to produce.... Fine, half a sextary of wine.

Tooting [Surrey]. Sunday After Ascension Day.

11 The court presented that the following had encroached on the lord's land, to wit,[5] William Cobbler, Maud Robin's widow (fined 12 d.), John Shepherd (fined 12 d.), Walter Reeve (fined 2 s.), William of Moreville (fined 12 d.), Hamo of Hageldon (fined 12 d.), Mabel Spendlove's widow (fined 6 d.). Therefore they are in mercy.

12 ... Roger Rede in mercy for detention of rent. Pledge, John of Stratham. Fine, 6 d.

13 William of Streatham is in mercy for not producing what he was pledge to produce. Fine, 12d.

Ruislip [Middlesex]. Tuesday after Ascension Day.

14 The court presents that Nicholas Brakespeare is not in a tithing[6] and holds

---

3 To "make his law" or "go to the law six-handed" means that he must bring five men of lawful reputation to swear with him that they believe he is a man who is telling the truth.
4 Presents a legal excuse for himself for not appearing in court when summoned to do so.
5 Namely.
6 All adult free males in England became a member of a "tithing" about the age 14. A tithing was a group of about ten men who were legally responsible for one another's actions. At the "Hundred" court, the local court like a township court, the sheriff would question the members of a tithing to report crimes and problems as well as locate people when they were needed in court.

land. Therefore let him be distrained.[7]

15 Breakers of the assize[8]: Alice Salvage's widow (fined 12 d.), Agnotta the Shepherd's mistress, Roger Canon (fined 6 d.), the wife of Richard Chayham, the widow of Peter Beyondgrove, the wife of Ralph Coke (fined 6 d.), Ailwin (fined 6 d.), John Shepherd (fined 6 d.), Geoffrey Carpenter, Roise the Miller's wife (fined 6 d.), William White, John Carpenter, John Bradif.

16 Roger Hamo's son gives 20 s. to have seisin[9] of the land which was his father's and to have an inquest of twelve as to a certain croft which Gilbert Bisuthe holds. Pledges, Gilbert Lamb, William John's son and Robert King.

17 Isabella Peter's widow is in mercy for a trespass which her son John had committed in the lord's wood. Fine, 18 d. Pledges, Gilbert Bisuthe and Richard Robin.

18 Richard Maleville is at his law against the lord [to prove] that he did not take from the lord's servants goods taken in distress to the damage and dishonour of his lord [to the extent of] 20 s. Pledges, Gilbert Bisuthe and Richard Hubert.

19 Hugh Tree in mercy for his beasts caught in the lord's garden. Pledges, Walter Hill and William Slipper. Fine, 6 d.

20 [The] twelve jurors say that Hugh Cross has right in the bank and hedge about which there was a dispute between him and William White. Therefore let him hold in peace and let William be distrained for his many trespasses. (Afterwards he made fine[10] for 12 s.) They say also that the hedge which is between the Widow Druet and William Slipper so far as the bank extends should be divided along the middle of the bank, so that the crest of the bank should be the boundary between them, for the crest was thrown up along the ancient boundary.

21 [The roll is torn in places for the next two entries]... son of Roger Clerk gives 20 s. to have seisin of the land which was his father's. Pledges, Gilbert...and Hugh Cross.

22 [Name missing] gives 13 s. 4d. to have seisin of the land which was his mother's beyond the wood. Pledges, William... and Robert Mareleward.

PLEAS OF THE MANORS OF THE ABBEY OF BEC FOR THE MARTINMAS TERM A.D. 1247 Weedon Beck [Northamptonshire]. Vigil of St. Michael

23 Richard le Boys of Aldeston has sworn fealty for the land which was his

---

7 "Distrained" means that some part of Nicholas' property will be taken into the custody of the court to motivate him to join a tithing like any law abiding landholder ought to.
8 "Breakers of the assize" sold ale or bread that did not meet the established standards of quality and price.
9 Lawful possession.
10 Made Payment.

father's and has found pledges for 4 s. as his relief, to wit, William Clerk of the same place, Godfrey Elder and Roger Smith.

24 Elias Deynte in full court resigned his land and William Deynte his son was put in seisin of it and swore fealty and found the same pledges for 5 s. as his relief. Afterwards he paid.

25 The township presents that they suspect Robert Dochy and William Tale because they made fine with the knights, [who formed the jury] before the justices [in eyre][11] when they were accused of larceny.

26 Breakers of the assize: William Paris, Richard Cappe, Maud widow of Robert Carter, Walter Carter, Roger Smith, Richard Guy's son, William Green, Gilbert Vicar's son, Guy Lawman.

27 William Green and Guy Lawman have gallons which are too small.

28 John Mercer will give three chickens yearly at Martinmas for having the lord's patronage and he is received into a tithing.

Wretham [Norfolk]. Friday after the feast of S. Michael

30 Gilbert Richard's son gives 5 s. for license to marry a wife. Pledge, Seaman. Term [for payment,] the Purification.

Tooting [Surrey]. Tuesday after the feast of S. Denis.

31 William Jordan in mercy for bad ploughing on the lord's land. Pledge, Arthur. Fine, 6 d.

32 John Shepherd in mercy for encroaching beyond the boundary of his land. Pledge, Walter Reeve. Fine, 6 d.

33 ... Elias of Streatham in mercy for default of service in the autumn. Fine, 6 d.

34 Bartholomew Chaloner who was at his law against Reginald Swain's son has made default in his law. Therefore he is in mercy and let him make satisfaction to Reginald for his damage and dishonour with 6 s. Pledges, William Cobbler and William Spendlove. Fine, 6 gallons.

35 Ralph of Morville gives a half-mark on the security of Jordan of Streatham and William Spendlove to have a jury to inquire whether he be the next heir to the land which William of Morville holds. And [the] twelve jurors come and say that he has no right in the said land but that William Scot has greater right in the said land than any one else. And the said William [Scot] gives 1 mark on the security of Hamo of Hageldon, William of Morville, Reginald Swain and Richard Leaware that he may have seisin of the said land after the death of

---

11 The Justices in eyre were the king's justices that went from county to county in England on a regular circuit.

William of Morville in case he [William Scot] shall survive him [William of Morville].

36 Afterwards came the said William Scot and by the lord's leave quit-claimed all the right that he had in the said land with its appurtenances to a certain William son of William of Morville, who gives 20 s. to have seisin of the said land and is put in seisin of it and has sworn fealty. Walter the serjeant is to receive the pledges.

Deverill [Wiltshire]. Saturday after the feast of S. Leonard.

37 ... Arnold Smith is in mercy for not producing the said William Scut whose pledge he was.

38 The parson of the church is in mercy for his cow caught in the lord's meadow. Pledges, Thomas Guner and William Coke.

39 From William Cobbe, William Coke and Walter Dogskin 2 s. for the ward of seven pigs belonging to Robert Gentil and for the damage that they did in the lord's corn. [Maitland believes that they were amerced for not guarding the lord's crops]

40 From Martin Shepherd 6 d. for the wound that he gave Pekin.

St, Thomas Aquinas
Faith and Reason in the *Summa Against the Gentiles*
1259–1264

Thomas Aquinas (1225–1274 CE) was a Catholic theologian and philosopher. Born to a noble family, Aquinas excelled in his studies in Italy and Paris. Though his family resisted his decision to enter the Dominican monastic order, Aquinas's writings marked the pinnacle of Medieval Scholastic thought. His most famous work, *Summa Theologica* (Summary of Theology), though unfinished, covered a range of topics—such as natural law and the nature and existence of God—and aimed to reconcile reason with faith, and the ideas of Aristotle with Christian Scriptures. Pope John XXII canonized Aquinas in 1323, and in the sixteenth century the Catholic Church declared Aquinas's ideas to be official doctrine.

Source: Fathers of the English Dominican Province, trans., Thomas Aquinas, *Summa Theologica* (New York Benziger Bros. 1947–48).

1. Would you describe Aquinas' Scholastic form of writing as "theoretical" or "applied"?

2. What is Aquinas's purpose in discussing natural law?

QUESTION #95: OF HUMAN LAW
Article 4:
Whether Isidore's division of human laws is appropriate?

Objection 1. It would seem that Isidore wrongly divided human statutes or human law (Etym. v, 4, seqq.). For under this law he includes the "law of nations," so called, because, as he says, "nearly all nations use it." But as he says, "natural law is that which is common to all nations." Therefore the law of nations is not contained under positive human law, but rather under natural law.

Objection 2. Further, those laws which have the same force, seem to differ not formally but only materially. But "statutes, decrees of the commonalty, senatorial decrees," and the like which he mentions (Etym. v, 9), all have the same force. Therefore they do not differ, except materially. But art takes no notice of such a distinction: since it may go on to infinity. Therefore this division of human laws is not appropriate.

Objection 3. Further, just as, in the state, there are princes, priests and soldiers, so are there other human offices. Therefore it seems that, as this division includes "military law," and "public law," referring to priests and magistrates; so also it should include other laws pertaining to other offices of the state.

Objection 4. Further, those things that are accidental should be passed over. But it is accidental to law that it be framed by this or that man. Therefore it is unreasonable to divide laws according to the names of lawgivers, so that one be called the "Cornelian" law, another the "Falcidian" law, etc.

On the contrary, The authority of Isidore (Objection 1) suffices.

I answer that, A thing can of itself be divided in respect of something contained in the notion of that thing. Thus a soul either rational or irrational is contained in the notion of animal: and therefore ani-mal is divided properly and of itself in respect of its being rational or irrational; but not in the point of its being white or black, which are entirely beside the notion of animal. Now, in the notion of human law, many things are contained, in respect of any of which human law can be divided properly and of itself. For in the first place it belongs to the notion of human law, to be derived from the law of nature, as explained above (2). In this respect positive law is divided into the "law of nations" and "civil law," according to the two ways in which something may be derived from the law of nature, as stated above (2). Because, to the law of nations belong those things which are derived from the law of nature, as conclusions from premises, e.g., just buyings and sellings, and the like, without which men cannot live together, which is a point of the law of nature, since man is by nature a social animal, as is proved in Polit. i, 2. But those things which are derived from the law of nature by way of particular determination, belong to the civil law, according as each state decides on what is best for itself.

Secondly, it belongs to the notion of human law, to be ordained to the common good of the state. In this respect human law may be divided according to the different kinds of men who work in a special way for the common good: e.g., priests, by praying to God for the people; princes, by governing the people; soldiers, by fighting for the safety of the people. Wherefore certain special kinds of law are adapted to these men.

Thirdly, it belongs to the notion of human law, to be framed by that one who governs the community of the state, as shown above (90, 3). In this respect, there are various human laws according to the various forms of government. Of these, according to the Philosopher (Polit. iii, 10) one is "monarchy," i.e., when the state is governed by one; and then we have "Royal Ordinances." Another form is "aristocracy," i.e., government by the best men or men of highest rank; and then we have the "Authoritative legal opinions" [Responsa Prudentum] and "Decrees of the Senate" [Senatus consulta]. Another form is "oligarchy," i.e., government by a few rich and powerful men; and then we have "Praetorian," also called "Honorary," law. Another form of government is that of the people, which is called "democracy," and there we have "Decrees of the commonalty" [Plebiscita]. There is also tyrannical government, which is altogether corrupt, which, therefore, has no corresponding law. Finally, there is a form of government made up of all these, and which is the best: and in this respect we have law sanctioned by the "Lords and Commons," as stated by Isidore (Etym. v, 4, seqq.).

Fourthly, it belongs to the notion of human law to direct human actions. In this respect, according to the various matters of which the law treats, there are various kinds of laws, which are sometimes named after their authors: thus we have the "Lex Julia" about adultery, the "Lex Cornelia" concerning assassins, and so on, differentiated in this way, not on account of the authors, but on account of the matters to which they refer.

Reply to Objection 1. The law of nations is indeed, in some way, natural to man, in so far as he is a reasonable being, because it is derived from the natural law by way of a conclusion that is not very remote from its premises. Wherefore men easily agreed thereto. Nevertheless it is distinct from the natural law, especially it is distinct from the natural law which is common to all animals.

The Replies to the other Objections are evident from what has been said.

Marco Polo, excerpt from *Travels*
c. 1300

One of the most famous medieval European travelers was the Italian merchant, Marco Polo (1254–1324 CE). He wrote a very detailed and accurate description of his travels to and around Asia that in many ways remains unsurpassed. His father and uncle had made an earlier trip through the Mongol lands, meeting Kublai Khan, the Mongol ruler of China, who gave them a lavish reception. Marco accompanied his uncle on the long second trip (1271–1295) in which Marco also met Kublai Khan. Marco remained in the khan's service for seventeen years as an administrator in many parts of China, before he and his uncle finally returned home with their accumulated wealth.

Source: Marco Polo, *Travels*, ed. by Henry Yule (London, 1870).

Focus Questions:

1. What are the dangers of the trip?
2. What might the "spirit voices" be?
3. Consider who and what makes up a caravan.

"When a man is riding through this desert by night and for some reason—falling asleep or anything else—he gets separated from his companions and wants to rejoin them, he hears spirit voices talking to him as if they were his companions, sometimes even calling him by name. Often these voices lure him away from the path and he never finds it again, and many travelers have got lost and died because of this. Sometimes in the night travelers hear a noise like the clatter of a great company of riders away from the road; if they believe that these are some of their own company and head for the noise, they find themselves in deep trouble when daylight comes and they realize their mistake. There were some who, in crossing the desert, have seen a host of men coming towards them and, suspecting that they were robbers, returning, they have gone hopelessly astray...Even by daylight men hear these spirit voices, and often you fancy you are listening to the strains of many instruments, especially drums, and the clash of arms. For this reason bands of travelers make a point of keeping very close together. Before they go to sleep they set up a sign pointing in the direction in which they have to travel, and round the necks of all their beasts they fasten little bells, so that by listening to the sound they may prevent them from straying off the path."

Guilds: Regulating the Craft
1347

Medieval tradesmen, craftsmen, and merchants organized themselves into "guilds", associations that maintained a monopoly, guaranteed the quality of the group's production, and regulated prices for its products. The following articles, passed in 1347, regulated the "Spurriers" (spur-makers) in London, and they illustrate the guild's principles and standards as they related to this craft.

Source: Articles of the Spurriers" in Henry Thomas Riley, ed., *Memorials of London and London Life, A.D. 12761419* (London: Longmans, Green, and Co., 1868), pp. 226–28, 239–40.

FOCUS QUESTIONS:

1. How did the guild attempt to create a monopoly for its members and to protect the industry as a whole?
2. How did they ensure the quality of the ultimate product of their labor?

ARTICLES OF THE LONDON SPURRIERS, 1347

Be it remembered, that on Tuesday, the morrow of St. Peter's Chains [1 August], in the 19th year of the reign of King Edward the Third etc., the Articles underwritten were read before John Hamond, Mayor, Roger de Depham, Recorder, and the other Aldermen; and seeing that the same were deemed befitting, they were accepted and enrolled, in these words:

"In the first place,—that no one of the trade of Spurriers shall work longer than from the beginning of the day until curfew rung out at the Church of St. Sepulchre, without Neugate; by reason that no man can work so neatly by night as by day.

And many persons of the said trade, who compass how to practise deception in their work, desire to work by night rather than by day: and then they introduce false iron, and iron that has been cracked, for tin, and also, they put gilt on false copper, and cracked.

And further, many of the said trade are wandering about all day, without working at all at their trade; and then, when they have become drunk and frantic, they take to their work, to the annoyance of the sick and of all their neighbourhood, as well as by reason of the broils that arise between them and the strange folks who are dwelling among them.

And then they blow up their fires so vigorously, that their forges begin all at once to blaze; to the great peril of themselves and of all the neighbourhood around. And then too, all the neighbours are much in dread of the sparks, which so vigorously issue forth in all directions from the mouths of the chimneys in their forges.

By reason whereof, it seems unto them that working by night [should be put an end to,] in order such false work and such perils to avoid; and therefore, the Mayor and Aldermen do will, by assent of the good folks of the said trade, and for the common profit, that from henceforth such time for working, and such false work made in the trade, shall be forbidden.

And if any person shall be found in the said trade to do to the contrary hereof, let him be amerced, the first time in 40 d [pence]., one half thereof to go to the use of the Chamber of the Guildhall of London, and the other half to the use of the said trade; the second time, in half a mark, and the third time, in 10 s. [shillings], to the use of the same Chamber and trade; and the fourth time, let him forswear the trade for ever.

"Also,—that no one of the said trade shall hang his spurs out on Sunday, or on other days that are Double Feasts; but only a sign indicating his business: and such spurs as they shall so sell, they are to show and sell within their shops, without exposing them without, or opening the doors or windows of their shops, on the pain aforesaid.

"Also,—that no one of the said trade shall keep a house or shop to carry on his business, unless he is free of the City; and that no one shall cause to be sold, or exposed for sale, any manner of old spurs for new ones; or shall garnish them, or change them for new ones.

"Also,—that no one of the said trade shall take an apprentice for a less term than seven years; and such apprentice shall be enrolled, according to the usages of the said city."Also,—that if any one of the said trade, who is not a freeman, shall take an apprentice for a term of years, he shall be amerced, as aforesaid. "Also,—that no one of the said trade shall receive the apprentice, serving-man, or journeyman, of another in the same trade, during the term agreed upon between his master and him; on the pain aforesaid.

"Also,—that no alien of another country, or foreigner of this country, shall follow or use the said trade, unless he is enfranchised before the Mayor, Aldermen, and Chamberlain; and that, by witness and surety of the good folks of the said trade, who will undertake for him as to his loyalty and his good behaviour.

"Also,—that no one of the said trade shall work on Saturdays, after None has been rung out in the City; and not from that hour until the Monday morning following."

"For the Honor of the Guild": Social and Civic Responsibilities 1421–1425

Each of these documents pertains to a different guild, functioning in Florence at roughly the same period. The first lists the articles regulating the local wine merchants, the second is a petition from the silk guild to the Florentine government, and the last is a decree passed by the *Lana* (Wool) guild. Each of these three sources reveals another dimension of the guilds, extending beyond the simple regulation of their industry.

Source: *The Society of Renaissance Florence: A Documentary Study*, ed.Gene Brucker, (Harper and Row, Inc., 1972), 90–94.

Focus Questions:

1. What did the members of these guilds think of their civic obligations—and prestige—within the city as a whole?
2. How did rivalry among the guilds express itself in Florentine society?

The Corporation of Wine Merchants

[Chapter 18] It is also decreed and ordained that the consuls [of the guild] are required, by their oath, to force all of the wine sellers... who sell at retail in the city and *contado* of Florence to swear allegiance to this guild and for this guild. And for this purpose they must make a monthly search through the city and the suburbs of Florence, and if they find anyone who is not matriculated in the guild, they must require him to swear allegiance.... And whoever, as has been said, is engaged in this trade, even though he is not... matriculated in the guild... is considered to be a member of the guild.... And each newly matriculated wine seller... must pay... 5 lire to the guild treasurer... as his matriculation fee.... If, however, he is a father or son of a guild member, then he is not required to pay anything.

[Chapter 20] The consuls, treasurer, and notary of the guild are required to assemble together wherever they wish... to render justice to whoever demands it of the men of this guild, against any and all those... who sell wine at retail... in the city, *contado*, and district of Florence.

... [They must] hear, take cognizance of, make decisions, and act on everything which pertains to their office, and accept every appeal which is brought before them by whosoever has any claim upon any member of the guild.... They must record [these acts] in their protocols and render justice with good faith and without fraud on one day of each week.

With respect to these disputes, the consuls are required to proceed in the following manner. If any dispute or quarrel is brought against any member of the guild... and it involves a sum of 3 Florentine lire di piccolo or less, this dispute is to be decided summarily by the consuls, after the parties have sworn an oath, in favor of whoever appears to be more honest and of better reputation.... If the dispute involves 60 soldi or more, the consuls, after receiving the complaint, are required to demand that... the defendant appear to reply to the complaint.... [Witnesses are to be called and interrogated in such major disputes, and the consuls must announce their judgment within one month.]

[Chapter 21] It is decreed and ordained that each wine-seller shall come to the assembly of the guild as often as he is summoned by the consuls.... The consuls are required to levy a fine of 10 soldi... against whoever violates this [rule], and the same penalty is to be incurred by anyone who fails to respond to the consuls' order to come to the guild's offering in a church.... And if necessity requires that the members of the guild assemble under their banner to stand guard, or to go on a march, by day or night, in the city and *contado* of Florence or elsewhere, every member of the guild is required to appear in person, with or without arms as ordered, with their standard-bearer and under their banner, or pay a fine of 10 lire.

[Chapter 35] For the honor of the guild and of the members of the guild, it is decreed and ordained that whenever any member of the guild dies, all guild members in the city and suburbs who are summoned by the messenger of the guild... are required to go to the service for the dead man, and to stay there until he is buried....

And the consuls are required to send the guild messenger, requesting and inviting the members of the guild to participate in the obsequies for the dead.

A CHARITABLE ENTERPRISE, 1421

... This petition is presented with all due reverence to you, lord priors, on behalf of your devoted sons of the guild of Por Santa Maria [the silk guild] and the merchants and guildsmen of that association. It is well known to all of the people of Florence that this guild has sought, through pious acts, to conserve... and also to promote your republic and this guild. It has begun to construct a most beautiful edifice in the city of Florence and in the parish of S. Michele Visdomini, next to the piazza called the "Frati de' Servi." [This building is] a hospital called S.Maria degli Innocenti, in which shall be received those who, against natural law, have been deserted by their fathers or their mothers, that is, infants, who in the vernacular are called *gittatelli* [literally, castaways; foundlings]. Without the help and favor of your benign lordships, it will not be possible to transform this laudable objective into reality nor after it has been achieved, to preserve and conserve it.

And since [we] realized that your lordships and all of the people are, in the highest degree, committed to works of charity, [we have] decided to have recourse to your clemency, and to request, most devotedly, all of the things which are described below. So on behalf of the above-mentioned guild, you are humbly petitioned... to enact a law that this guild of Por Santa Maria and its members and guildsmen-as founders, originators, and principals of this hospital-are understood in perpetuity to be... the sole patrons, defenders, protectors, and supporters of this hospital as representatives of, and in the name of, the *popolo* and Commune of Florence.

Item, the consuls of the guild... have authority to choose supervisors and governors of the hospital and of the children and servants.

GUILD RIVALRY, 1425

The above-mentioned consuls, assembled together in the palace of the [Lana]1 guild in sufficient numbers and in the accustomed manner for the exercise of their office... have diligently considered the law approved by the captains of the society of the blessed Virgin Mary of Orsanmichele. This law decreed, in effect, that for the ornamentation of that oratory, each of the twenty-one guilds of the city of Florence... in a place assigned to each of them by the captains of the society, should construct... a tabernacle, properly and carefully decorated, for the honor of the city and the beautification of the oratory. The consuls have considered that all of the guilds have finished their tabernacles, and that those constructed by the Calimala and Cambio guilds, and by other guilds, surpass in beauty and ornamentation that of the Lana guild. So it may truly be said that this does not redound to the honor of the Lana guild, particularly when one considers the magnificence of that guild which has always sought to be the master and the superior of the other guilds.

For the splendor and honor of the guild, the lord consuls desire to provide a remedy for this.... They decree that through the month of August, the existing lord consuls and their successors in office, by authority of the present provision, are to construct, fabricate, and remake a tabernacle and a statue of the blessed Stephen, protomartyr, protector and defender of the renowned Lana guild, in his honor and in reverence to God. They are to do this by whatever ways and means they choose, which will most honorably contribute to the splendor of the guild, so that this tabernacle will exceed, or at least equal, in beauty and decoration the more beautiful ones. In the construction of this tabernacle and statue, the lord consuls... may spend... up to 1,000 florins. And during this time, the lord consuls may commission that statue and tabernacle to the person or persons, and for that price or prices, and with whatever agreement and time or times which seem to them to be most useful for the guild.

The Ideal Merchant's Wife
c. 1450

Leon Battista Alberti (1404-1472) was the epitome of the Renaissance man in his native Florence. An architect, theoretician of art, mathematician, philosopher, and writer, Alberti also constructed a humorous dialogue between two Florentine merchants. In this scene, an old but very rich man gloats over the superb choice he has made in a wife. Alberti's audiences would have seen where this story was tending; May-December marriages like these were always bound to end in disaster for the older partner, blinded by love to his wife's true nature. However, the account is good evidence for what (at least in Alberti's opinion) a man of this class would have been seeking in his marriage.

Source: *Not in God's Image: Women in History from the Greeks to the Victorian,* eds. Julia O'Faolain, and Lauro Martines, (New York: Harper and Row, 1973), pp. 187–89.

FOCUS QUESTIONS:

1. Can this relationship be compared with that between Euphiletus and his wife?

2. How does this man express confidence in his wife's abilities?

3. Is there any element of fear in his description of her virtues?

After my wife had been settled in my house a few days, and after her first pangs of longing for her mother and family had begun to fade, I took her by the hand and showed her around the whole house. I explained that the loft was the place for grain and that the stores of wine and wood were kept in the cellar. I showed her where things needed for the table were kept, and so on, through the whole house. At the end there were no household goods of which my wife had not learned both the place and the purpose. Then we returned to my room, and, having locked the door, I showed her my treasures, silver, tapestry, garments, jewels, and where each thing had its place....

Only my books and records and those of my ancestors did I determine to keep well sealed.... These my wife not only could not read, she could not even lay hands on them. I kept my records at all times... locked up and arranged in order in my study, almost like sacred and religious objects. I never gave my wife permission to enter that place, with me or alone. I also ordered her, if she ever came across any writing of mine, to give it over to my keeping at once. To take away any taste she might have for looking at my notes or prying into my private affairs, I often used to express my disapproval of bold and forward females who try too hard to know about things outside the house and about the concerns of their husband and of men in general....

[Husbands] who take counsel with their wives... are madmen if they think true prudence or good counsel lies in the female brain.... For this very reason I have always tried carefully not to let any secret of mine be known to a woman. I did not doubt that my wife was most loving, and more discreet and modest in her ways than any, but I still considered it safer to have her unable, and not merely unwilling, to harm me.... Furthermore, I made it a rule never to speak with her of anything but household matters or questions of conduct, or of the children. Of these matters I spoke a good deal to her....

When my wife had seen and understood the place of everything in the house, I said to her, 'My dear wife... you have seen our treasures now, and thanks be to God they are such that we ought to be contented with them. If we know how to preserve them, these things will serve you and me and our children. It is up to you, therefore, my dear wife, to keep no less careful watch over them than I.'

... She said she would be happy to do conscientiously whatever she knew how to do and had the skill to do, hoping it might please me. To this I said, 'Dear wife, listen to me. I shall be most pleased if you do just three things: first, my wife, see that you never want another man to share this bed but me. You understand.' She blushed and cast down her eyes. Still I repeated that she should never receive anyone into that room but myself. That was the first point. The second, I said, was that she should take care of the household, preside over it with modesty, serenity, tranquillity, and peace. That was the second point. The third thing, I said, was that she should see that nothing went wrong in the house.

... I could not describe to you how reverently she replied to me. She said her mother had taught her only how to spin and sew, and how to be virtuous and obedient. Now she would gladly learn from me how to rule the family and whatever I might wish to teach her.

Then she and I knelt down and prayed to God to give us the power to make good use of those possessions which he, in his mercy and kindness, had allowed us to enjoy. We also prayed... that he might grant us the grace to live together in peace and harmony for many happy years, and with many male children, and that he might grant to me riches, friendship, and honor, and to her, integrity, purity, and the character of a perfect mistress of the household. Then, when we had stood up, I said to her: 'My dear wife, to have prayed God for these things is not enough.... I shall seek with all my powers to gain what we have asked of God. You, too, must set your whole will, all your mind, and all your modesty to work to make yourself a person whom God has heard.... You should realize that in this regard nothing is so important for yourself, so acceptable to God, so pleasing to me, and precious in the sight of your children as your chastity. The woman's character is the jewel of her family; the mother's purity has always been a part of the dowry she passes on to her daughters; her purity has always far outweighed her beauty.... Shun every sort of dishonor, my dear wife. Use every means to appear to all people as a highly respectable woman. To seem less would be to offend God, me, our children, and yourself.'

.... Never, at any moment, did I choose to show in word or action even the least bit of self-surrender in front of my wife. I did not imagine for a moment that I could hope to win obedience from one to whom I had confessed myself a slave. Always, therefore, I showed myself virile and a real man.

CHAPTER 8

The Late Middle Ages – Crisis and Recovery

How They Died:
Coroner's Rolls from the 14ᵗʰ Century
1322–1337

The Coroner's Office was established in London in 1194, as part of the general legal reform of the English kingdom by Henry II. This official was charged with investigating episodes of sudden or unnatural death, and the goal was to satisfy the community at large that the death could be explained. Thereby, the community's psychological needs could be met—but it was also the Coroner's duty to determine whether criminal charges should be brought or financial compensation be assessed. The documents below are from a remarkable series of Coroners' Reports in the 1320s and 1330s. Within these odd (and often tragic) little stories are nuggets that can be used by social historians attempting to reconstruct life in the Late Medieval period.

Source: Calendar of Coroners Rolls of the City of London,1300–1378. ed. R. R. Sharpe, London: Richard Clay and Sons, 1913), pp. 56–57, 63–69, 86–87, 127, 183. Language has been modernized by the editors.

FOCUS QUESTIONS:

1. What do these documents tell us about the living conditions for various classes in London in this period?
2. What do the homicide cases suggest about criminality in this era?

1. ON THE DEATH OF ROBERT. SON OF JOHH de ST. BOTULPH

Saturday before the Feast of St. Margaret [20 July] in the year [16 Edward II, A.D. 1322], information was given to the... Coroner and Sheriffs that a certain Robert, son of John de St. Botulph, a boy seven years old, lay dead of a death other than his rightful death in a certain shop which the said Robert held of

Richard de Wirhale in the parish of St. Michael de Paternosterchurch in the Ward of Vintry. Thereupon the Coroner and Sheriffs proceeded there and, having summoned good men of that Ward and of the three nearest Wards, namely Douuegate, Queenhithe and Cordewanerstreet, they diligently inquired how it happened. The jurors say that when on the Sunday next before the Feast of St. Dunstan [19 May], [Robert son of] John, Richard son of John de Chesthunt, and two other boys, names unknown, were playing on certain pieces of timber in a lane called "Kyrounelane" in the Ward of Vintry, a certain piece fell on [Robert] and broke his right leg. In the course of time Johanna, his mother, arrived, and rolled the timber off him, and carried him to a shop where he lingered until Friday... when he died at the hour of Prime of the broken leg and of no other felony, nor do they suspect anyone of the death, but only the accident and the fracture. Being asked who were present when it happened, they say the aforesaid Robert, Richard son of John de Chesthunt and two boys whose names they know not and no others.

Four neighbors attached, namely:

Richard Daske, by Peter Cosyn and Roger le Roper.

Anketin de Gisors, by Robert de Wynton and Andrew de Gloucester.

Thomas le Roper, by Richard de Colyngstoke and Thomas atte March.

John Amys, by John de Shirbourne and John de Lincoln.

2. ON THE DEATH OF NICHOLAS. SERVANT TO SIMON de KNOTTYNGLEY

On Monday in Pentecost week the year [A.D. 1324], it happened that Nicholas, the servant of Simon de Knottyngley, lay killed before the gate of the house of William de Pomfreit in the high street in the parish of St. Botulph de Bisshopsgate.... On hearing this, the... Coroner and Sheriffs proceeded there, and having summoned good men of that Ward and of the three nearest Wards..., they diligently inquired how it happened. The jurors say that on that Monday, at break of day, William de la March, the late palfrey-man [a type of groom] of Henry de Percy, Thomas the servant of Henry de Percy's cook, John the servant to Henry Krok, who was Henry's esquire, assaulted, beat and wounded Nicholas in the house held by Alice de Witteney, a courtesan, whose landlord was John de Assheby.... William de la March struck Nicholas with a knife called an "Irishknife" under the right breast and penetrating to the belly, inflicting a wound an inch long and in depth half through the body. [Nicholas] thus wounded went from there to the place where he was found dead, where he died at daybreak of the same day. Being asked what became of the said William, Thomas and John, the jurors say that they immediately fled, but where they went or who received them they know not, nor do they suspect any one except those three. Being asked as to their goods and chattels, the jurors say that they had none, so far as could be ascertained. Being asked who first found the corpse, they say it was Thomas, son of John le Marshall, who raised the cry so that the country came. The corpse was viewed on which the wound appeared. [Order] to the Sheriff to attach the said William, Thomas and John as soon as they be found in their bailiwick.

Afterwards the William de la March was captured by Adam de Salisbury, the Sheriff and committed to Newgate [prison]. William has a surcoat which is confiscated [because of] his flight, worth two shillings, for which Adam de Salisbury the Sheriff [is responsible].

Four neighbors attached, namely:

John Assheby, by Thomas Starling and Walter de Stanes.

Walter de Bedefunte, by Walter de Northampton and John le Barber.

William de Pomfreit, by William de Chalke and Roger Swetyng.

Adam le Fuitz Robert, by Eustace le Hattere and Thomas de Borham.

3. ON THE DEATH OF THOMAS le POUNTAGER

On Saturday the Feast of St. Laurence [10 Aug.] the year [A.D. 1325], it happened that a certain Thomas, son of John le Pountager, lay drowned in the water of the Thames before the wharf of Richard Dorking in the parish of St. Martin, in the Ward of Vintry. On hearing this, the Coroner and Sheriffs proceeded there, and having summoned good men of that Ward and of the three nearest Wards... they diligently inquired how it happened. The jurors say that when on the preceding Friday, at dusk, Thomas had placed himself on the quay of Edward le Blount to bathe in the Thames, he was accidentally drowned, no one being present; that he remained in the water until Saturday, when at the third hour John Fleg a boatman discovered his corpse and raised the cry so that the country came. The corpse viewed on which no wound or bruise appeared.

The above John Fleg, the finder of the body, attached by Robert de Lenne and Robert de Taunton. Four neighbors attached [their names are listed in the report].

4. ON THE DEATH OF JOHANNA, DAUGHTER OF BERNARD OF IRLAUNDE

Friday after the Feast of St. Dunstan [19 May] the year [A.D. 1322], it happened that Johanna daughter of Bernard de Irlaunde, a child one month old, lay dead of a death other than her rightful death, in a shop held by the said Bernard... in the parish of St. Michael, in the Ward of Queenhithe. On hearing this, the Coroner and Sheriffs proceeded there, and having summoned good men of that Ward and of the three nearest Wards..., they diligently inquired how it happened. The jurors say that when on the preceding Thursday, before the hour of Vespers,

Johanna was lying in her cradle alone, the shop door being open there entered a certain sow which mortally bit the right side of the head of Johanna. At length there came Margaret, … Johanna's mother, and raised the cry and snatched up Johanna and kept her alive until midnight Friday when she died of the said bite and of no other felony. Being asked who were present, [the jurors] say, "No one except Margaret," nor do they suspect [any other cause] except the bite . the corpse of the said Johanna viewed on which no [other?] hurt appeared [sic]. The sow appraised by the jurors at 13 d. for which Richard Costantin, the Sheriff; [is responsible]. The above Margaret who found the body attached by John de Bedford and Andrew de Gloucester. Four neighbors attached [their names are listed in the report].

5. ON THE DEATH OF MATILDA CAMBERSTER AND MARGERY HER DAUGHTER

Friday after the Feast of St. Ambrose [4 April, 1337], information given to the Coroner and Sheriffs, that Matilda la Cambester and Margery her daughter aged one mouth, lay dead of a death other than their rightful death in a shop in the rent of the Prior of Tortyton in the parish of St Swythin in the Ward of Walbrok. Thereupon they proceeded there, and having summoned good men of that Ward, they diligently inquired how it happened. The jurors… say that on the preceding Thursday, after the hour of curfew when Matilda and Margery lay asleep in the shop a lighted candle which Matilda had negligently left on the wall, fell down among some straw and set fire to the shop so that the said Matilda and Margery were suffocated and burnt before the neighbors knew anything about it. The bodies viewed, &c. Four neighbors attached [their names are listed in the report].

6. ON THE DEATH OF LUCY FAUKES

On Monday before the Feast of St. Michael [29 Sept., 1322], it happened that a certain Lucy Faukes lay dead of a death other than her rightful death in a certain shop which Richard le Sherman held of John Priour, senior, in the parish of St. Olave in the Ward of Alegate. On hearing this, the Coroner and Sheriffs proceeded thither, and having summoned good men of that Ward and of the three nearest Wards, … they diligently inquired how it happened. The jurors say that on Sunday before the Feast of St. Matthew [2 Sept., 1322], about the hour of curfew, Lucy came to the shop in order to pass the night there with… Richard le Sherman and Cristina his wife, as she oftentimes was accustomed, and because Lucy was clad in good clothes, Richard and Cristina began to quarrel with her in order to obtain a reason for killing her for her clothes. At length Robert took up a staff called 'Balstaf;' and with the force and assistance of Cristina, struck her on the top of the head, and mortally broke and crushed the whole of her head, so that she died at once. Richard and Cristina stripped Lucy of her clothes, and immediately fled, but where they went or who received them, [the jurors] do not know. Being asked who were present when this happened, they say, "No one except the said Richard, Cristina and Lucy." Nor do they suspect anyone of the death except Richard and Cristina. Being asked about the goods and chattels of Richard and Cristina, the jurors say that they had nothing except what they took away with them. Being asked who found the dead Lucy's dead body, they say a certain Giles le Portor who raised the cry so that the country came. Order to the Sheriffs to attach the said Richard and Cristina when found in their bailiwick.

... Four neighbors attached [their names are listed in the report].

Flagellants Attempt to Ward Off the Black Death
1349

Although "flagellation" (beating oneself with a whip) had been practiced as a means of spiritual discipline by monks long before, it did not emerge as a public group activity until the mid-13th-century. While Europe was besieged by the Black Death (1347-1350), the Brotherhood of Flagellants (which also included women) resorted to ever more spectacular public flagellation. The movement probably originated in Eastern Europe and took root most deeply in German-speaking areas. As we see from the following report of Robert of Avesbury, however, they had also crossed into England.

Source: *Medieval England as Viewed by Contemporaries* ,*ed*. W. O. Hassall, (New York: Torch-books,1965, © 1957), pp. 157–58.

Focus Questions:

1. What did the Flagellants think was the source and cause of the Plague?

2. How might their behavior have made matters worse for the English?

About Michaelmas 1349 over six hundred men came to London from Flanders, mostly of Zeeland and Holland origin. Sometimes at St. Paul's and sometimes at other points in the city they made two daily public appearances wearing cloths from the thighs to the ankles, but otherwise stripped bare. Each wore a cap marked with a red cross in front and behind. Each had in his right hand a scourge with three tails. Each tail had a knot and through the middle of it there were sometimes sharp nails fixed. They marched naked in a file one behind the other and whipped themselves with these scourges on their naked and bleeding bodies. Four of them would chant in their native tongue and another four would chant in response like a litany. Thrice they would all cast themselves on the ground in this sort of procession, stretching out their hands like the arms of a cross. The singing would go on and, the one who was in the rear of those thus prostrate acting first, each of them in turn would step over the others and give one stroke with his scourge to the man lying under him. This went on from the first to the last until each of them had observed the ritual to the full tale of those on the ground. Then each put on his customary garments and always wearing their caps and carrying their whips in their hands they retired to their lodgings. It is said that every night they performed the same penance.

The Lollard Conclusions
1394

The followers of Wycliffe were called "Lollards", perhaps a derivation from the Dutch word "Lollaerd", meaning "mumbler", "grumbler", or similar. These Lollards translated the Latin Bible into English, and circulated a list of demands for Church reform in 1394. However, in 1401, a statute was passed entitled *"De heretico comburendo"* ("On the Necessity of Burning the Heretic"), and Lollards were rounded up and simultaneously hanged and burned. A group of them led an unsuccessful revolt in London in 1414 called "Oldcastle's Rebellion", and many of their ideas would re-emerge in the Protestant Reformation.

Source: *Documents of the Christian Church,* ed. Henry Bettenson (New York: Oxford University Press, 1970), 175–179.

Focus Questions:

1. Compare this document with the Unam Sanctam of Boniface VIII.
2. Why are the Lollards so concerned with "idolatry"? In what form does it appear, in their opinion?
3. Why are these demands couched in such extreme language? Would this have been effective in the 15th century?

1. That when the Church of England began to go mad after temporalities, like its great step-mother the Roman Church, and churches were authorized by appropriation in divers places, faith, hope, and charity began to flee from our Church, because pride, with its doleful progeny of moral sins, claimed this under title of truth. This conclusion is general, and proved by experience, custom, and manner or fashion, as you shall afterwards hear.

2. That our usual priesthood which began in Rome, pretended to be of power more lofty than the angels, is not that priesthood which Christ ordained for His apostles. This conclusion is proved because the Roman priesthood is bestowed with signs, rites, and pontifical blessings, of small virtue, nowhere exemplified in Holy Scripture, because the bishop's ordinal and the New

Testament scarcely agree, and we cannot see that the Holy Spirit, by reason of any such signs, confers the gift, for He and all His excellent gifts cannot consist in any one with mortal sin. A corollary to this is that it is a grievous play for wise men to see bishops trifle with the Holy Spirit in the bestowal for orders, because they give the tonsure in outward appearance in the place of white hearts[1]; and this is the unrestrained introduction of antichrist into the Church to give colour to idleness.

3. That the law of continence enjoined on priests, which was first ordained to the prejudice of women, brings sodomy into all the Holy Church, but we excuse ourselves by the Bible because the decree says that we should not mention it, though suspected. Reason and experience prove this conclusion: reason, because the good living of ecclesiastics must have a natural outlet or worse; experience, because the secret proof of such men is that they find delight in women, and when thou hast proved such a man mark him well, because he is one of them. A corollary to this is that private religions and the originators or beginning of this sin would be specially worthy of being checked, but God of His power with regard to secret sin sends open vengeance in His Church.

4. That the pretended miracle of the sacrament of bread drives all men, but a few, to idolatry, because they think that the Body of Christ which is never away from heaven could by power of the priest's word be enclosed essentially in a little bread which they show the people; but God grant that they might be willing to believe what the evangelical doctor[1] says in his Trialogus (iv. 7), that the bread of the altar is habitually the Body of Christ, for we take it that in this way any faithful man and woman can by God's law perform the sacrament of that bread without any such miracle. A final corollary is that although the Body of Christ has been granted eternal joy, the service of Corpus Christi, instituted by Brother Thomas [Aquinas], is not true but is fictitious and full of false miracles. It is no wonder; because Brother Thomas, at that time holding with the pope, would have been willing to perform a miracle with a hen's egg; and we know well that any falsehood openly preached turns to the disgrace of Him who is always true and without any defect.

5. That exorcisms and blessings performed over wine, bread, water and oil, salt, wax, and incense, the stones of the altar, and church walls, over clothing, mitre, cross, and pilgrims' staves, are the genuine performance of necromancy rather than of sacred theology. This conclusion is proved as follows, because by such exorcisms creatures are honoured as being of higher virtue than they are in their own nature, and we do not see any change in any creature which is so exorcized, save by false faith which is the principal characteristic of the Devil's art. A corollary: that if the book of exorcising holy water, read in church, were entirely trustworthy we think truly that the holy water

1 Alborum cervorum= 'white harts'! 1 I.e. Wycliffe, who in the Trialogus('Three-cornered Discussion'—between Truth, Falsehood, and Prudence) expounded his views on the Eucharist.

used in church would be the best medicine for all kinds of illnesses—sores, for instance; whereas we experience the contrary day by day.

6. That king and bishop in one person, prelate and judge in temporal causes, curate and officer in secular office, puts any kingdom beyond good rule. This conclusion is clearly proved because the temporal and spiritual are two halves of the entire Holy Church. And so he who has applied himself to one should not meddle with the other, for no one can serve two masters. It seems that hermaphrodite or ambidexter would be good names for such men of double estate. A corollary is that we, the procurators of God in this behalf, do petition before Parliament that all curates, as well superior as inferior, be fully excused and should occupy themselves with their own charge and no other.

7. That special prayers for the souls of the dead offered in our Church, preferring one before another in name, are a false foundation of alms, and for that reason all houses of alms in England have been wrongly founded. This conclusion is proved by two reasons: the one is that meritorious prayer, and of any effect, ought to be a work proceeding from deep charity, and perfect charity leaves out no one, for 'Thou shalt love thy neighbour as thyself.' And so it is clear to us that the gift of temporal good bestowed on the priesthood and houses of alms is a special incentive to private prayer which is not far from simony. For another reason is that special prayer made for men condemned is very displeasing to God. And although it be doubtful, it is probable to faithful Christian people that founders of a house of alms have for their poisonous endowment passed over for the most part to the broad road. The corollary is: effectual prayer springing from perfect love would in general embrace all whom God would have saved, and would do away with that well-worn way or merchandise in special prayers made for the possessionary mendicants and other hired priests, who are a people of great burden to the whole realm, kept in idleness: for it has been proved in one book, which the king had, that a hundred houses of alms would suffice in all the realm, and from this would rather accrue possible profit to the temporal estate.

8. That pilgrimages, prayers, and offerings made to blind crosses or roods, and to deaf images of wood or stone, are pretty well akin to idolatry and far from alms, and although these be forbidden and imaginary, a book of error to the lay folk, still the customary image of the Trinity is specially abominable. This conclusion God clearly proves, bidding alms to be done to the needy man because they are the image of God, and more like than wood or stone; for God did not say, 'let us make wood or stone in our likeness and image,' but man; because the supreme honour which clerks call latria appertains to the Godhead only; and the lower honour which clerks call dulia appertains to man and angel and to no inferior creature. A corollary is that the service of the cross, performed twice in any year in our church, is full of idolatry, for if that should, so might the nails and lance be so highly honoured; then would the

lips of Judas be relics indeed if any were able to possess them. But we ask you, pilgrim, to tell us when you offer to the bones of saints placed in a shrine in any spot, whether you relieve the saint who is in joy, or that almshouse which is so well endowed and for which men have been canonized, God knows how. And to speak more plainly, a faithful Christian supposes that the wounds of that noble man, whom men call St Thomas, were not a case of martyrdom.

9. That auricular confession which is said to be so necessary to the salvation of a man, with its pretended power of absolution, exalts the arrogance of priests and gives them opportunity of other secret colloquies which we will not speak of; for both lords and ladies attest that, for fear of their confessors, they dare not speak the truth. And at the time of confession there is a ready occasion for assignation, that is for 'wooing,' and other secret understandings leading to mortal sins. They themselves say that they are God's representatives to judge of every sin, to pardon and cleanse whomsoever they please. They say that they have the keys of heaven and of hell, and can excommunicate and bless, bind and loose, at their will, so much so that for a drink, or twelve pence, they will sell the blessing of heaven with charter and close warrant sealed with the common seal. This conclusion is so notorious that it needs not any proof. It is a corollary that the pope of Rome, who has given himself out as treasurer of the whole Church, having in charge that worthy jewel of Christ's passion together with the merits of all saints in heaven, whereby he grants pretended indulgence from penalty and guilt, is a treasurer almost devoid of charity, in that he can set free all that are prisoners in hell at his will, and cause that they should never come to that place. But in this any Christian can well see there is much secret falsehood hidden away in our Church.

10. That manslaughter in war, or by pretended law of justice for a temporal cause, without spiritual revelation, is expressly contrary to the New Testament, which indeed is the law of grace and full of mercies. This conclusion is openly proved by the examples of Christ's preaching here on earth, for he specially taught a man to love his enemies, and to show them pity, and not to slay them. The reason is this, that for the most part, when men fight, after the first blow, charity is broken. And whoever dies without charity goes the straight road to hell. And beyond this we know well that no clergyman can by Scripture or lawful reason remit the punishment of death for one mortal sin and not for another; but the law of mercy, which is the New Testament, prohibits all manner of manslaughter, for in the Gospel: 'It was said unto them of old time, Thou shalt not kill.' The corollary is that it is indeed robbery of poor folk when lords get indulgences from punishment and guilt for those who aid their army to kill a Christian people in distant lands for temporal gain, just as we too have seen soldiers who run into heathendom to get them a name for the slaughter of men; much more do they deserve ill thanks from the King of

Peace, for by our humility and patience was the faith multiplied, and Christ Jesus hates and threatens men who fight and kill, when He says: 'He who smites with the sword shall perish by the sword.'

11. That the vow of continence made in our Church by women who are frail and imperfect in nature, is the cause of bringing in the gravest horrible sins possible to human nature, because, although the killing of abortive children before they are baptized and the destruction of nature by drugs are vile sins, yet connection with themselves or brute beasts of any creature not having fife surpasses them in foulness to such an extent as that they should be punished with the pains of hell. The corollary is that, widows and such as take the veil and the ring, being delicately fed, we could wish that they were given in marriage, because we cannot excuse them from secret sins.

12. That the abundance of unnecessary arts practised in our realm nourishes much sin in waste, profusion, and disguise. This, experience and reason prove in some measure, because nature is sufficient for a man's necessity with few arts. The corollary is that since St Paul says: 'having food and raiment, let us be therewith content,' it seems to us that goldsmiths and armourers and all kinds of arts not necessary for a man, according to the apostle, should be destroyed for the increase of virtue; because although these two said arts were exceedingly necessary in the old law, the New Testament abolishes them and many others.

This is our embassy, which Christ has bidden us fulfil, very necessary for this time for several reasons. And although these matters are briefly noted here they are however set forth at large in another book, and many others besides, at length in our own language, and we wish that these were accessible to all Christian people. We ask God then of His supreme goodness to reform our Church, as being entirely out of joint, to the perfectness of its first beginning.

[Foxe's translation of some contemporary verses added to the foregoing document]

The English nation doth lament of these vile men their sin, Which Paul doth plainly dignify by idols to begin.

But Gehazites full ingrate from sinful Simon sprung, This to defend, though priests in name, make bulwarks great and strong. Ye princes, therefore, whom to rule the people God hath placed With justice' sword, why see ye not this evil great defaced?

The Execution of Heretics: Saints and Witches
1389–1427

Lollards were by no means the only people to have been executed as heretics in the period. In the later Middle Ages, many changes rocked generally placid societies, including the devastating mortality of the Black Death, rural migration to cities, disruption in the Church's hierarchy, and new technologies, discoveries, and ideas. Increasing uncertainty placed marginal people at further risk and made everyone more suspicious of those who seemed to threaten accepted authority and stability. The following accounts illustrate how some people were condemned in Florence for dubious behavior—or the appearance of it.

Source: *The Society of Renaissance Florence: A Documentary Study*, ed. Gene Brucker, (Harper and Row, Inc., 1972), pp. 253–57, 270–73.

Focus Questions:

1. How are both stories predicated upon an acceptance of supernatural forces and their ability to control human behavior?

2. Why are the victims encouraged to "recant" their beliefs and "confess" to their crimes?

3. How is sexuality used against the defendants? Were women particularly vulnerable to charges like this?

THE EXECUTION OF FRA MICHELE OF CALCI, 1389

[April 30, 1389] This is the condemnation of Giovanni, called Fra Michele di Berti of Calci, in the territory of Pisa, a man of low condition, evil conversation, life, and reputation, and a heretic against the Catholic faith, against whom we have proceeded by means of inquisition.... It has come to our attention that this Giovanni... with the spirit and intent of being a heretic, had relations with the Fraticelli, called the Little Brothers of Poverty, heretics and schismatics and denounced by the Holy Roman Church, and that he joined that depraved sect in a place called the grotto of the Dieci Yoffensi, in which place they congregated and stayed.... With the intention of proclaiming this heresy and of contaminating faithful Christians, the accused came to the city of Florence and in public places he did maintain, affirm, and preach the heretical teachings hereby stated: Item, that Christ, our Redeemer, possessed no property either individually or in common but divested himself of all things, as the Holy Scripture testifies. Item, that Christ and his Apostles, according to the Scriptures, denounced the taking, holding, or exchanging of goods as against divine law.

Item, that Pope John XXII [d. 1334] of blessed memory was a heretic and lost all power and ecclesiastical authority as pope and as a heretic had no authority to appoint bishops or prelates, and that all prelates so appointed by him do not legally hold their office and that they sin by pretending to do so.

Item, that all cardinals, prelates, and clerics who accepted the teaching of John XXII on apostolic poverty, and who should resist these teachings and who do not resist, are also heretics and have lost all authority as priests of Christ.

Item, that this Giovanni, a heretic and schismatic, not content with all this mentioned above, but desiring also the damnation of others, in the months of March and April sought to persuade many men and women of the city of Florence, to induce them to believe inland to enter the above-mentioned sect of the Fraticelli. He told them about the above-mentioned sect; with false words and with erroneous reasons he claimed that this sect was the true religion and the true observance of the rule and life of the blessed Francis; and that all those who observe this doctrine and life are in a state of grace, and that all other friars and priests are heretics and schismatics and are damned.

And since this Giovanni appeared before us and our court and confessed to the above-mentioned charges... and refused to recant or to reject these teachings, we hereby decree that unless this Giovanni gives up his false teaching and beliefs, that as an example to others, he be taken to the place of justice and there he is to be burned with fire and the flames of fire so that he shall die and his spirit be separated from his body.

Now everything which I here describe, I who write both saw or heard. Fra Michele, having come into the courtyard, waited attentively to hear the condemnation. And the vicar [general of the bishop] spoke: "The bishop and the Inquisitor have sent me here to tell you that if you wish to return to the Holy Church and renounce your errors, then do so, in order that the people may see that the church is merciful." And Fra Michele replied, "I believe in the poor crucified Christ, and I believe that Christ, showing the way to perfection, possessed nothing...." Having read his confession, the judge turned his back upon Fra Michele... and the guards seized him and with great force pushed him outside of the gate of the judge's palace. He remained there alone, surrounded by scoundrels, appearing in truth as one of the martyrs. And there was such a great crowd that one could scarcely see. And the throng increased in size, shouting: "You don't want to die!" And Fra Michele replied, "I will die for Christ." And the crowd answered: "Oh! You aren't dying for Christ! You don't believe in God!" And Fra Michele replied: "I believe in God, in the Virgin Mary, and in the Holy Church!" And someone said to him, "You wretch! The devil is pushing you from behind!"

And when he arrived in the district of the Proconsolo, there was a great press of people who came to watch. And one of the faithful cried: "Fra Michele!

Pray to God for us...." When he arrived at S. Giovanni, they shouted to him: "Repent, repent! You don't want to die." And he said:

"I have repented of my sins...." And at the Mercato Vecchio, they shouted even louder: "Save yourself! Save yourself!" And he replied, "Save yourselves from damnation." And at the Mercato Nuovo, the shouts grew louder:

"Repent, repent!" And he replied, "Repent of your sins; repent of your usury and your false merchandising....And at the Piazza del Grano, there were many women in the windows of the houses who cried to him: "Repent, repent!" And he replied, "Repent of your sins, your usury, your gambling, your fornication...." When he arrived at S. Croce, near the gate of the friars, the image of St. Francis was shown to him and he raised his eyes to heaven and said, "St. Francis, my father, pray to Christ for me."

And then moving toward the gate of Justice, the crowd cried in unison: "Recant, recant! You don't want to die!" And he replied, "Christ died for us." And some said to him, mocking: "Ho, you're not Christ and you don't have to die for us." And he replied, "I wish to die for Him." And then another shouted, "Ho, you're not among pagans," and he answered, "I wish to die for the truth....

And when he arrived at the gate near the place of execution, one of the faithful began to cry, "Remain firm, martyr of Christ, for soon you will receive the crown...."And arriving at the place of execution, there was a great turmoil and the crowd urged him to repent and save himself and he refused.... And the guards pushed the crowd back and formed a circle of horsemen around the pyre so that no one could enter. I myself did not enter but climbed upon the river bank to see, but I was unable to hear.... And he was bound to the stake... and the crowd begged him to recant, except one of the faithful, who comforted him. And they set fire to the wood... and Fra Michele began to recite the Te Deum.... And when he had said, "In your hands, 0 Lord, I commend my spirit," the fire burned the cords which bound him and he fell dead... to the earth.

And many of the onlookers said, "He seems to be a saint." Even his enemies whispered it... and then they slowly began to return to their homes. They talked about Michele and the majority said that he was wrong and that no one should speak such evil of the priests. And some said, "He is a martyr," and others said, "He is a saint," and still others denied it. And there was a greater tumult and disturbance in Florence than there had ever been.

CONDEMNATION OF A WITCH (JUNE 7, 1427)

...We condemn... Giovanna called Caterina, daughter of Francesco called El Toso, a resident of the parish of S. Ambrogio of Florence... who is a magician, witch, and sorceress, and a practitioner of the black arts.

It happened that Giovanni Ceresani of the parish of S. Jacopo tra le Fosse was passing by her door and stared at her fixedly. She thought that she would draw the chaste spirit of Giovanni to her for carnal purposes by means of the black arts.... She went to the shop of Monna Gilia, the druggist, and purchased from her a small amount of lead... and then she took a bowl and placed the lead in it and put it on the fire so that the lead would melt. With this melted lead she made a small chain and spoke certain words which have significance for this magical and diabolical art (and which, lest the people learn about them, shall not be recorded).... All this which was done and spoken against Giovanni's safety by Giovanna was so powerful that his chaste spirit was deflected to lust after her, so that willynilly he went several times to her house and there he fulfilled her perfidious desire.

With the desire of doing further harm to Giovanni's health through the black arts, and so persisting in what she had begun, she acquired a little gold, frankincense, and myrrh, and then took a little bowl with some glowing charcoal inside, and having prepared these ingredients and having lit the candle which she held in her left hand, she genuflected before the image and placed the bowl at the foot of the figure. Calling out the name of Giovanni, she threw the gold, frankincense, and myrrh upon the charcoal. And when the smoke from the charcoal covered the whole image, Giovanna spoke certain words, the tenor of which is vile and detestable, and which should be buried in silence lest the people be given information for committing sin.

When she realized that what she had done against Giovanni's health was not sufficient to satisfy completely her insatiable lust, she learned from a certain priest that... if water from the skulls of dead men was distilled and given with a little wine to any man, that it was a most valid test.... Night and day, that woman thought of nothing but how she could give that water to Giovanni to drink.... She visited the priest and bought from him a small amount of that water... and that accursed woman gave Giovanni that water mixed with wine to drink. After he drank it, Giovanni could think of nothing but satisfying his lust with Giovanna. And his health has been somewhat damaged, in the opinion of good and worthy [men].

In the time when Giovanna was menstruating, she took a little of her menses, that quantity which is required by the diabolical ceremonies, and placed it in a small beaker, and then poured it into another flask filled with wine and gave it to Giovanni to drink. And on account of this and the other things described above, Giovanni no longer has time for his affairs as he did in the past, and he has left his home and his wife and son... And does only what pleases Giovanna....

On several occasions, Giovanna had intercourse with a certain Jacopo di Andrea, a doublet-maker, of the parish of S. Niccolo. Desiring to possess his chaste spirit totally for her lust and against his health, Giovanna... thought to give

Jacopo some of her menses, since she knew that it was very efficacious.... Having observed several diabolical rites, she took the beaker with the menses... and gave it to Jacopo to drink. After he had drunk, she uttered these words among others: "I will catch you in my net if you don't flee." ... When they were engaged in the act of intercourse, she placed her hand on her private parts... and after uttering certain diabolical words, she put a finger on Jacopo's lips.... Thereafter, in the opinion of everyone, Jacopo's health deteriorated and he was forced by necessity to obey her in everything.

Several years ago, Giovanna was the concubine of Niccolo di Ser Casciotto of the parish of S. Giorgio, and she had three children by him. Having a great affection for Niccolo, who was then in Hungary, she wanted him to return to her in Florence.... So she planned a diabolical experiment by invoking a demon, to the detriment of Niccolo's health.... She went to someone who shall not be identified... and asked him to go to another diabolical woman, a sorceress (whose name shall not be publicized, for the public good), and asked her to make for Giovanna a wax image in the form of a woman, and also some pins and other items required by this diabolical experiment.... Giovanna took that image and placed it in a chest in her house. When, a few days later, she had to leave that house and move to another, she left the image in the chest. Later it was discovered by the residents of that house, who burned it.

She collected nine beans, a piece of cloth, some charcoal, several olive leaves which had been blessed and which stood before the image of the Virgin Mary, a coin with a cross, and a grain of salt. With these in her hand she genuflected... [before the image] and recited three times the Pater Noster and the Ave Maria, spurning the divine prayers composed for the worship of God and his mother the Virgin Mary. Having done this, she placed these items on a piece of linen cloth and slept over them for three nights. And afterwards, she took them in her hand and thrice repeated the Pater Noster and the Ave Maria.... And thus Giovanna knew that her future husband would not love her. And so it happened, for after the celebration and the consummation of the marriage, her husband Giovanni stayed with her for a few days, and then left her and has not yet returned. [Giovanna confessed to these crimes and was beheaded.]

Propositions of John Wycliffe, as Described in the Church's Condemnation
1415

Born around 1328, John Wycliffe (also spelled Wyclif, and many other ways) taught theology and philosophy at Oxford and was a forceful advocate of Church reform. He believed that the Bible was the highest spiritual authority and that the sacraments were not necessary for salvation. He insisted that the Bible would only be useful, if translated into English, and he set some of his students to this task. His beliefs were drawn up by the Church and condemned as a group in 1382, but he was allowed to live in retirement until his death in 1384. However, his positions were again listed and condemned by the Council of Constance in 1415. In response, his body was dug up in 1428, and his ashes were burned and scattered in the Thames.

Source: *Documents of the Christian Church,* ed. Henry Bettenson (New York: Oxford University Press, 1970), 172–173.

FOCUS QUESTIONS:

1. Compare this statement with Eugenius IV's pronouncement on the Seven Sacraments.
2. If this is an accurate reflection of Wycliffe's beliefs, was his position on the Church too extreme?

I.2 That the material substance of bread and the material substance of wine remain in the Sacrament of the altar.

2. That the accidents of bread do not remain without a subject (substance) in the said Sacrament.

3. That Christ is not in the Sacrament essentially and really, in his own corporeal presence.

4. That if a bishop or priest be in mortal sin he does not ordain, consecrate or baptize.

5. That it is not laid down in the Gospel that Christ ordained the Mass.

6. That God ought to obey the devil.

7. That if a man be duly penitent any outward confession is superfluous and useless.

10. That it is contrary to Holy Scripture that ecclesiastics should have possessions.

14. That any deacon or priest may preach the word of God apart from the authority of the Apostolic See or a Catholic bishop.

15. That no one is civil lord, or prelate, or bishop, while he is in mortal sin.

16. That temporal lords can at their will take away temporal goods from the church, when those who hold them are sinful (habitually sinful, not sinning in one act only).

17. That the people can at their own will correct sinful lords.

18. That tithes are mere alms, and that parishioners can withdraw them at their will because of the misdeeds of their curates.

20. That he who gives alms to friars is by that fact excommunicate.

21. That any one who enters a private religion (i.e. religious house], either of those having property or of mendicants, is rendered more inapt and unfit for the performance of the commands of God.

22. That holy men have sinned in founding private religions.

23. That the religious who live in private religions are not of the Christian religion.

24. That friars are bound to gain their livelihood by the labour of their hands, and not by begging.

28. That the confirmation of young men, the ordination of clerics, the consecration of places are reserved for the Pope and bishops on account of the desire for temporal gain and honour.

30. That the excommunication of the Pope or of any prelate is not to be feared, because it is the censure of antichrist.

34. That all of the order of mendicants are heretics.

35. That the Roman Church is the synagogue of Satan, and the Pope is not the next and immediate vicar of Christ and the Apostles.

42. That it is fatuous to believe in the indulgences of the Pope and the bishops.

43. That all oaths made to corroborate human contracts and civil business are unlawful.

PART 3

The West in
Transformation (1350 – 1700)

CHAPTER 9

The Renaissance

Petrarch:
Rules for the Successful Ruler
c. 1350

Petrarch (1304-1374) was one of the first "humanists" who made his living as a public writer, receiving patronage from the wealthy political leaders of the Italian city-states. His concerns, more than those of his medieval predecessors, were secular, though he did not entirely ignore religion, especially in later life. He encouraged the scholars of his day to re-examine classical literature, reviving the style and substance of intellectual production that had ruled before Christianity became the dominant religion of the Roman Empire. In this excerpt, he duly praises his patron, and then he speaks more generally about how one ought to rule a state. Like Dante a generation before him, he used the vernacular language and helped make Italian a literary language.

Source: Francesco Petrarca, *How a Ruler Ought to Govern His State*, trans. Benjamin G. Kohl, cited in *The Earthly Republic: Italian Humanists on Government and Society*, ed. Benjamin G. Kohl and Ronald G. Witt, (University of Pennsylvania Press, 1981, © 1978), 35–80, passim.

FOCUS QUESTIONS:

1. What examples and sources are used to support Petrarch's claims about good government?

2. How highly does he esteem the writings of the ancient Greeks and Romans?

The first quality is that a lord should be friendly, never terrifying, to the good citizens, even though it is inevitable that he be terrifying to evil citizens if he is to be a friend to justice. "For he does not carry a sword without good cause, since he is a minister of God," as the Apostle says. Now nothing is more foolish, nothing is more destructive to the stability of the state, than to wish to be dreaded by everyone. Many princes, both in antiquity and in modern times, have wanted nothing more than to be feared and have believed that nothing is more useful than fear and cruelty in maintaining their power. Concerning this belief we have an example in the case of the barbaric emperor named Maximinus. In fact, nothing is farther from the truth than these opinions; rather, it is much more advantageous to be loved than to be feared, unless we are speaking of the way in which a devoted child fears a good father. Any other kind of fear is diametrically opposed to what a ruler should desire. Rulers in general want to reign for a long time and to lead their lives in security, but to be feared is opposed to both of these desires, and to be loved is consistent with both.

* * *

What I can say is that the nature of public love is the same as private love. Seneca says: "I shall show you a love potion that is made without medicines, without herbs, without the incantations of any poison-maker. If you want to be loved, love." There it is. Although many other things could be said, this saying is the summation of everything. What is the need for magical arts, what for any reward or labor? Love is free; it is sought out by love alone. And who can be found with such a steely heart that he would not want to return an honorable love? "Honorable" I say, for a dishonorable love is not love at all, but rather hatred hidden under the guise of love. Now to return love to someone who loves basely is to do nothing other than to compound one crime with another and to become a part of another person's disgraceful deceit.

* * *

Indeed, from the discussion of this topic nothing but immense and honorable pleasure ought to come to you since you are so beloved by your subjects that you seem to them to be not a lord over citizens but the "father of your country." In fact this was the title of almost all of the emperors of antiquity; some of them bore the name justly, but others carried it so unjustly that nothing more perverse can be conceived. Both Caesar Augustus and Nero were called "father of his country." The first was a true father, the second was an enemy of both his country and of religion. But this title really does belong to you.

* * *

You should know, moreover, that to merit this kind of esteem you must always render justice and treat your citizens with goodwill. Do you really want to be a father to your citizens? Then you must want for your subjects what you want for your own children.

* * *

Now I shall speak of justice, the very important and noble function that is to give to each person his due so that no one is punished without good reason. Even when there is a good reason for punishment you should incline to mercy, following the example of Our Heavenly Judge and Eternal King. For no one of us is immune from sin and all of us are weak by our very nature, so there is no one of us who does not need mercy.

* * *

Indeed, I do not deny, nor am I ignorant of, the fact that the lord of a city ought to take every precaution to avoid useless and superfluous expenditures. In this way he will not exhaust the treasury and have nothing left for necessary expenditures. Therefore, a lord should spend nothing and do nothing whatsoever that does not further the beauty and good order of the city over which he rules. To put it briefly, he ought to act as a careful guardian of the state, not as its lord. Such was the advice that the Philosopher gave at great length in his *Politics*, advice that is found to be very useful and clearly consistent with justice.[1] Rulers who act otherwise are to be judged as thieves rather than as defenders and preservers of the state.

* * *

From these concerns, however, derives not just the happiness of the people, but the security of the ruling class as well. For no one is more terrifying than a starving commoner of whom it has been said: "the hungry pleb knows no fear." Indeed, there are not just ancient examples but contemporary ones, especially from recent events in the city of Rome, which bear out this saying.[2]

* * *

Among those honored for their abilities in governing, the first place ought to go to learned men. And among these learned men, a major place should go to those whose knowledge in law is always very useful to the state. If, indeed, love of and devotion to justice is added to their knowledge of law, these citizens are (as Cicero puts it) "learned not just in the law, but in justice."[3] However, there are those who follow the law but do no justice, and these are unworthy to bear the name of the legal profession. For it is not enough simply to have knowledge; you must want to use it. A good lawyer adds good intentions to his legal knowledge. Indeed, there have been many lawyers who have added luster to ancient Rome

---

1 Aristotle Politica5.9, 1314b40ff, which Petrarch knew only in medieval Latin translation.
2 An allusion to a revolt—caused by famine—by the lower classes of Rome against the senatorial families in 1353, just before the return to the city of the demagogic Cola di Rienzo. See F. Gregorovius, History of the City of Rome in the Middle Ages, trans. A. Hamilton, 8 vols. (London, 1898), 6:337ff.
3 Cicero Orationes Philippicae9.5.10.

and other places: Adrianus Julius Celsus, Salvius Julianus, Neratius Priscus, Antonius Scaevola, Severus Papinianus, Alexander Domitius Ulpianus, Fabius Sabinus, Julius Paulus, and many others.[4] And you too (as much as our own times permit) have by the patronage of your university added honor to your country. There are other kinds of learned men, some of whom you can depend on for advice and learned conversation, and (as Alexander used to say) invent literary tales.[5] One reads that Julius Caesar, in like fashion, used to confer Roman citizenship on doctors of medicine and on teachers of the liberal arts.[6] Now, among learned men there is no doubt that we ought to give preference to those who teach the knowledge of sacred things (or what we call theology), provided that these men have kept themselves free from any foolish sophistries.

* * *

That very wise emperor Augustus used to bestow patronage on learned men to encourage them to remain in Rome, and hope of such a reward stimulated others to study, for at that time Roman citizenship was a highly valued honor. Indeed, when St. Paul claimed that he was a Roman citizen, the tribune judging the case said to him: "I myself have at a high price obtained this status."[7]

* * *

Even if it were not written in any book, still death is certain, as our common nature tells us. Now I do not know whether it is because of human nature or from some longstanding custom that at the death of our close friends and relatives we can scarcely contain our grief and tears, and that our funeral services are often attended by wailings and lamentations. But I do know that scarcely ever has this propensity for public grief been so deep-rooted in other cities as it is in yours. Someone dies—and I do not care whether he is a noble or a commoner, the grief displayed by the commoners is certainly no less manifest, and perhaps more so, than that of the nobles, for the plebs are more apt to show their emotions and less likely to be moved by what is proper; as soon as he breathes his last, a great howling and torrent of tears begins. Now I am not asking you to forbid expressions of grief. This would be difficult and probably impossible, given human nature. But what Jeremiah says is true: "You should not bemoan the dead, nor bathe the corpse in tears."[8] As the great poet Euripides wrote in Crespontes: "Considering the evil of our present existence, we ought to lament at our birth and rejoice at our death."[9] But these philosophic opinions are not well known, and, in any case, the common people would find them unthinkable and strange.

---

4 Petrarch derived this list of famous legal experts from the time of the Roman Empire mainly from his reading of the Scriptores historiae Augusta passim.
5 Scriptores historiae Augustae18.34.6.
6 Seutonius Divus Julius42.
7 Acts 22:28.
8 Jeremiah 22:10.
9 Cf. Cicero Tusculane disputationes1.48.115, quoting Euripides.

Therefore, I will tell you what I am asking. Take an example: Some old dowager dies, and they carry her body into the streets and through the public squares accompanied by loud and indecent wailing so that someone who did not know what was happening could easily think that here was a madman on the loose or that the city was under enemy attack. Now, when the funeral cortege finally gets to the church, the horrible keening redoubles, and at the very spot where there ought to be hymns to Christ or devoted prayers for the soul of the deceased in a subdued voice or even silence, the walls resound with the lamentations of the mourners and the holy altars shake with the wailing of women. All this simply because a human being has died. This custom is contrary to any decent and honorable behavior and unworthy of any city under your rule. I wish you would have it changed. In fact, I am not just advising you, I am (if I may) begging you to do so. Order that wailing women should not be permitted to step outside their homes; and if some lamentation is necessary to the grieved, let them do it at home and do not let them disturb the public thoroughfares.

I have said to you perhaps more than I should, but less than I would like to say. And if it seems to you, illustrious sir, that I am mistaken in one place or another, I beg your pardon, and I ask you to consider only the good advice. May you rule your city long and happily. Farewell. Arquà, the 28th of November.

Advice to Lorenzo de Medici:
On Wifely Duties
1416

Francesco Barbaro wrote *On Wifely Duties* for the benefit of his friend and fellow aristocrat, Lorenzo de Medici, on the occasion of the latter's marriage in 1416. He hoped to teach the youth of Florence through de Medici's example—and through the Medicis' circulation of his treatise. He also wanted to stress the importance of marriage in the maintenance of the aristocratic ruling families of his native Venice, in particular, and to the Italian city-states, more generally.

Source: Francesco Barbaro, *On Wifely Duties*, trans. Benjamin G. Kohl, cited in *The Earthly Republic: Italian Humanists on Government and Society*, ed. Benjamin G. Kohl and Ronald G. Witt, (University of Pennsylvania Press, 1981, © 1978), 189–230, passim.

Focus Questions:

1. What behaviors will ensure a good and healthy marriage in Renaissance Italy?

2. Do these differ from expected behaviors in other historical periods?

CHAPTER ONE: ON THE FACULTY OF OBEDIENCE

This is now the remaining part to be done here, in which if wives follow me, either of their own free will or by the commands of their husbands, no one will be so unfair as to think that I have not so established the duties of the wife that youth can enjoy peace and quiet the whole life long. Therefore, there are three things that, if they are diligently observed by a wife, will make a marriage praiseworthy and admirable: love for her husband, modesty of life, and diligent and complete care in domestic matters. We shall discuss the first of these, but before this I want to say something about the faculty of obedience, which is her master and companion, because nothing more important, nothing greater can be demanded of a wife than this.

If a husband, excited to anger, should scold you more than your ears are accustomed to hear, tolerate his wrath silently. But if he has been struck silent by a fit of depression, you should address him with sweet and suitable words, encourage, console, amuse, and humor him. Those who work with elephants do not wear white clothes, and those who work with wild bulls are right not to wear red; for those beasts are made ever more ferocious by those colors. Many authors report that tigers are angered by drums and made violent by them. Wives ought to observe the same thing; if, indeed, a particular dress is offensive to a husband, then we advise them not to wear it, so that they do not give affront to their husbands, with whom they ought to live peacefully and pleasantly.

The wife who is angry with her husband because of jealousy and is considering a separation should ask herself this question: If I put myself in a workhouse because I hate a whore, what could make her far happier and more fortunate than this? She would see me almost shipwrecked, while at the same time she was sailing with favorable winds and securely casting her anchor into my marriage bed?

It was considered very good for domestic peace and harmony if a wife kept her husband's love with total diligence. At the olympic games that were dedicated to the great god Jupiter and attended by all of Greece, Gorgias used his eloquence to urge a union of all the Greeks. Melanthus said: Our patron attempts to persuade us that we should all join together in a league, but he cannot bring himself and his wife and her maid—who are only three people—to a mutual agreement (for the wife was very jealous because Gorgias was wildly enamoured of her maid). Likewise, Philip was for a long time displeased with the queen Olympias and Alexander. And when Demaratus of Corinth returned from Greece, Philip eagerly and closely questioned him about the union of the Greeks. Demaratus said to him:"Philip, I consider it a very bad thing that you are spending all your energy in bringing peace and concord to all of Greece when you are not yet reconciled with your own wife and son."Therefore, if any woman wants to govern her children and servants, she should make sure that she is, first of all, at peace with her husband. Otherwise, it will seem that she wants to imitate the very things that she is trying to correct in them. In order that a wife does her duty and brings peace and harmony to her household, she must agree to the first principle that she does not disagree with her husband on any point. But of this enough has been said.

CHAPTER TWO: ON LOVE

In the first place, let wives strive so that their husbands will clearly perceive that they are pensive or joyful according to the differing states of their husbands' fortunes. Surely congratulations are proper in times of good fortune, just as consolations are appropriate in times of adversity. Let them openly discuss whatever is bothering them, provided it is worthy of prudent people, and let them feign nothing, dissemble nothing, and conceal nothing. Very often sorrow and trouble of mind are relieved by means of discussion and counsel that ought to be carried out in a friendly fashion with the husband. If a husband shares all the pressures of her anxieties he will lighten them by participating in them and make their burden lighter; but if her troubles are very great or deeply rooted, they will be relieved as long as she is able to sigh in the embrace of her husband. I would like wives to live with their husbands in such a way that they can always be in agreement, and if this can be done, then, as Pythagoras defines friendship, the two are united in one.

I therefore would like wives to evidence modesty at all times and in all places. They can do this if they will preserve an evenness and restraint in the movements of the eyes, in their walking, and in the movement of their bodies; for the wandering of the eyes, a hasty gait, and excessive movement of the hands and other parts of the body cannot be done without loss of dignity, and such actions are always joined to vanity and are signs of frivolity.

Moreover, I earnestly beg that wives observe the precept of avoiding immoderate laughter. This is a habit that is indecent in all persons, but it is especially hateful in a woman. On the other hand, women should not be censured if they laugh a little at a good joke and thus lapse somewhat from their serious demeanor. Demosthenes used to rehearse his legal speeches at home in front of a mirror so that with his own eyes he could judge what he should do and what he should avoid in delivering his speeches at court. We may well apply this practice to wifely behavior. I wish that wives would daily think and consider what the dignity, the status of being a wife requires, so that they will not be lacking in dignified comportment.

We who follow a middle way should establish some rather liberal rules for our wives. They should not be shut up in their bedrooms as in a prison but should be permitted to go out, and this privilege should be taken as evidence of their virtue and propriety. Still, wives should not act with their husbands as the moon does with the sun; for when the moon is near the sun it is never visible, but when it is distant it stands resplendent by itself. Therefore, I would have wives be seen in public with their husbands, but when their husbands are away wives should stay at home. By maintaining an honest gaze in their eyes, they can communicate most significantly as in painting, which is called silent poetry. They also should maintain dignity in the motion of their heads and the other movements of their bodies. Now that I have spoken about demeanor and behavior, I shall now speak of speech.

CHAPTER FOUR: ON SPEECH AND SILENCE

Isocrates warns men to speak on those matters that they know well and about which they cannot, on account of their dignity, remain silent. We commend women to concede the former as the property of men, but they should consider the latter to be appropriate to themselves as well as to men. Loquacity cannot be sufficiently reproached in women, as many very learned and wise men have stated, nor can silence be sufficiently

applauded. For this reason women were prohibited by the laws of the Romans from pleading either criminal or civil law cases.

CHAPTER EIGHT: ON DOMESTIC MATTERS AND THE MANAGEMENT OF HOUSEHOLD SERVANTS

We are interested in the care of our property and the diligence proper to our servants and staff because it is necessary to have both property and servants, without whose help family life itself cannot exist. Surely it is in these two things that the management of domestic matters primarily is involved, for unless a wife imposes her own judgment and precepts on these matters, the operation of the household will have no order and will be in great disarray. Men are naturally endowed with strength of mind and body; both for these and other reasons, they provision their homes by their labor, industry, and willingness to undergo hardships. Conversely, I think we may infer that since women are by nature weak they should diligently care for things concerning the household. For weakness can never be separated from cares nor cares from vigilance. What is the use of bringing home great wealth unless the wife will work at preserving, maintaining, and utilizing it?

They ought to attend, therefore, to governing their households just as Pericles daily attended to the affairs of Athens.[1] And they ought always to consider how well they are doing so that they will never be deficient in their care, interest, and diligence in household matters. They will surely be successful in this matter if they do what they should do, that is, if they are accustomed to stay at home and oversee everything there.

1 Cf. Xenophon Oeconomicus 7.3.5.

So that a wife's duty might be commended to posterity, there were affixed to the bronze statue of Gaia Caecilia, the daughter of Tarquinius, an ordinary shoe and a distaff and spindle, so that those objects might in some way signify that her diligent work at home ought to be imitated by future generations.[2] What neglectful landowner can hope to have hard-working peasants? What slothful general can make his soldiers vigilant for the state? Therefore, if a wife would like to have her maids working hard at home, she should not merely instruct them with words but she ought also by her actions to demonstrate, indicate, and show what they should be doing. Indeed, there is surely nothing more excellent in household affairs than that everything be put in its place, because there is nothing more beautiful, more useful than order, which is always of the greatest importance. We consider that an army or chorus can be called anything but an army or chorus unless its organization is well preserved.[3] I would have wives imitate the leaders of bees, who supervise, receive, and preserve whatever comes into their hives, to the end that, unless necessity dictates otherwise, they remain in their honeycombs where they develop and mature beautifully. Wives may send their maids and manservants abroad if they think this would be useful to them. But if, indeed, these servants are required at home, they should urge, order, and require their presence. Wives should also consider it their duties to see to it that no harm comes to their husbands' winecellars, pantries, and oil cellars.

It is now proper to speak, as we have promised, about servants, who, provided they are not neglected, can add great luster to our houses and be useful and pleasant. So they will be if wives will instruct them carefully and if they will not get angry with them before, having warned them, they discover that they have made the same mistakes. I should like that wives, in these matters as in others, follow the example of the leaders of the bees, who allow no one under their control to be lazy or negligent.[4]

Thrifty wives constantly ought to seek out and appoint sober stewards for the provisions and address them courteously and be generous of them, so that by the great interest of the mistress the industry of the steward daily increases. They should feed their servants so that they will satisfy both their human needs and reward their constant labor. Wives should clothe their servants comfortably as befits the season, climate, and place. Moreover, as Hesiod advises, they should always be careful that servants are not separated from their children and families,[5] for servants will always find a way to stay together with their own family, even secretly. Furthermore, servants will be very grateful if especially good medical care is provided when a member of their family is taken sick. For these acts of humanity, this solicitiousness will make servants very conscientious and hardworking for the household.

---

2 Cf. Plutarch Quaestiones Romanae 30; Moralia 271E.
3 Cf. Xenophon Oeconomicus 1.3.
4 Cf. Xenophon Oeconomicus 7.33.
5 Probably an allusion to Hesiod Opera et Dies 373.

After their offspring have passed their infancy, mothers should use all their skill, care, and effort to ensure that their children are endowed with excellent qualities of mind and body. First they should instruct them in their duty toward Immortal God, their country, and their parents, so that they will be instilled from their earliest years with those qualities that are the foundation of all other virtues. Only those children who fear God, obey the laws, honor their parents, respect their superiors, are pleasant with their equals and courteous to their inferiors, will exhibit much hope for themselves. Children should meet all people with a civil demeanor, pleasant countenance, and friendly words. But they should be on the most familiar terms with only the best people. Thus they will learn moderation in food and drink so that they may lay, as it were, the foundation of temperance for their future lives. They should be taught to avoid these pleasures that are dishonorable, and they should apply their efforts and thoughts to those matters that are the most becoming and will be useful and pleasant when they become older. If mothers are able to instruct their children in these matters, their offspring will much more easily and better receive the benefit of education.

Mothers should often warn their children to abstain from excessive laughter and to avoid words that denote a rash character. That is the mark of stupidity, the evidence of passion. Moreover, children should be warned not ever to speak on those matters that are base in the act. Therefore, mothers should restrain them from vulgar or cutting words. If their children should say anything that is obscene or licentious, mothers should not greet it with a laugh or a kiss, but with a whip.

Moreover, they should teach their children not to criticize anyone because of his poverty or the low birth of his lineage or other misfortunes, for they are sure to make bitter enemies from such actions or develop an attitude of arrogance. Mothers should teach their children sports in which they so willingly learn to exert themselves that, if the occasion arises, they can easily bear even more difficult hardships. I would have mothers sharply criticized for displays of anger, greed, or sexual desire in the presence of their offspring, for these vices weaken virtue. If mothers act appropriately, their children will learn from infancy to condemn, avoid, and hate these most filthy mistresses and they will take care to revere the names of God and will be afraid to take them in vain. For whoever has been taught at an early age to despise the Divinity, will they not as adults surely curse Him? Therefore, it is of great importance to train children from infancy so that they never swear. Indeed, those who swear readily because of some misfortune are not deserving of trust, and those who readily swear very often unwittingly betray themselves. Mothers ought to teach their children to speak the truth.

Therefore, my Lorenzo, your compatriots ought to be stirred by your example and follow you with great enthusiasm, for in Ginevra you have taken a wife who is a virgin well endowed with virtue charm, a noble lineage, and great wealth. What more outstanding, more worthy model could I propose than yours? What more shining, more worthy example than yours, since in this outstanding city of Florence you are most eminently connected through your father, grandfather, and ancestors? You have taken a wife whose great wealth the entire world indeed admires but whose chastity, constancy, and prudence all men of goodwill esteem highly. They consider that you are blessed and happy to have her as a wife, and she is to have you as a husband. Since you have contracted such an outstanding and fine marriage, these same men ask God Immortal that you will have the best children who will become very honored citizens in your state. These matters might perhaps seem negligible since I am treating them, but indeed they are, in their own fashion, borne out in your marriage. Thus, surely young men who follow your example will profit more than only by following my precepts; just as laws are much more likely to be observed in a city when they are obeyed by its ruler, so, since your own choice of a wife is consistent with my teachings, we may hope that these precepts will be followed by the youth.

Lorenzo Valla Skewers the Supposed "Donation of Constantine"
c. 1440

The "Donation of Constantine" was a document forged by the papal bureaucracy in the mid 8th century, at a time when the Church was attempting to demonstrate its claim to temporal power against a growing power-base in the Frankish kingdom. In this document, Constantine the Great surrenders his Empire to the Pope, Sylvester I (314-335 CE), in exchange for his curing him of leprosy. (Neither event actually occurred, of course.) In fairness to the papal court, however, the forging of documents was not an unusual practice at the time, especially when it was believed that the text *ought* to have existed anyway. However, the document was written in an extremely poor Latin, with several easily-spotted errors, and it had been exposed as a forgery as early as the 15th century. Nevertheless, using all the skills he could muster as a "philologist" (a student of language), the remarkably gifted writer Lorenzo Valla (1406-1457) blasted the papacy for laying claim to the Empire in a bogus text. Working for a king who wished to stymie the papacy, Valla unloaded all the vitriol he could muster at the Church hierarchy, and especially at the hypothetical monk who had created the document in the first place. In his treatise, Valla quoted from the forgery, and then attacked its writer.

Source: *The Treatise of Lorenzo Valla on the Donation of Constantine*, translated by Christopher B. Coleman (New Haven: Yale University Press, 1922), pp. 25, 27, 95, 97, 131, and 133.

FOCUS QUESTIONS:

1. How does Valla express his outrage, and what rhetorical forms does he employ?
2. How does he use the tools of "humanism" to do so?

I know that for a long time now men's ears are waiting to hear the offense with which I charge the Roman pontiffs. It is, indeed, an enormous one, due either to supine ignorance, or to gross avarice which is the slave of idols, or to pride of empire of which cruelty is ever the companion. For during some centuries now, either they have not known that the Donation of Constantine is spurious and forged, or else they themselves forged it, and their successors walking in the same way of deceit as their elders have defended as true what they knew to be false, dishonoring the majesty of the pontificate, dishonoring the memory of ancient pontiffs, dishonoring the Christian religion, confounding everything with murders, disasters and crimes. They say the city of Rome is theirs, theirs the kingdom of Sicily and of Naples, the whole of Italy, the Gauls, the Spains, the Germans, the Britons, indeed the whole West; for all these are contained in the instrument of the Donation itself. So all these are yours, supreme pontiff? And it is your purpose to recover them all? To despoil all kings and princes of the West of their cities or compel them to pay you a yearly tribute, is that your plan?

I, on the contrary, think it fairer to let the princes despoil you of all the empire you hold. For, as I shall show, that Donation whence the supreme pontiffs will have their right derived was unknown equally to Sylvester and to Constantine....

How in the world – this is much more absurd, and impossible in the nature of things – could one speak of Constantinople as one of the patriarchal sees, when it was not yet a patriarchate, nor a see, nor a Christian city, nor named Constantinople, nor founded, nor planned! For the "privilege" was granted, so it says, the third day after Constantine became a Christian; when as yet Byzantium, not Constantinople, occupied that site. I am a liar if this fool does not confess as much himself. For toward the end of the "privilege" he writes:

"Wherefore we have perceived it to be fitting that our empire and our royal power should be transferred in the regions of the East; and that in the province of Bizantia [sic], in the most fitting place, a city should be built in our name; and that our empire should there be established."

But if he was intending to transfer the empire, he had not yet transferred it; if he was intending to establish his empire there, he had not yet established it; if he was planning to build a city, he had not yet built it. Therefore he could not have spoken of it as a patriarchal see, as one of the four sees, as Christian, as having this name, nor as already built. According to the history [the Life of Sylvester] which Palea cites as evidence, he had not yet even thought of founding it. And this beast, whether Palea or some one else who Palea follows, does not notice that he contradicts this history, in which it is said that Constantine issued the decree concerning the founding of the city, not on his own initiative, but at a command received in his sleep from God, not at Rome but at Byzantium, not within a few days [of his conversion] but several years after, and that he learned its name by revelation in a dream. Who then does not see that the man who wrote the "privilege" lived long after the time of Constantine, and in his effort to embellish his falsehood forgot that earlier he had said that these events took place at Rome on the third day after Constantine was baptized? So the trite old proverb applies nicely to him, "Liars need good memories."

And how is it that he speaks of a province of "Byzantia," when it was a town, Byzantium by name? The place was by no means large enough for the erection of so great a city; for the old city of Byzantium was included within the walls of Constantinople. And this man says the [new] city is to be built on the most fitting place in it! Why does he choose to put Thrace, in which Byzantium lies, in the East, when it lies to the north? I suppose Constantine did not know the place which he had chosen for the building of the city, in what latitude it was, whether it was a town or a province, nor how large it was!...

"If any one, moreover – which we do not believe – prove a scorner in this matter, he shall be condemned and shall be subject to eternal damnation; and shall feel the holy apostles of God, Peter and Paul, opposed to him in the present and in the future life. And he shall be burned in the lower hell and shall perish with the devil and all the impious."

This terrible threat is the usual one, not of a secular ruler, but of the early priests and flamens, and nowadays, of ecclesiastics. And so this is not the utterance of Constantine, but of some fool of a priest who, stuffed and pudgy, knew neither what to say nor how to say it, and, gorged with eating and heated with wine, belched out these wordy sentences which convey nothing to another, but turn against the author himself. First he says, "shall be subject to eternal damnation," then as though more could be added, he wishes to add something else, and to eternal penalties he joins penalties in the present life; and after he frightens us with God's condemnation, he frightens us with the hatred of Peter, as though it were something still greater. Why he should add Paul, and why Paul alone, I do not know. And with his usual drowsiness he returns again to eternal penalties, as though he had not said that before. Now if these threats and curses were Constantine's, I in turn would curse him as a tyrant and destroyer of my country, and would threaten that I, as a Roman, would take vengeance on him. But who would be afraid of the curse of an overly avaricious man, and one saying a counterfeit speech after the manner of actors, and terrifying people in the role of Constantine? This is being a hypocrite in the true sense, if we press the Greek word closely; that is, hiding your own personality under another's.

Marriage in the Renaissance: A Serious Business
1464–1465

The formation of marriage ties in Medieval and Renaissance Florence was not simply a matter of love—or, rather, it was very rarely about love. Particularly among
long-established elites, blood and family ties were valued more than almost anything
else. In the following excerpt, we see some of the honor, prestige, and property that
were at stake in marriage negotiations in 14th century Italy.

Source: "Letters from Alessandra Strozzi in Florence to her son Filippo in
Naples" Alessandra Macinghi Strozzi, Lettere di una gentildonna flo-
rentina,ed. C. Guasti, (Florence, 1877), 394–95, 458–59, 463–65, 475–76,
cited in *The Society of Renaissance Florence: A Documentary Study*, ed.
Gene Brucker, (New York: Harper and Row, Inc., 1972), 37–40.

Focus Questions:

1. What was the role of women in arranging suitable marriages? Is this surprising?

2. What factors, in this mother's opinion, create a good marriage?

MARRIAGE NEGOTIATIONS: THE STROZZI, 1464-65

[April 20, 1464]... Concerning the matter of a wife [for Filippo], it appears to
me that if Francesco di Messer Guglielmino Tanagli wishes to give his daughter,
that it would be a fine marriage.... Now I will speak with Marco [Parenti,
Alessandra's son-in-law], to see if there are other prospects that would be better,
and if there are none, then we will learn if he wishes to give her [in marriage]....
Francesco Tanagli has a good reputation, and he has held office, not the highest,
but still he has been in office. You may ask: "Why should he give her to someone
in exile?" There are three reasons. First, there aren't many young men of good
family who have both virtue and property. Secondly, she has only a small dowry,
1,000 florins, which is the dowry of an artisan.... Third, I believe that he will give
her away, because he has a large family and he will need help to settle them....

[July 26, 1465]... Marco Parenti came to me and told me that for some time,
he has been considering how to find a wife for you.... There is the daughter of
Francesco di Messer Guglielmino Tanagli, and until now there hasn't been anyone who is better suited for you than this girl. It is true that we haven't discussed
this at length, for a reason which you understand. However, we have made secret
inquiries, and the only people who are willing to make a marriage agreement
with exiles have some flaw, either a lack of money or something else. Now
money is the least serious drawback, if the other factors are positive.... Francesco
is a good friend of Marco and he trusts him. On S. Jacopo's day, he spoke to him

discreetly and persuasively, saying that for several months he had heard that we were interested in the girl and... that when we had made up our minds, she will come to us willingly. [He said that] you were a worthy man, and that his family had always made good marriages, but that he had only a small dowry to give her, and so he would prefer to send her outside of Florence to someone of worth, rather than to give her to someone here, from among those who were available, with little money.... He invited Marco to his house and he called the girl down.... Marco said that she was attractive and that she appeared to be suitable. We have information that she is affable and competent. She is responsible for a large family (there are twelve children, six boys and six girls), and the mother is always pregnant and isn't very competent....

[August 17, 1465]... Sunday morning I went to the first mass at S. Reparata... to see the Adimari girl, who customarily goes to that mass, and I found the Tanagli girl there. Not knowing who she was, I stood beside her.... She is very attractive, well proportioned, as large or larger than Caterina [Alessandra's daughter].... She has a long face, and her features are not very delicate, but they aren't like a peasant's. From her demeanor, she does not appear to me to be indolent.... I walked behind her as we left the church, and thus I realized that she was one of the Tanagli. So I am somewhat enlightened about her....

[August 31, 1465]... I have recently received some very favorable information [about the Tanagli girl] from two individuals.... They are in agreement that whoever gets her will be content.... Concerning her beauty, they told me what I had already seen, that she is attractive and well-proportioned. Her face is long, but I couldn't look directly into her face, since she appeared to be aware that I was examining her... and so she turned away from me like the wind.... She reads quite well... and she can dance and sing.... Her father is one of the most respected young men of Florence, very civilized in his manners. He is fond of this girl, and it appears that he has brought her up well.

So yesterday I sent for Marco and told him what I had learned. And we talked about the matter for a while, and decided that he should say something to the father and give him a little hope, but not so much that we couldn't withdraw, and find out from him the amount of the dowry.... Marco and Francesco [Tanagli] had a discussion, about this yesterday (I haven't seen him since), and Marco should inform you about it one of these days, and you will then understand more clearly what should follow. May God help us to choose what will contribute to our tranquillity and to the consolation of us all....

[September 13, 1465]... Marco came to me and said that he had met with Francesco Tanagli, who had spoken very coldly, so that I understand that he had changed his mind. They say that he wants to discuss the matter with his brother-in-law, Messer Antonio Ridolfi.... And he [Francesco] says that it would be a serious matter to send his daughter so far away [to Naples], and to a house that might be described as a hotel. And he spoke in such a way that it is clear that he has changed his mind. I believe that this is the result of the long delay in our replying to him, both yours and Marco's. Two weeks ago, he could have given him a little hope. Now this delay has angered him, and he has at hand some prospect that is more attractive.... I am very annoyed by this business; I can't recall when I have been so troubled. For I felt that this marriage would have satisfied our needs better than any other we could have found....

[Filippo Strozzi eventually married Fiametta di Donato Adimari, in 1466.]

Niccoló Machiavelli
From the *Discourses on Livy*
1513–1517

Born in 1469, Niccolò Machiavelli found a job in the bureaucracy of the Florentine Republic in 1498, loving the opportunity to examine political intrigue, diplomatic exchanges, and the nitty-gritty of policy creation at close quarters. However, as part of a general peace treaty in Italy in 1512, the Medici were restored to Florence and Machiavelli lost his job. Moreover, he was soon arrested, drawn by the rope, and tortured; after demonstrating his innocence, he was released and, for the next 14 years, wrote a series of letters, treatises, and even a comedy, much of it in the effort to rehabilitate himself with Florence's ruling elite. From this enforced exile came one of the most remarkable pieces of political theory ever to have been created, The *Discourses on Livy*, a portion of which was written up as a separate treatise entitled The Prince. Experience had taught him that "the ends justify the means", and he believed that history demonstrated the same phenomenon.

Source: The *Discourses* (Penguin Classics), translation by Leslie Walker, ed. Bernard Crick (New York: Penguin Books, 1983), 131–135.

Focus Questions:

1. Under what conditions is a powerful tyrant necessary?
2. What sorts of examples does Machiavelli use in his argument? How does he derive general principles from them?

That it is necessary to be the Sole Authority if one would constitute a Republic afresh or would reform it thoroughly regardless of its Ancient Institutions

To some it will appear strange that I have got so far in my discussion of Roman history without having made any mention of the founders of that republic or of either its religious or its military institutions. Hence, that I may not keep the minds of those who are anxious to hear about such things any longer in suspense, let me say that many perchance will think it a bad precedent that the founder of a civic state, such as Romulus, should first have killed his brother, and then have acquiesced in the death of Titus Tatius, the Sabine, whom he had chosen as his colleague in the kingdom. They will urge that, if such actions be justifiable, ambitious citizens who are eager to govern, will follow the example of their prince and use violence against those who are opposed to their authority. A view that will hold good provided we leave out of consideration the end which Romulus had in committing these murders.

One should take it as a general rule that rarely, if ever, does it happen that a state, whether it be a republic or a kingdom, is either well-ordered at the outset or radically transformed vis-à-vis its old institutions unless this be done by one person. It is likewise essential that there should be but one person upon whose mind and method depends any similar process of organization. Wherefore the prudent organizer of a state whose intention it is to govern not in his own interests but for the common good, and not in the interest of his successors but for the sake of that fatherland which is common to all, should contrive to be alone in his authority. Nor will any reasonable man blame him for taking any action, however extraordinary, which may be of service in the organizing of a kingdom or the constituting of a republic. It is a sound maxim that reprehensible actions may be justified by their effects, and that when the effect is good, as it was in the case of Romulus, it always justifies the action. For it is the man who uses violence to spoil things, not the man who uses it to mend them, that is blameworthy.

The organizer of a state ought further to have sufficient prudence and virtue not to bequeath the authority he has assumed to any other person, for, seeing that men are more prone to evil than to good, his successor might well make ambitious use of that which he had used virtuously. Furthermore, though but one person suffices for the purpose of organization, what he has organized will not last long if it continues to rest on the shoulders of one man, but may well last if many remain in charge and many look to its maintenance. Because, though the many are incompetent to draw up a constitution since diversity of opinion will prevent them from discovering how best to do it, yet when they realize it has been done, they will not agree to abandon it.

That Romulus was a man of this character, that for the death of his brother and of his colleague he deserves to be excused, and that what he did was done for the common good and not to satisfy his personal ambition, is shown by his having at once instituted a senate with which he consulted and with whose views his decisions were in accord. Also, a careful consideration of the authority which Romulus reserved to himself will show that all he reserved to himself was the command of the army in time of war and the convoking of the senate. It is clear, too, that when the Tarquins were expelled and Rome became free, none of its ancient institutions were changed, save that in lieu of a permanent king there were appointed each year two consuls. This shows that the original institutions of this city as a whole were more in conformity with a political and self-governing state than with absolutism or tyranny.

I might adduce in support of what I have just said numberless examples, for example Moses, Lycurgus, Solon and other founders of kingdoms and republics who assumed authority that they might formulate laws to the common good; but this I propose to omit since it is well known. I shall adduce but one further example, not so celebrated but worth considering by those who are contemplating the drawing up of good laws. It is this. Agis, King of Sparta, was considering how to confine the activities of the Spartans to the limits originally set for them by the laws of Lycurgus, because it seemed to him that it was owing to their having deviated from them in part that this city had lost a good deal of its ancient virtue, and, in consequence, a good deal of its power and of its empire. He was, however, while his project was still in the initial stage, killed by the Spartan ephors, who took him to be a man who was out to set up a tyranny. But Cleomenes, his successor in that kingdom, having learned from some records and writings of Agis which he had discovered, what was the latter's true mind and intention, determined to pursue the same plan. He realized, however, that be could not do this for the good of his country unless he became the sole authority there, and, since it seemed to him impossible owing to man's ambition to help the many against the will of the few, he took a suitable opportunity and had all the ephors killed and anybody else who might obstruct him. He then renewed in their entirety the laws of Lycurgus. By so doing he gave fresh life to Sparta, and his reputation might thereby have become as great as that of Lycurgus if it had not been for the power of the Macedonians and the weakness of other Greek republics. For, after Sparta had thus been reorganized, it was attacked by the Macedonians, and, since its forces proved to be inferior and it could get no outside help, it was defeated, with the result that Cleomenes' plans, however just and praiseworthy, were never brought to completion. All things considered, therefore, I conclude that it is necessary to be the sole authority if one is to organize a state, and that Romulus' action in regard to the death of Remus and Titus Tatius is excusable, not blameworthy.

Benvenuto Cellini: The Life of an Artist
1558–1562

Benvenuto Cellini (1500-1571) was an artist who made his living as a goldsmith in Renaissance Florence and Rome. He was also quite a talented musician. The following excerpt, from his autobiography written between 1558 and 1562, describes his life and work as an artist. It was not published until the 18ᵗʰ century, when it became quite popular.

Source: Benvenuto Cellini, *The Life of Benvenuto Ceillini*, 4th edition, trans. J. A. Symonds, cited in ed. John L. Beatty and Oliver A. Johnson, Heritage of Western Civilization,vol. 1, 7th edition, (Englewood Cliffs, NJ: Prentice Hall, 1991), 397–411, passim.

FOCUS QUESTIONS:

1. What interest did the Madonna Porzia have in this rising young artist?
2. What does this document reveal about the artistic ambience of Rome in this period?

II

It is true that men who have laboured with some show of excellence, have already given knowledge of themselves to the world; and this alone ought to suffice them; I mean the fact that they have proved their manhood and achieved renown. Yet one must needs live like others; and so in a work like this there will always be found occasion for natural bragging, which is of divers kinds, and the first is that a man should let others know he draws his lineage from persons of worth and most ancient origin.

When I reached the age of fifteen, I put myself, against my father's will, to the goldsmith's trade with a man called Antonio, son of Sandro, known commonly as Marcone the goldsmith. He was a most excellent craftsman and a very good fellow to boot, high-spirited and frank in all his ways. My father would not let him give me wages like the other apprentices; for having taken up the study of this art to please myself, he wished me to indulge by whim for drawing to the full. I did so willingly enough; and that honest master of mine took marvellous delight in my performances. He had an only son, a bastard, to whom he often gave his orders, in order to spare me. My liking for the art was so great, or, I may truly say, my natural bias, both one and the other, that in a few months I caught up the good, nay, the best young craftsmen in our business, and began to reap the fruits of my labours. I did not, however, neglect to gratify my good father from time to time by playing on the flute or cornet. Each time he heard me, I used to make his tears fall accompanied with deep-drawn sighs of satisfaction. My filial piety often made me give him that contentment, and induced me to pretend that I enjoyed the music too.

XIV

[... Later, after traveling to Rome, he entered a new workshop]

"Welcome to my workshop; and do as you have promised; let your hands declare what man you are." He gave me a very fine piece of silver plate to work on for a cardinal. It was a little oblong box, copied from the prophyry sarcophagus before the door of the Rotonda. Beside what I copied, I enriched it with so many elegant masks of my invention, that my master went about showing it through the art, and boasting that so good a piece of work had been turned out from his shop. It was about half a cubit in size, and was so constructed as to serve for a salt-cellar at table. This was the first earning that I touched at Rome, and part of it I sent to assist my good father; the rest I kept for my own use, living upon it while I went about studying the antiquities of Rome, until my money failed, and I had to return to the shop for work.

After undertaking some new commissions, I took it into my head, as soon as I had finished them, to change my master; I had indeed been worried into doing so by a certain Milanese, called Pagolo Arsago. My first master, Firenzuola, had a great quarrel about this with Arsago, and abused him in my presence; whereupon I took up speech in defence of my new master. I said that I was born free, and free I meant to live, and that there was no reason to complain of him, far less of me, since some few crowns of wages were still due to me; also that I chose to go, like a free journeyman, where it pleased me, knowing I did wrong to no man. My new master then put in with his excuses, saying that he had not asked me to come, and that I should gratify him by returning to Firenzuola. To this I replied that I was not aware of wronging the latter in any way, and as I had completed his commissions, I chose to be my own master and not the man of others, and that he who wanted me must beg me of myself. Firenzuola cried: "I don't intend to beg you of yourself; I have done with you; don't show yourself again upon my premises." I reminded him of the money he owed me. He laughed me in the face; on which I said that if I knew how to use my tools in handicraft as well as he had seen, I could be quite as clever with my sword in claiming the just payment of my labour. While we were exchanging these words, an old man happened to come up, called Maestro Antonio, of San Marino. He was the chief among the Roman goldsmiths, and had been Firenzuola's master. Hearing what I had to say, which I took good care that he should understand, he immediately espoused my cause, and bade Firenzuola pay me. The dispute waxed warm, because Firenzuola was an admirable swordsman, far better than he was a goldsmith. Yet reason made itself heard; and I backed my cause with the same spirit, till I got myself paid. In course of time Firenzuola and I became friends, and at his request I stood godfather to one of his children.

XV

I went on working with Pagolo Arsago, and earned a good deal of money, the greater part of which I always sent to my good father. At the end of two years, upon my father's entreaty, I returned to Florence, and put myself once more under Francesco Salimbene, with whom I earned a great deal, and took continual pains to improve in my arts. I renewed my intimacy with Francesco di Filippo; and though I was too much given to pleasure, owing to that accursed music, I never neglected to devote some hours of the day or night to study.

XIX

During that time I went to draw sometimes in Michel Agnolo's chapel, and sometimes in the house of Agostino Chigi of Siena, which contained many incomparable paintings by the hand of that great master Raffaello., This I did on feast-days, because the house was then inhabited by Messer Gismondo, Agostino's brother. They plumed themselves exceedingly when they saw young men of my sort coming to study in their palaces. Gismondo's wife, noticing my frequent presence in that house-she was a lady as courteous as could be, and of surpassing beauty-came up to me one day, looked at my drawings, and asked me if I was a sculptor or a painter; to whom I said I was a goldsmith. She remarked that I drew too well for a goldsmith; and having made one of her waiting-maids bring a lily of the finest diamonds set in gold, she showed it to me, and bade me value it. I valued it at 800 crowns. Then she said that I had very nearly hit the mark, and asked me whether I felt capable of setting the stones really well. I said that I should much like to do so, and began before her eyes to make a little sketch for it, working all the better because of the pleasure I took in conversing with so lovely and agreeable a gentlewoman. When the sketch was finished, another Roman lady of great beauty joined us; she had been above, and now descending to the ground-floor, asked Madonna Porzia what she was doing there. She answered with a smile: "I am amusing myself by watching this worthy young man at his drawing; he is as good as he is handsome." I had by this time acquired a trifle of assurance, mixed, however, with some honest bashfulness; so I blushed and said: "Such as I am, lady, I shall ever be most ready to serve you." The gentlewoman, also slightly blushing, said: "You know well that I want you to serve me"; and reaching me the lily, told me to take it away; and gave me besides twenty golden crowns which she had in her bag, and added: "Set me the jewel after the fashion you have sketched, and keep for me the old gold in which it is now set." On this the Roman lady observed: "If I were in that young man's body, I should go off without asking leave." Madonna Porzia replied that virtues rarely are at home with vices, and that if I did such a thing, I should strongly belie my good looks of an honest man. Then turning round, she took the Roman lady's hand, and with a pleasant smile said: "Farewell, Benvenuto." I stayed on a short while at the drawing I was making, which was a copy of a Jove by Raffaello. When I had finished it and left the house, I set myself to making a little model of wax, in order to show how the jewel would look when it was completed. This I took to Madonna Porzia, whom I found with the same Roman lady. Both of them were highly satisfied with my work, and treated me so kindly that, being somewhat emboldened, I promised the jewel should be twice as good as the model.

Accordingly I set hand to it, and in twelve days I finished it in the form of a fleur-de-lys, as I have said above, ornamenting it with little masks, children, and animals, exquisitely enamelled, whereby the diamonds which formed the lily were more than doubled in effect.

XX

While I was working at this piece, Lucagnolo, of whose ability I have before spoken, showed considerable discontent, telling me over and over again that I might acquire far more profit and honour by helping him to execute large plate, as I had done at first. I made him answer that, whenever I chose, I should always be capable of working at great silver pieces; but that things like that on which I was now engaged were not commissioned every day; and beside their bringing no less honour than large silver plate, there was also more profit to be made by them. He laughed me in the face, and said: "Wait and see Benvenuto; for by the time that you have finished that work of yours, I will make haste to have finished this vase, which I took in hand when you did the jewel; and then experience shall teach you what profit I shall get from my vase, and what you will get from your ornament." I answered that I was very glad indeed to enter into such a competition with so good a craftsman as he was, because the end would show which of us was mistaken. Accordingly both the one and the other of us, with a scornful smile upon our lips, bent our heads in grim earnest to the work, which both were now desirous of accomplishing; so that after about ten days, each had finished his undertaking with the great delicacy and artistic skill.

So he took his vase and carried it to the Pope, who was very well pleased with it, and ordered at once that he should be paid at the ordinary rate of such large plate. Meanwhile I carried mine to Madonna Porzia, who looked at it with astonishment, and told me I had far surpassed my promise. Then she bade me ask for my reward whatever I liked; for it seemed to her my desert was so great that if I craved a castle she could hardly recompense me; but since that was not in her hands to bestow, she added laughing that I must beg what lay within her power. I answered that the greatest reward I could desire for my labour was to have satisfied her ladyship. Then, smiling in my turn, and bowing to her, I took my leave, saying I wanted no reward but that. She turned to the Roman lady and said: "You see that the qualities we discerned in him are companied by virtues, and not vices." They both expressed their admiration, and then Madonna Porzio continued: "Friend Benvenuto, have you never heard it said that when the poor give to the rich, the devil laughs?" I replied: "Quite true! and yet, in the midst of all his troubles, I should like this time to see him laugh"; and as I took my leave, she said that this time she had no will to bestow on him that favour.

When I came back to the shop, Lucagnolo had the money for his vase in a paper packet; and on my arrive he cried out: "Come and compare the price of your jewel with the price of my plate." I said that he must leave things as they were till the next day, because I hoped that even as my work in its kind was not less excellent than his, so I should be able to show him quite an equal price for it.

XXI

On the following, Madonna Porzia sent a major-domo of hers to my shop, who called me out, and putting into my hands a paper packet full of money from his lady, told me that she did not choose the devil should have his whole laugh out; by which she hinted that the money sent me was not the entire payment merited by my industry, and other messages were added worthy of so courteous a lady. Lucagnolo, who was burning to compare his packet with mine, burst into the shop, then in the presence of twelve journeymen and some neighbors, eager to behold the result of this competition, he seized his packet, scornfully exclaiming "Ou! Ou!" three or four times, while he poured his money on the counter with a great noise. They were twenty-five crowns in giulios; and he fancied that mine would be four or five crowns di moneta. I for my part, stunned and stifled by his cries, and by the looks and smiles of the bystanders, first peeped into my packet; then, after seeing that it contained nothing but gold, I retired to one end of the counter, and keeping my eyes lowered and making no noise at all, I lifted it with both hands suddenly above my head, and emptied it like a mill hopper. My coin was twice as much as his; which caused the onlookers, who had fixed their eyes on me with some derision, to turn round suddenly to him and say: "Lucagnolo, Benvenuto's pieces, being all of gold and twice as many as yours, make a far finer effect." I thought for certain that, what with jealousy and what with shame, Lucagnolo would have fallen dead upon the spot; and though he took the third part of my gain, since I was a journeymen (for such is the custom of the trade, two-thirds fall to the workman and one-third to the masters of the shop), yet inconsiderate envy had more power in him than avarice: it ought indeed to have worked quite the other way; he being a peasant's son from Iesi. He cursed his art and those who taught it to him, vowing that thenceforth he would never work at large plate, but give his whole attention to those whoreson gewgaws, since they were so well paid. Equally engaged on my side, I answered that every bird sang its own note; that he talked after the fashion of the hovels he came from; but that I dared swear that I should succeed with ease in making his lubberly lumber, while he would never be successful in my whoreson gewgaws. Thus I flung off in a passion, telling him that I would soon show him that I spoke truth. The bystanders openly declared against him, holding him for a lout, as indeed he was, and me for a man, as I had proved myself.

XXIII

While I was pushing forward Salamanca's vase, I had only one little boy as help, whom I had taken at the entreaty of friends, and half against my own will, to be my workman. He was about fourteen years of age, bore the name of Paulino, and was son to a Roman burgess, who lived upon the income of his property. Paulino was the best-mannered, the most honest, and the most beautiful boy I ever saw in my whole life. His modest ways and actions, together with his superlative beauty and his devotion to myself, bred in me as great an affection for him as a man's breast can hold. This passionate love led me often-times to delight the lad with music; for I observed that his marvellous features, which by complexion wore a tone of modest melancholy, brightened up, and when I took my cornet, broke into a smile so lovely and sweet, that I do not marvel at the silly stories which the Greeks have written about the deities of heaven. Indeed, if my boy had lived in those times, he would probably have turned their heads still more. He had a sister, named Faustina, more beautiful, I verily believe, than that Faustina about whom the old books gossip so. Sometimes he took me to their vineyard, and, so far as I could judge, it struck me that Paulino's good father would have welcomed me as a son-in-law. This affair led me to play more than I was used to do.

It happened at that time that one Giangiacomo of Cesena, a musician in the Pope's band, and a very excellent performer, sent word through Lorenzo, the trumpeter of Lucca, who is now in our Duke's service, to inquire whether I was inclined to help them at the Pope's Ferragosto, playing soprano with my cornet in some motets of great beauty selected by them for that occasion. Although I had the greatest desire to finish the vase I had begun, yet, since music has a wondrous charm of its own, and also because I wished to please my old father, I consented to join them. During eight days before the festival we practised two hours a day together; then on the first of August we went to the Belvedere, and while Pope Clemente was at table, we played those carefully studied motets so well that his Holiness protested he had never heard music more sweetly executed or with better harmony of parts. He sent for Giangiacomo, and asked him where and how he had procured so excellent a cornet for soprano, and inquired particularly who I was. Giangiacomo told him my name in full. Whereupon the Pope said: "So, then, he is the son of Maestro Giovanni?" On being assured I was, the Pope expressed his wish to have me in his service with the other bandsmen. Giangiacomo replied: "Most blessed Father, I cannot pretend for certain that you will get him, for his profession, to which he devotes himself assiduously, is that of a goldsmith, and he works in it miraculously well, and earns by it far more than he could do by playing." To this the Pope added: "I am the better inclined to him now that I find him possessor of a talent more than I expected. See that he obtains the same salary as the rest of you; and tell him from me to join my service, and that I will find work enough by the day for him to do at his other trade." Then stretching out his hand, he gave him a hundred golden crowns of the Camera in a handkerchief, and said: "Divide these so that he may take his share."

CHAPTER 10

Reformations and Counter-Reformations

The Act of Supremacy
1534

In England, the Protestant Reformation unfolded as an act of state when King Henry VIII (r. 1509-1547), in conjunction with the English Parliament, broke all ties with the Catholic Church and established a Protestant Church of England or the Anglican Church. The English break with the Catholic Church was not tied to the reforms of Luther or Calvin, but more motivated by Henry's desire for an annulment of his marriage to Catherine of Aragon. Henry sought to override Pope Clement VII's refusal to grant an annulment so he could marry Anne Boleyn (1507-1536) who he believed would be able to provide him with a male heir. This act, passed by the English Parliament, formally established the Church of England as an independent institution from the Catholic Church.

Source: Statutes of the Realm, vol. 3, (London, 1810-28), 436-39.

Focus Questions:

1. What did this act accomplish, and by what authority or power?
2. What was the relationship between church and state in England as a result of this act?
3. How and why was this tied to the Protestant Reformation?

ALBEIT the king's majesty justly and rightfully is and ought to be the supreme head of the Church of England, and so is recognized by the clergy of this realm in their Convocations, yet nevertheless for corroboration and confirmation thereof, and for increase of virtue in Christ's religion within this realm of England, and to repress and extirp all errors, heresies, and other enormities and abuses heretofore used in the same: be it enacted by authority of this present Parliament, that the king our sovereign lord, his heirs and successors, kings of this realm, shall be taken, accepted, and reputed the only supreme head in earth of the Church of England, called Anglicana Ecclesia; and shall have and enjoy, annexed and united to the imperial crown of this realm, as well the title and style thereof, as all honours, dignities, preeminences, jurisdictions, privileges, authorities, immunities, profits, and commodities to the said dignity of supreme head of the same Church belonging and appertaining; and that our said sovereign lord, his heirs and successors, kings of this realm, shall have full power and authority from time to time to visit, repress, redress, reform, order, correct, restrain, and amend all such errors, heresies, abuses, offences, contempts, and enormities, whatsoever they be, which by any manner spiritual authority or jurisdiction ought or may lawfully be reformed, repressed, ordered, redressed, corrected, restrained, or amended, most to the pleasure of Almighty God, the increase of virtue in Christ's religion, and for the conservation of the peace, unity, and tranquillity of this realm; any usage, custom, foreign law, foreign authority, prescription, or any other thing or things to the contrary hereof notwithstanding.

The Council of Trent
1545–1563

The Protestant Reformation coincided with a reform movement within the Catholic Church, which reaffirmed the main tenants of Catholic beliefs and practices while it also addressed corruption and abuses. The Catholic reform also answered the challenges to Catholic beliefs and practices made by the many Protestant reformers. Drawing on the longstanding practice in the Catholic Church of calling church councils, Pope Paul II (pose 1534-1549) called such an assembly of biblical scholars and high-ranking clergy to help popes define Catholic doctrine and practice. This Catholic Reformation church council to meet in Trent, on and off, from 1545 to 1563 and ultimately issued this treatise affirming Catholic teachings and practices.

Source: John L. Beatty and Oliver A. Johnson, eds., *The Heritage of Western Civilization* (Prentice Hall: Upper Saddle River, N.J., 1991), 452-460.

FOCUS QUESTIONS:

1. Why did the Council of Trent consider the issues excerpted here? What did they hope to achieve by doing so?

2. In what ways and to what extent were these discussions and resolutions in reaction to the criticisms of Protestant Reformers? How and why?

DECREE TOUCHING THE OPENING OF THE COUNCIL

Doth it please you-unto the praise and glory of the holy and undivided Trinity, Father, and Son, and Holy Ghost; for the increase and exaltation of the Christian faith and religion; for the extirpation of heresies; for the peace and union of the Church; for the reformation of the Clergy and Christian people; for the depression and extinction of the enemies of the Christian name-to decree and declare that the sacred and general council of Trent do begin, and hath begun? They answered: It pleaseth us.

DECREE CONCERNING ORIGINAL SIN

That our Catholic faith, without which it is impossible to please God, may, errors being purged away, continue in its own perfect and spotless integrity, and that the Christian people may not be carried about with every wind of doctrine; whereas that old serpent, the perpetual enemy of mankind, amongst the very many evils with which the Church of God is in these our times troubled, has also stirred up not only new, but even old, dissensions touching original sin, and the remedy thereof; the sacred and holy, oecumenical and general Synod of Trent,—lawfully assembled in the Holy See presiding therein,—wishing now to come to the reclaiming of the erring, and the confirming of the wavering—following the testimonies of the sacred Scriptures, of the holy Fathers, or the most approved councils, and the judgement and consent of the Church itself, ordains, confesses, and declares these things touching the said original sin:

1. If any one does not confess that the first man, Adam, when he had transgressed the commandment of God in Paradise, immediately lost the holiness and justice wherein he had been constituted; and that he incurred, through the offense of that prevarication, the wrath and indignation of God, and consequently death, with which God had previously threatened him, and, together with death, captivity under his power who thenceforth had the empire of death, that is to say, the devil, and that the entire Adam, through that offence of prevarication, was changed, in body and soul, for the worse; let him be anathema.

3. If any one asserts, that this sin of Adam—which in its origin is one, and being transfused into all by propagation, not by imitation, is in each one as his own—is taken away either by the powers of human nature, or by any other remedy than the merit of the one mediator our Lord Jesus Christ, who hath reconciled us to God in his own blood, made unto us justice, sanctification, and redemption; or if he denies that the said merit of Jesus Christ is applied, both to adults and to infants, by the sacrament of baptism rightly administered in the form of the Church; let him be anathema....

ON THE SACRAMENTS IN GENERAL

Canon I. If any one saith, that the sacraments of the New Law were not all instituted by Jesus Christ, our Lord; or, that they are more, or less, than seven, to wit, Baptism, Confirmation, the Eucharist, Penance, Extreme Unction, Order, and Matrimony; or even that any one of these seven is not truly and properly a sacrament; let him be anathema.

Canon IV. If any one saith, that the sacraments of the New Law are not necessary unto salvation, but superfluous; and that, without them, or without the desire thereof, men obtain of God, through faith alone, the grace of justification;- though all (the sacraments) are not indeed necessary for every individual; let him be anathema.

Canon VI. If any one saith, that the sacraments of the New Law do not contain the grace which they signify; or, that they do not confer that grace on those who do not place an obstacle thereunto; as though they were merely outward signs of grace or justice received through faith, and certain marks of the Christian profession, whereby believers are distinguished amongst men from unbelievers; let him be anathema. Canon X. If any one saith, that all Christians have power to administer the word, and all the sacraments; let him be anathema.

ON THE MOST HOLY SACRAMENT OF THE EUCHARIST

Canon I. If any one deny, that, in the sacrament of the most holy Eucharist, are contained truly, really, and substantially, the body and blood together with the soul and divinity of our Lord Jesus Christ. and consequently the whole Christ: but saith that He is only therein as in a sign, or in figure, or virtue: let him be anathema. Canon II. If anyone saith that in the sacred and holy sacrament of the Eucharist, the substance of the bread and wine remains conjointly with the body and blood of our Lord Jesus Christ, and denieth that wonderful and singular conversion of the whole substance of the bread into the Body, and of the whole substance of the wine into the Blood—the species only of the bread and wine remaining—which conversion indeed the Catholic Church most aptly calls transubstantiation; let him be anathema.

ON THE ECCLESIASTICAL HIERARCHY, AND ON ORDINATION

... If any one affirm, that all Christians indiscriminately are priests of the New Testament. or that they are all mutually endowed with an equal spiritual power, he clearly does nothing but confound the ecclesiastical hierarchy; which is as an army set in array....

.... It decree, that all those who, being only called and instituted by the people, or by the civil power and magistrate, ascend to the exercise of these ministrations, and those who of their own rashness assume them to themselves, are not ministers of the Church, but are to be looked upon as thieves and robbers, who have not entered by the door. These are the things which it hath seemed good to the sacred Synod to teach the faithful of Christ in general terms, touching the sacrament of Order.

ON THE SACRAMENT OF MATRIMONY

Canon IX. If anyone saith, that clerics constituted in sacred orders or Regulars, who have solemnly professed chastity, are able to contract marriage, and that being contracted it is valid. notwithstanding the ecclesiastical law, or vow: and that the contrary is nothing else than to condemn marriage: and, that all who do not feel that they have the gift of chastity; even though they have made a vow thereof, may contract marriage: let him be anathema: seeing that God refuses not that gift to those who ask for it rightly; neither does He suffer us to be tempted above that which we are able.

Canon X. If anyone saith that the marriage state is to be placed above the state of virginity and of celibacy, and that it is not better and more blessed to remain in virginity, or in celibacy, than to be united in matrimony; let him be anathema.

ON THE INVOCATION, VENERATION AND RELICS OF SAINTS, AND ON SACRED IMAGES

The holy Synod enjoins on all bishops and others who sustain the office and charge of teaching, that, agreeably to the usage of the Catholic and Apostolic Church, received from the primitive times of the Christian religion, and agreeably to the consent of the holy Fathers, and to the decrees of sacred Councils, they especially instruct the faithful diligently concerning the intercession and invocation of saints; the honour (paid) to relics; and the legitimate use of images; teaching them that the saints who reign together with Christ, offer up their own prayers to God for men, that it is good and useful supplicantly to invoke them, and to have recourse to their prayers, aid, (and) help for obtaining benefits from God, through His Son, Jesus Christ, our lord, who is alone Redeemer and Saviour; but that they think impiously, who denies that the saints, who enjoy eternal happiness in heaven, are to be invocated or who assert either that they do not pray for men; or, that the invocation of them to pray for each of us even in particular is idolatry or that it is repugnant to the word of God; and is opposed to the honour of the one mediator between God and me, Christ Jesus; or that it is foolish to supplicate, vocally or mentally, those who reign in heaven. Also, that the holy bodies of holy martyrs, and of others now living with Christ.... They who affirm that veneration and honour are not due to the relics of saints; or, that these, and other sacred monuments, are uselessly honoured by the faithful; and that the places dedicated to the memories of the saints are in vain visited with the view of obtaining their aid; are wholly to be condemned, as the Church has already long since condemned, and now also condemns.

CARDINALS AND ALL PRELATES OF THE CHURCHES SHALL BE CONTENT WITH MODEST FURNITURE AND A FRUGAL TABLE: THEY SHALL NOT ENRICH THEIR RELATIVES OR DOMESTICS OUT OF THE PROPERTY OF THE CHURCH

... Wherefore, after the example of our fathers in the Council of Carthage, it not only orders that bishops be content with modest furniture, and a frugal table and diet, but that they also give heed that in the rest of their manner of living, and in their whole house, there be nothing seen that is alien from this holy institution, and which does not manifest simplicity, zeal toward God, and a contempt of vanities. Also, it wholly forbids them to enrich their own kindred or domestics out of the revenues of the church.... It would seem to be a shame, if they did not at the same time shine so pre-eminent in virtue and in the discipline of their lives, as deservedly to draw upon themselves the eyes of all men.

DECREE CONCERNING INDULGENCES

Whereas the power of conferring Indulgences was granted by Christ to the Church; and she has, even in the most ancient times, used the said power, delivered unto her of God; the sacred holy Synod teaches, and enjoins, that the use of Indulgences for the Christian people most salutary, and approved of by the authority of sacred Councils, is to be retained in the Chruch; and It condemns with anathema those who either assert, that they are useless; or who deny that there is in the Church the power of granting them. In granting them, however, it desires that, in accordance with the ancient and approved custom in the Church, moderation be observed; lest by excessive facility. Ecclesiastical discipline be enervated. And being desirous that the abuses which have crept therein, and by occasion of which this honourable name of Indulgences is blasphemed by heretics, be amended and corrected....

Anonymous, " The Execution of Archbishop Cranmer" 1556

Henry VIII (r. 1509-1547) named Thomas Cranmer (1489-1556) to head the Church of England (Anglican Church) as archbishop of Canterbury. Cranmer served in the same post during the following reign of Edward VI (r. 1547-1543). After Edward VI's short reign, his half sister Mary I (r.1553-1558) ascended to the throne. A devout Catholic in the tradition of her mother Catherine of Argon, Mary pushed for policies that suppressed the Protestant Church of England and restored the Catholic Church as the official state church. This shift brought Archbishop Cranmer into conflict with Queen Mary and the English government as he fought to defend and maintain the Anglican Church. As a consequence of his outspoken refusal to accept Mary's religious policies, he was arrested, put on trial, and executed in 1556.

Source: John Casey, Eyewitness to History (New York: Avon Books, 1997), 96-99.

FOCUS QUESTIONS:

1. What was the author's view of Cranmer, and how did that shape his account of Cranmer's conviction and execution?
2. How was Cranmer's trial and execution related to changing religious policies in England and in Europe?

But that I know for our great friendships, and long continued love, you look even of duty that I should signify to you of the truth of such things as here chanceth among us; I would not at this time have written to you the unfortunate end, and doubtful tragedy, of Thomas Cranmer late bishop of Canterbury: because I little pleasure take in beholding of such heavy sights. And, when they are once overpassed, I like not to rehearse them again; being but a renewing of my woe, and doubling my grief. For although his former life, and wretched end, deserves a greater misery, (if any greater might have chanced than chanced unto him), yet, setting aside his offences to God and his country, and beholding the man without his faults, I think there was none that pitied not his case, and bewailed not his fortune, and feared not his own chance, to see so noble a prelate, so grave a counsellor, of so long continued honour, after so many dignities, in his old years to be deprived of his estate, adjudged to die, and in so painful a death to end his life. I have no delight to increase it. Alas, it is too much of itself, that ever so heavy a case should betide to man, and man to deserve it.

But to come to the matter: on Saturday last, being 21 of March, was his day appointed to die. And because the morning was much rainy, the sermon appointed by Mr Dr Cole to be made at the stake, was made in St Mary's church: whither Dr Cranmer was brought by the mayor and aldermen, and my lord Williams: with whom came divers gentlemen of the shire, sit T. A. Bridges, sit John Browne, and others. Where was prepared, over against the pulpit, an high place for him, that all the people might see him. And, when he had ascended it, he kneeled him down and prayed, weeping tenderly: which moved a great number to tears, that had conceived an assured hope of his conversion and repentance...

When praying was done, he stood up, and, having leave to speak, said, 'Good people, I had intended indeed to desire you to pray for me; which because Mr Doctor hath desired, and you have done already, I thank you most heartily for it. And now will I pray for myself, as I could best devise for mine own comfort, and say the prayer, word for word, as I have here written it.' And he read it standing: and after kneeled down, and said the Lord's Prayer; and all the people on their knees devoutly praying with him...

And then rising, he said, 'Every man desireth, good people, at the time of their deaths, to give some good exhortation, that other may remember after their deaths, and be the better thereby. So I beseech God grant me grace, that I may speak something, at this my departing, whereby God may be glorified, and you edified...

'And now I come to the great thing that troubleth my conscience more than any other thing that ever I said or did in my life: and that is, the setting abroad of writings contrary to the truth. Which here now I renounce and refuse, as things written with my hand, contrary to the truth which I thought in my heart, and written for fear of death, and to save my life, if it might be: and that is, all such bills, which I have written or signed with mine own hand since my degradation: wherein I have written many things untrue. And forasmuch as my hand offended in writing contrary to my heart, therefore my hand shall first be punished: for if I may come to the fire, it shall be first burned. And as for the pope, I refuse him, as Christ's enemy and antichrist, with all his false doctrine.'

And here, being admonished of his recantation and dissembling, he said, "Alas, my lord, I have been a man that all my life loved plainness, and never dissembled till now against the truth; which I am most sorry for it." He added hereunto, that, for the sacrament, he believed as he had taught in his book against the bishop of Winchester. And here he was suffered to speak no more...

Then was he carried away; and a great number, that did run to see him go so wickedly to his death, ran after him, exhorting him, while time was, to remember himself. And one Friar John, a godly and well learned man, all the way travelled with him to reduce him. But it would not be. What they said in particular I cannot tell, but the effect appeared in the end: for at the stake he professed, that he died in all such opinions as he had taught, and oft repented him of his recantation.

Coming to the stake with a cheerful countenance and willing mind, he put off his garments with haste, and stood upright in his shirt: and a bachelor of divinity, named Elye, of Brazen-nose college, laboured to convert him to his former recantation, with the two Spanish friars. And when the friars saw his constancy, they said in Latin one to another 'Let us go from him: we ought not to be nigh him: for the devil is with him.' But the bachelor in divinity was more earnest with him: unto whom he answered, that, as concerning his recantation, he repented it right sore, because he knew it was against the truth; with other words more. Whereby the Lord Williams cried, 'Make short, make short.' Then the bishop took certain of his friends by the hand. But the bachelor of divinity refused to take him by the hand, and blamed all others that so did, and said, he was sorry that ever he came in his company. And yet again he required him to agree to his former recantation. And the bishop answered, (shewing his hand), 'This was the hand that wrote it, and therefore shall it suffer first punishment.'

Fire being now put to him, he stretched out his right hand, and thrust it into the flame, and held it there a good space, before the fire came to any other part of his body; where his hand was seen of every man sensibly burning, crying with a loud voice, 'This hand hath offended.' As soon as the fire got up, he was very soon dead, never stirring or crying all the while.

His patience in the torment, his courage in dying, if it had been taken either for the glory of God, the wealth of his country, or the testimony of truth, as it was for a pernicious error, and subversion of true religion, I could worthily have commended the example, and matched it with the fame of any father of ancient time: but, seeing that not the death, but cause and quarrel thereof, commendeth the sufferer, I cannot but much dispraise his obstinate stubbornness and sturdiness in dying, and specially in so evil a cause. Surely his death much grieved every man; but not after one sort. Some pitied to see his body so tormented with the fire raging upon the silly carcass, that counted not of the folly. Other that passed not much of the body, lamented to see him spill his soul, wretchedly, without redemption, to be plagued for ever. His friends sorrowed for love; his enemies for pity: strangers for a common kind of humanity, whereby we are bound one to another. Thus I have enforced myself, for your sake, to discourse this heavy narration, contrary to my mind: and, being more than half weary, I make a short end, wishing you a quieter life, with less honour; and easier death, with more praise.

Catherine Zell,
"Letter to Ludwig Rabus"
1556–1558

With their emphasis on marriage and rejection of celibacy for clergy, Protestant churches significantly redefined roles for men and women in their institutions. While the Catholic Church affirmed celibacy for its priests at the Council of Trent, Protestant churches encouraged their preachers and pastors to marry. The author of this document, Catherine Zell (c. 1497-c. 1563) married an ex-Catholic priest who became a Lutheran minister in Strasbourg, in 1523. As a couple, they were active proponents of the more radical Protestant movement in central Europe (Calvinist and Zwingli followers) which brought them into conflict with Catholics as well as fellow Lutheran Protestants. The following excerpt is from one of Catherine Zell's letters to a young Lutheran minister, Ludwig Rabus, who publicly criticized the Zell's for their actions and beliefs. Zell published her correspondence, including this letter, after the death of her husband in an effort to defend and explain their opinions, beliefs, and work.

Source: Julia O'Faolain and Lauro Martines, eds., *Not in God's Image* (New York: Harper and Row, Inc., 1973), 203-206.

FOCUS QUESTIONS:

1. What does Zell's letter say about the role of women in the Protestant movement?
2. According to Zell, what religious groups experienced persecution in Strasbourg? Why?
3. What does her letter tell us about the Protestant Reformation as it unfolded in the Strasbourg area?

I, Catherine Zell, wife of the late lamented Mathew Zell, who served in Strasbourg, where I was born and reared and still live, wish you peace and enhancement in God's grace.

From my earliest years I turned to the Lord, who taught and guided me, and I have at all times, in accordance with my understanding and His grace, embraced the interests of His church and earnestly sought Jesus. Even in youth this brought me the regard and affection of clergymen and others much concerned with the church, which is why the pious Mathew Zell wanted me as a companion in marriage; and I, in turn, to serve the glory of Christ, gave devotion and help to my husband, both in his ministry and in keeping his house....

Ever since I was ten years old I have been a student and a sort of church mother, much given to attending sermons. I have loved and frequented the company of learned men, and I conversed much with them, not about dancing, masquerades, and worldly pleasures but about the kingdom of God.

Yet I resisted and struggled against that kingdom. Then, as no learned man could find a way of consoling me in my sins, prayers and physical suffering, and as none could make me sure of God's love and grace, I fell gravely ill in body and spirit. I became like that poor woman of the Gospel who, having spent all she had on doctors to no avail, heard speak of Christ, went to Him, and was healed. As I foundered, devoured by care and anxiety, vainly searching for serenity in the practices of the church, God took pity on me. From among our people He drew out and sent forth Martin Luther. This man so persuaded me of the ineffable goodness of our Lord Jesus Christ that I felt myself snatched from the depths of hell and transported to the kingdom of heaven. I remembered the Lord's words to Peter: 'Follow me and I shall make you a fisher of men'. Then did I labor day and night to cleave to the path of divine truth....

While other women decorated their houses and ornamented themselves, going to dances, wedding parties, and giving themselves to pleasure, I went into the houses of poor and rich alike, in all love, faith, and compassion, to care for the sick and the confined and to bury the dead. Was that to plant anxiety and turmoil in the church of Strasbourg?...

Consider the poor Anabaptists, who are so furiously and ferociously persecuted. Must the authorities everywhere be incited against them, as the hunter drives his dog against wild animals? Against those who acknowledge Christ the Lord in very much the same way we do and over which we broke with the papacy? Just because they cannot agree with us on lesser things, is this any reason to persecute them and in them Christ, in whom they fervently believe and have often professed in misery, in prison, and under the torments of fire and water?

Governments may punish criminals, but they should not force and govern belief which is a matter for the heart and conscience not for temporal authorities. [Urges Rabus to consult the leading reformers on this question and provides him, ironically, with a list.] ... When the authorities pursue one, they soon bring forth tears, and towns and villages are emptied...

Strasbourg does not offer the example of an evil town but rather the contrary-charity, compassion, and hospitality for the wretched and poor. Within its walls, God be thanked, there remains more than one poor Christian whom certain people would have liked to see cast out. Old Mathew Zell would not have approved of that: he would have gathered the sheep, not destroyed them....

Whether they were Lutherans, Zwinglians, Schwenkfeldians, or poor Anabaptist brethren, rich or poor, wise or foolish, according to the word of St. Paul, all came to us [to the Zells in Strasbourg]. We were not compelled to hold the same views and beliefs that they did, but we did owe to all a proof of love, service, and generosity: our teacher Christ has taught us that....

Acts of Uniformity
1559

Elizabeth I became queen of England (r. 1533-1603) during a period of severe religious and political turmoil which was the result of the wild fluctuations of the religious policies of her predecessors. Her father, Henry VIII (r. 1509-1547), broke away from the Catholic Church with the support of the English Parliament and established a Protestant Church of England in the 1520s, but her half sister Mary I (r.1553-1558) instigated ruthless policies that attempted to bring back the Catholic Church and eliminate Protestantism in England. Working with the English Parliament, Elizabeth sought to restore religious order through policies that brought together Catholics and Protestants in England under a reinstated Church of England. Elizabeth envisioned this as a religious and political compromise that would establish a state church that was independent from the Catholic Church, Protestant in name, but would retain many of the same rituals and beliefs familiar to English churchgoers. This act, passed by the English Parliament, launched Elizabeth's religious policies by providing clear guidelines for services, institutions, and personnel of the reinstated Church of England nationwide.

Source: Henry Bettenson, ed., *Documents of the Christian Church* (New York: Oxford University Press, 1970), 235-239.

FOCUS QUESTIONS:

1. What did Elizabeth and the English Parliament hope to accomplish with the passage of this act?
2. How did this act fit into the larger context of the Reformation in England and church-state relations?

Where at the death of our late sovereign lord King Edward VI there remained one uniform order of common service and prayer, and of the administration of sacraments, rites, and ceremonies in the Church of England, which was set forth in one book, intituled: The Book of Common Prayer, and Administration of Sacraments, and other rites and ceremonies in the Church of England; authorized by Act of Parliament holden in the fifth and sixth years of our said late sovereign lord King Edward VI, intituled: An Act for the uniformity of common prayer, and administration of the sacraments; the which was repealed and taken away by Act of Parliament in the first year of the reign of our late sovereign lady Queen Mary, to the great decay of the due honour of God, and discomfort to the professors of the truth of Christ's religion:

Be it therefore enacted by the authority of this present Parliament, that the said statute of repeal, and everything therein contained, only concerning the said book, and the service, administration of sacraments, rites, and ceremonies contained or appointed in or by the said book, shall be void and of none effect, from and after the feast of the Nativity of St John Baptist next coming; and that the said book, with the order of service, and of the administration of sacraments, rites, and ceremonies, with the alterations and additions therein added and appointed by this statute, shall stand and be, from and after the said feast of the Nativity Of St John Baptist, in full force and effect, according to the tenor and effect of this statute; anything in the aforesaid statute of repeal to the contrary notwithstanding.

And further be it enacted by the queen's highness, with the assent of the Lords and Commons in this present Parliament assembled, and by authority of the same, that all and singular ministers in any cathedral or parish church, or other place within this realm of England, Wales, and the marches of the same, or other the queen's dominions, shall from and after the feast of the Nativity of St John Baptist next coming be bounden to say and use the Matins, Evensong, celebration of the Lord's Supper and administration of each of the sacraments, and all their common and open prayer, in such order and form as is mentioned in the said book, so authorized by Parliament in the said fifth and sixth years of the reign of King Edward VI, with one alteration or addition of certain lessons to be used on every Sunday in the year,[1] and the form of the Litany altered and corrected,[2] and two sentences only added in the delivery of the sacrament to the communicants,[3] and none other or otherwise.

And that if any manner of parson, vicar, or other whatsoever minister, that ought or should sing or say common prayer mentioned in the said book, or minister the sacraments, from and after the feast of the Nativity of St John Baptist next coming, refuse to use the said common prayers, or to minister the sacraments in such cathedral or parish church, or other places as he should use to minister the same, in such order and form as they be mentioned and set forth in the said book, or shall, wilfully or obstinately standing in the same, use any other rite, ceremony, order, form, or manner of celebrating of the Lord's Supper, openly or privily, or Matins, Evensong, administration of the sacraments, or other open prayers, than is mentioned and set forth in the said book (open prayer in and throughout this Act, is meant that prayer which is for other to come unto, or hear, either in common churches or private chapels or oratorios, commonly called the service of the Church), or shall preach, declare, or speak anything in the derogation or depraving of the said book, or anything therein contained, or of any part thereof, and shall be thereof lawfully convicted, according to the laws of this realm, by verdict of twelve men, or by his own confession, or by the notorious evidence of the fact, shall lose and forfeit to the queen's highness, her heirs and successors, for his first offence, the profit of all his spiritual benefices or promotions coming or arising in the one whole year next after his conviction; and also that the person so convicted shall for the same offence suffer imprisonment by the space of six months, without ball or mainprize.

And if any such person once convicted of any offence concerning the premises, shall after his first conviction eftsoons offend, and be thereof, in form aforesaid, lawfully convicted, that then the same person shall for his second offence suffer imprisonment by the space of one whole year, and also shall therefor be deprived, ipso facto, of all his spiritual promotions; and that it shall be lawful to all patrons or donors of all and singular the same spiritual promotions, or of any of them, to present or collate to the same, as though the person and persons so offending were dead.

And that if any such person or persons, after he shall be twice convicted in form aforesaid, shall offend against any of the premises the third time, and shall

---

1 Proper Lessons for Sundays were given in 1st P.B. of Edw. VI (1549), but omitted in the 1552 Book.

2 The more important changes were: the omission of the deprecation, 'From the tyranny of the bishop of Rome and all his detestable enormities,' which appeared in 1549 and 1552, and the inclusion of the Prayer of the Queen's Majesty, and the Prayer for the Clergy and People, which have been, since 1662, included in Morning and Evening Prayer.

3 In the 1549 Book the words of administration were, 'The body (blood) of our Lord Jesus Christ which Was given (shed) for thee, preserve thy body and soul unto everlasting life.' In 1552 there was substituted, 'Take and eat this (Drink this) in remembrance that Christ died (Christ's blood was shed) for thee, and feed on him in thy heart by faith with thanksgiving (and be thankful).' The two forms were combined in 1559 and retained thus in 1662.

be thereof, in form aforesaid, lawfully convicted, that then the person so offending and convicted the third time, shall be deprived, ipso facto, of all his spiritual promotions, and also shall suffer imprisonment during his life.

And if the person that shall offend, and be convicted in form aforesaid, concerning any of the premises, shall not be beneficed, nor have any spiritual promotion, that then the same person so offending and convicted shall for the first offence suffer imprisonment during one whole year next after his said conviction, without bail or mainprize. And if any such person, not having any spiritual promotion, after his first conviction shall eftsoons offend in anything concerning the premises, and shall be, in form aforesaid, thereof lawfully convicted, that then the same person shall for his second offence suffer imprisonment during his life.

And it is ordained and enacted by the authority aforesaid, that if any person or persons whatsoever, after the said feast of the Nativity of St John Baptist next coming, shall in any interludes, plays, songs, rhymes, or by other open words, declare or speak anything in the derogation, depraving, or despising of the same book, or anything therein contained, or any part thereof, or shall, by open fact, deed, or by open threatenings, compel or cause, or otherwise procure or maintain, any parson, vicar, or other minister in any cathedral or parish church, or in chapel, or in any other place, to sing or say any common or open prayer, or to minister any sacrament otherwise, or in any other manner and form, than is mentioned in the said book; or that by any of the said means shall unlawfully interrupt or let any parson, vicar, or other minister in any cathedral or parish church, chapel, or any other place, to sing or say common and open prayer, or to minister the sacraments or any of them, in such manner and form as is mentioned in the said book; that then every such person, being thereof lawfully convicted in form abovesaid, shall forfeit to the queen our sovereign lady, her heirs and successors, for the first offence a hundred marks.

And if any person or persons, being once convicted of any such offence, eftsoons offend against any of the last recited offences, and shall, in form aforesaid, be thereof lawfully convicted, that then the same person so offending and convicted shall, for the second offence, forfeit to the queen our sovereign lady, her heirs and successors, four hundred marks.

And if any person, after he, in form aforesaid, shall have been twice convicted of any offence concerning any of the last recited offences, shall offend the third time, and be thereof, in form abovesaid, lawfully convicted, that then every person so offending and convicted shall for his third offence forfeit to our sovereign lady the queen all his goods and chattels, and shall suffer imprisonment during his life.

And if any person or persons, that for his first offence concerning the premises shall be convicted, in form aforesaid, do not pay the sum to be paid by virtue of his conviction, in such manner and form as the same ought to be paid, within six weeks next after his conviction; that then every person so convicted, and so not paying the same, shall for the same first offence, instead of the said sum, suffer imprisonment by the space of six months, without bail or mainprize. And if any person or persons, that for his second offence concerning the premises shall be convicted in form aforesaid, do not pay the said sum to be paid by virtue of his conviction and this statute, in such manner and form as the same ought to be paid, within six weeks next after his said second conviction; that then every person so convicted, and not so paying the same, shall, for the same second offence, in the stead of the said sum, suffer imprisonment during twelve months, without bail or mainprize.

And that from and after the said feast of the Nativity of St John Baptist next coming, all and every person and persons inhabiting within this realm, or any other the queen's majesty's dominions, shall diligently and faithfully, having no lawful or reasonable excuse to be absent, endeavour themselves to resort to their parish church or chapel accustomed, or upon reasonable let thereof, to some usual place where common prayer and such service of God shall be used in such time of let, upon every Sunday and other days ordained and used to be kept as holy days, and then and there to abide orderly and soberly during the time of the common prayer, preachings, or other service of God there to be used and ministered; upon pain of punishment by the censures of the Church, and also upon pain that every person so offending shall forfeit for every such offence twelve pence, to be levied by the churchwardens of the parish where such offence shall be done, to the use of the poor of the same parish, of the goods, lands, and tenements of such offender, by way of distress.

And for due execution hereof, the queen's most excellent majesty, the Lords temporal (sic), and all the Commons, in this present Parliament assembled, do in God's name earnestly require and charge all the archbishops, bishops, and other ordinaries, that they shall endeavour themselves to the uttermost of their knowledges, that the due and true execution hereof may be had throughout their dioceses and charges, as they will answer before God, for such evils and plagues wherewith Almighty God may justly punish His people for neglecting this good and wholesome law....

Anonymous Government Agent
"Arrest of Edmund Campion and his Associates"
1581

Edmund Campion (1540-1581) was part of the underground movement to preserve Catholicism in the face of Queen Elizabeth I's (r. 1533-1603) religious policies which required adherence to the state religion: The Church of England or Anglican Church.

In his early career, Campion was a professor at Oxford University as well as a minister in the Anglican Church. He had a change of heart around 1570, converted to Catholicism and went to Rome to become a Jesuit (Society of Jesus). He returned in England in 1580, as part of a group of Jesuits doing missionary work. They held secret and illegal Catholic services throughout England. Campion also authored a short pamphlet, entitled the "Ten Reasons," which denounced the Anglican Church and advocated the return of England to Catholicism. These actions led to his arrest, in July of 1581, and imprisonment in the Tower of London where he was subjected to torture. He was put on trial, convicted of treason, and executed. For his work in trying to preserve Catholicism in England, the Catholic Church made him a saint in 1970.

Source: John Casey, *Eyewitness to History* (New York: Avon Books, 1997), 121-127.

FOCUS QUESTIONS:

1. According to this report, why and how was Campion arrested? By whom?

2. What was the author of this report's view of Campion and his arrest? What were the author's sympathies and loyalties, and how did they affect his account of these events?

3. What larger historical events and trends in England at the same time provide context for understanding Campion's arrest?

It happened that after the receipt of our Commission, we consulted between ourselves, What way were best to take first? For we were utterly ignorant where, or in what place, certainly to find out the said Campion, or his compeers. And our consultation was shortly determined: for the greatest part of our travail and dealings in this service did lie chiefly upon mine own determination, by reason of mine acquaintance and knowledge of divers of the like sect.

It then presently came to my remembrance of certain acquaintance which I once had with one Thomas Cooper a cook, who, in November [1578] was two years, served Master Thomas Roper of [Orpington in] Kent; where, at that time, I in like manner served: and both of us, about the same month, departed the said Master Roper his service; I into Essex, and the said Cooper to Lyford in Berkshire, to one Master Yate. From whence, within one half year after, I was advertised in Essex, that the said Cook was placed in service; and that the said Master Yate was a very earnest Papist, and one that gave great entertainment to any of that sect.

Which tale, being told me in Essex two years before we entered [on] this journey, by God's great goodness, came to my memory but even the day before we set forth. Hereof I informed the said David Jenkins, being my fellow in Commission, and told him it would be our best way to go thither first: for that it was not meant that we should go to any place but where indeed I either had acquaintance; or by some means possible in our journey, could get acquaintance. And told him we would dispose of our journey in such sort as we might come to the said Master Yate's upon the Sunday about eight of the clock in the morning: 'where,' said I, 'if we find the said Cook, and that there be any Mass to be said there that day, or any massing Priest in the house; the Cook, for old acquaintance and for that he supposeth me to be a Papist, will bring me to the sight thereof.'

And upon this determination, we set from London the 14th day of July last; and came to the said Master Yate's house, the 16th of the same month, being Sunday, about the hour aforesaid.

Where, without the gates of the same house, we espied one of the servants of the house, who most likely seemed, by reason of his lying aloof, to be as it were a Scout Watcher, that they within might accomplish their secret matters more safely.

I called the said servant, and inquired of him for the said Thomas Cooper the Cook. Who answered, That he could not well tell, whether he were within or not.

I prayed him that he would friend me so much as to see; and told him my name.

The said servant did so, it seemed; for the Cook came forth presently unto us where we sat still upon horseback. And after a few such speeches, as betwixt friend and friend when they have been long asunder, were passed; still sitting upon our horses, I told him That I had longed to see him; and that I was then travelling into Derbyshire to see my friends, and came so far out of my way to see him. And said I, 'Now I have seen you, my mind is well satisfied; and so fare you well!'

'No,' saith he, 'that shall you not do before dinner.'

I made the matter very earnest to be gone; and he, more earnest and importune to stay me. But in truth I was as willing to stay as he to have me.

And so, perforce, there was no remedy but stay we must. And having lighted from horseback; and being by him brought into the house, and so into the buttery, and there caused to drink: presently after, the said Cook came and whispered with me, and asked, Whether my friend (meaning the said Jenkins) were within the Church or not? Therein meaning, Whether he were a Papist or no?

To which I answered, 'He was not; but yet,' said I, 'he is a very honest man, and one that wisheth well that way.'

Then said the Cook to me, 'Will you go up?' By which speech, I knew he would bring me to a Mass.

And I answered him and said, 'Yea, for God's sake, that let me do: for seeing I must needs tarry, let me take something with me that is good.'

And so we left Jenkins in the buttery; and I was brought by the Cook through the hall, the dining parlour, and two or three other odd rooms, and then into a fair large chamber: where there was, at the same instant, one Priest, called Satwell, saying Mass; two other Priests kneeling by, whereof one was Campion, and the other called Peters alias Collington; three Nuns, and 37 other people.

When Satwell had finished his Mass; then Campion he invested himself to say Mass, and so he did: and at the end thereof, made holy bread and delivered it to the people there, to every one some, together with holy water; whereof he gave me part also.

And then was there a chair set in the chamber something beneath the altar, wherein the said Campion did sit down; and there made a sermon very nigh an hour long: the effect of his text being, as I remember, 'That Christ wept over Jerusalem, &c.' And so applied the same to this our country of England for that the Pope his authority and doctrine did not so flourish here as the same Campion desired.

At the end of which sermon, I sat down unto the said Jenkins so soon as I could. For during the time that the Masses and the sermon were made, Jenkins remained still beneath in the buttery or hall; not knowing of any such matter until I gave him some intelligence what I had seen.

And so we departed, with as convenient expedition as we might, and came to one Master Fettiplace, a Justice of the Peace in the said country: whom we made privy of our doings therein; and required him that, according to the tenour of our Commission, he would take sufficient Power, and with us thither.

Whereupon the said Justice of Peace, within one quarter of an hour, put himself in a readiness, with forty or fifty men very well weaponed: who went, in great haste, together with the said Master Fettiplace and us, to the said Master Yate his house.

Where, at our coming upon the sudden, being about one of the clock in the afternoon of the same day, before we knocked at the gates which were then (as before they were continually accustomed to be) fast shut (the house being moated round about; within which moat was great store of fruit trees and other trees, with thick hedgerows: so that the danger for fear of losing of the said Campion and his associates was the more doubted); we beset the house with our men round about the moat in the best sort we could devise: and then knocked at the gates, and were presently heard and espied; but kept out by the space of half an hour.

In which time, as it seemeth, they had hidden Campion and the other two Priests in a very secret place within the said house; and had made reasonable purveyance for him as hereafter is mentioned: and then they let us into the house.

Where came presently to our sight, Mrs Yate, the good wife of the house; five Gentlemen, one Gentlewoman, and three Nuns: the Nuns being then disguised in Gentlewomen's apparel, not like unto that they heard Mass in. All which I well remembered to have seen, the same morning, at the Masses and Sermon aforesaid: yet every one of them a great while denied it. And especially the said Mistress Yate; who could not be content only to make a plain denial of the said Masses and the Priests: but, with great and horrible oaths, forsware the same, betaking herself to the Devil if any such there were; in such sort as, if I had not seen them with mine own eyes, I should have believed her.

But knowing certainly that these were but bare excuses, and that we should find the said Campion and his compeers if we made narrow search; I eftsoons put Master Fettiplace in remembrance of our Commission: and so he, myself, and the said Jenkins Her Majesty's Messenger, went to searching the house; where we found many secret corners.

Continuing the search, although with no small toil, in the orchards, hedges, and ditches, within the moat and divers other places; at the last found out Master Edward Yate, brother to the good man of the house, and two countrymen called Weblin and Mansfield, fast locked together in a pigeon house: but we could not find, at that time, Campion and the other two Priests whom we specially sought for.

It drew then something towards evening, and doubting lest we were not strong enough; we sent our Commission to one Master Foster, High Sheriff of Berkshire; and to one Master Wiseman, a justice of Peace within the same County; for some further aid at their hands.

The said Master Wiseman came with very good speed unto us the same evening, with ten or twelve of his own men, very able men and well appointed: but the said Master Foster could not be found, as the messenger that went for him returned us answer.

And so the said house was beset the same night with at the least three score men well weaponed; who watched the same very diligently.

And the next day, being Monday, in the morning very early, came one Master Christopher Lydcot, a Justice of Peace of the same shire, with a great sort of his own men, all very well appointed: who, together with his men, showed such earnest loyal and forward service in those affairs as was no small comfort and encouragement to all those which were present, and did bear true hearts and good wills to Her Majesty.

The same morning, began a fresh search for the said Priests; which continued with very great labour until about ten of the clock in the forenoon of the same day: but the said Priests could not be found, and every man almost persuaded that they were not there.

Yet still searching, although in effect clean void of any hope for finding of them, the said David Jenkins, by God's great goodness, espied a certain secret place, which he quickly found to be hollow; and with a pin of iron which he had in his hand much like unto a harrow tine, he forthwith did break a hole into the said place: where then presently he perceived the said Priests lying all close together upon a bed, of purpose there laid for them; where they had bread, meat, and drink sufficient to have relieved them three or four days together.

The said Jenkins then called very loudly, and said,'I have found the traitors!'; and presently company enough was with him: who there saw the said Priests, when there was no remedy for them but nolens volens, courteously yielded themselves.

Shortly after came one Master Reade, another justice of the Peace of the said shire, to be assistant in these affairs.

Of all which matters, news was immediately carried in great haste to the Lords of the Privy Council: who gave further Commission that the said Priests and certain others their associates should be brought to the Court under the conduction of myself and the said Jenkins; with commandment to the Sheriff to deliver us sufficient aid forth of his shire, for the safe bringing up of the said people.

After the rumour and noise for the finding out of the said Campion, Satwell, and Peters alias Collington, was in the said house something assuaged; and that the sight of them was to the people there no great novelty: then was the said High Sheriff sent for once again; who all that while had not been seen in this service. But then came, and received into his charge the said Priests and certain others from that day until Thursday following.

The fourth Priest which was by us brought up to the Tower, whose name is William Filbie, was not taken with the said Campion and the rest in the said house: but was apprehended and taken in our watch by chance, in coming to the said house to speak with the said Peters, as he said; and thereupon delivered likewise in charge to the Sheriff, with the rest.

Upon Thursday, the 20th day of July last, we set forwards from the said MasterYate his house towards the Court, with our said charge; being assisted by the said Master Lydcot and Master Wiseman, and a great sort of their men; who never left us until we came to the Tower of London. There were besides, that guarded us thither, 50 or 60 Horsemen; very able men and well appointed: which we received by the said Sheriff his appointment.

We went that day to Henley upon Thames, where we lodged that night.

And about midnight we were put into great fear by reason of a very great cry and noise that the said Filbie made in his sleep; which wakened the most that were that night in the house, and that in such sort that every man almost thought that some of the prisoners had been broken from us and escaped; although there was in and about the same house a very strong watch appointed and charged for the same. The aforesaid Master Lydcot was the first that came unto them: and when the matter was examined, it was found no more but that the said Filbie was in a dream; and, as he said, he verily thought one to be a ripping down his body and taking out his bowels.

The Edict of Nantes
1598

In France, the Huguenot church emerged out of the Protestant movement based on the teachings of Protestant reformer John Calvin. Many prominent and political powerful nobles in France became Huguenots. The ruling dynasty of France, however, the Valois family which included Henri II (r. 1547-59) and his sons Francis II (r. 1559-60, Charles IX (r. 1560-1574) and Henry III (1574-1589), remained staunchly Catholic and adopted sometimes violent policies to stem the growth of the Huguenot movement and suppress the political power of the nobility. The Huguenot nobles' quest for religious and political independence pitted them against the French kings and resulted in a series of civil wars in France, called the Wars of Religion (1562-98). The first French king from the Bourbon dynasty, Henry IV (r. 1589-1610) had been a Huguenot but ultimately converted to Catholicism once he became king. He negotiated the peace that ended the civil war and promulgated this edict which defined the rights of French Huguenots in France.

Source: Sidney Z. Ehler and John B. Morrall, eds. and trans., *Church and State Through the Centuries: A Collection of Historic Documents* (London: Burns and Gates, 1954), 185-188.

FOCUS QUESTIONS:

1. What rights did Huguenots have as a result of this edict? What were the limits on their rights?
2. Why was it necessary to specifically outline the status of Huguenots in France?
3. What larger events influenced and shaped the drafting of this edict? How?

Firstly, that the memory of everything done on both sides from the beginning of the month of March 1585, until our accession to the Crown and during the other previous troubles, and at the outbreak of them, shall remain extinct and suppressed, as if it were something which had never occurred. And it shall not be lawful or permissible to our Procurators-General or to any other persons, public or private, at any time or on any pretext whatsoever, to institute a case, lawsuit or action in any Court or judicial tribunals whatever [concerning those things].

We forbid all our subjects, of whatever rank and quality they may be, to renew the memory of these matters, to attack, be hostile to, injure or provoke each other in revenge for the past, whatever may be the reason and pretext; or to dispute, argue or quarrel about it, or to do violence, or to give offence in deed or word, but let them restrain themselves and live peaceably together as brothers, friends and fellow-citizens, on pain of being liable to punishment as disturbers of the peace and troublers of public quiet.

We ordain that the Catholic, Apostolic and Roman religion shall be restored and re-established in all places and districts of this our kingdom and the countries under our rule, where its practice has been interrupted, so that it can be peacefully and freely practiced there, without any disturbance or hindrance. We forbid very expressly all persons of whatever rank, quality or condition they may be, under the aforesaid penalties, to disturb, molest or cause annoyance to clerics in the celebration of the Divine worship, the enjoyment and receipt of tithes, fruits and revenues of their benefices, and all other rights and duties which belong to them; and we ordain that all those who during the disorders have come into possession of churches, houses, goods and revenues belonging to the said clerics, and who retain and occupy them, shall give back the entire possession and enjoyment of them, with such rights, liberties and safeguards as they had before they were seized. We also forbid very expressly those of the so-called Reformed religion to hold prayer meetings or any devotions of the aforesaid religion in churches, houses and dwellings of the above-said clerics....

And in order not to leave any cause for discords and disputes between our subjects, we have permitted and we permit those of the so-called Reformed religion to live and dwell in all the towns and districts of this our kingdom and the countries under one rule, without being annoyed, disturbed, molested or constrained to do anything against their conscience, or for this cause to be sought out in their houses and districts where they wish to live, provided that they conduct themselves in other respects according to the provisions of our present Edict....

We also permit those of the aforesaid religion to carry out and continue its practice in the towns and districts under our rule, where it was established and carried out publicly several distinct times in the year 1597, until the end of the month of March, notwithstanding all decrees and judgments to the contrary....

We forbid very expressly all those of the aforesaid religion to practice it in so far as ministration, regulation, discipline or public instruction of children and others is concerned, in this our kingdom and the countries under our rule, in matters concerning religion, outside the places permitted and conceded by the present Edict....

Books dealing with the matters of the aforesaid so-called Reformed religion shall not be printed and sold publicly, except in the towns and districts where the public exercise of the said religion is allowed. And with regard to other books which shall be printed in other towns, they shall be seen and inspected by our officials and theologians as laid down by our ordinances. We forbid very specifically the printing, publication and sale of all defamatory books, tracts and writings, under the penalties contained in our ordinances, instructing all our judges and officials to carry out this ruling strictly.

We ordain that there shall be no difference or distinction, because of the aforesaid religion, in the reception of students to be instructed in Universities, Colleges and schools, or of the sick and poor into hospitals, infirmaries and public charitable institutions....

In order to reunite more effectively the wills of our subjects, as is our intention, and to remove all future complaints, we declare that all those who profess or shall profess the aforesaid so-called Reformed religion are capable of holding and exercising all public positions, honours, offices and duties whatsoever, Royal, seigneurial, or offices in the towns of our kingdom, countries, lands and lordships subject to us, notwithstanding all contrary oaths, and of being admitted and received into them without distinction; it shall be sufficient for our courts of Parliament and other judges to ascertain and inquire concerning the life, morals, religion and honest behaviour of those who are or shall be appointed to offices, whether of one religion or the other, without enacting from them any oath other than that of well and faithfully serving the King in the exercise of their functions and keeping the ordinances, as has been perpetually the custom. During vacancies in the aforesaid positions, functions and offices, we shall make—in respect of those which shall be in our disposition—appointments without bias or discrimination of capable persons, as the unity of our subjects requires it. We declare also that members of the aforesaid so-called Reformed religion can be admitted and received into all Councils, conferences, assemblies and gatherings which are connected with the offices in question; they can not be rejected or prevented from enjoying these rights on grounds of the said religion....

And for greater security of the behaviour and conduct which we expect with regard to it [the Edict], we will, command and desire that all the Governors and Lieutenants-General of our provinces, Bailiffs, Seneschals asnd other ordinary judges in towns in our aforesaid kingdom, immediately after the reception of this Edict, swear to cause it to be kept and observed, each one in his own district; likewise the mayors, sheriffs, captains, consuls and magistrates of the towns, annual and perpetual. We also enjoin our said bailiffs, seneschals or their lieutenants and other judges, to cause the principal inhabitants from both religions in the above-mentioned towns to swear to respect the present Edict immediately after its publication. We place all those of the said towns in our protection and safe keeping, each religion being placed in the safe keeping of the other; and we wish them to be instructed respectively and by public acts to answer by due legal process any contraventions of our present Edict which shall be made in the said towns by their inhabitants, or to make known the said contraventions and put them into the hand of justice.

We command our beloved and loyal people who hold our Courts of Parliament, "Chambres des Comptes" and courts of aids that immediately after the present Edict has been received, they are bound, all business being suspended and under penalty of nullity for any acts which they shall make otherwise, to take an oath similar to the above and to make this our Edict to be published and registered in our above-mentioned Courts according to its proper form and meaning, purely and simply, without using any modifications, rectifications, declarations or secret registering and without waiting for further order or commandment from us; and we order our Procurators-General to demand and ensure immediately and without delay the aforesaid publication....

For such is our pleasure. As witness thereof we have signed the present enactment with our own hand, and in order that it may be sure and stable permanently, we have placed and affixed our Seal to it.

Given at Nantes in the month of April, in the year of grace 1598, the ninth year of our reign.

[Signed,] Henry

CHAPTER 11

The Development of Early-Modern States and Societies

Jean Bodin,
Six Books of the Commonwealth,
"The True Attributes of Sovereignty"

Jean Bodin (ca. 1530–1596 CE) was a French political theorist and lawyer. Bodin studied civil law at the University of Toulouse, taught and practiced law, and in 1571 served in the household of the king's brother. The events and turmoil of sixteenth-century France heavily influenced his thought, which was devoted to the maintenance of order. He is most well known for identifying and recognizing the impor-tance of the state's sovereignty. In Six Books of the Commonwealth (1576), Bodin contended that the state, preferably in the form of a monarch, held supreme power. He favored religious toleration and also wrote about the state's role in finance and trade.

Source: Jean Bodin, "The True Attributes of Sovereignty," *Six Livres de la Republique (Six Books of the Commonwealth).*

FOCUS QUESTIONS:

1. According to Bodin, what kind of rights of sovereignty does a sovereign possess?
2. To Bodin, what is the difference between custom and law?

SIX BOOKS OF THE COMMONWEALTH BOOK I, CHAPTER X: THE TRUE ATTRIBUTES OF SOVEREIGNTY

The first attribute of the sovereign prince therefore is the power to make law binding on all his subjects in general and on each in particular. But to avoid any ambiguity one must add that he does so without the consent of any superior, equal, or inferior being necessary. If the prince can only make law with the consent of a superior he is a subject; if of an equal he shares his sovereignty; if of an inferior, whether it be a council of magnates or the people, it is not he who is sovereign. The names of the magnates that one finds appended to a royal edict are not there to give force to the law, but as witnesses, and to make it more acceptable…When I say that the first attribute of sovereignty is to give law to all in general and each in particular, I mean by this last phrase the grant of privileges. I mean by a privilege a concession to one or a small group of individuals which concerns the profit or loss of those persons only…

It may be objected however that not only have magistrates the power of issuing edicts and ordinances, each according to his competence and within his own sphere of jurisdiction, but private citizens can make law in the form of general or local custom. It is agreed that customary law is as binding as statute law. But if the sovereign prince is author of the law, his subjects are the authors of custom. But there is a difference between law and custom. Custom establishes itself gradually over a long period of years, and by common consent, or at any rate the consent of the greater part. Law is made on the instant and draws its force from him who has the right to bind all the rest. Custom is established imperceptibly and without any exercise of compulsion. Law is promulgated and imposed by authority, and often against the wishes of the subject. For this reason Dion Chrysostom compared custom to the king and law to the tyrant. Moreover law can break custom, but custom cannot derogate from the law, nor can the magistrate, or any other responsible for the administration of law, use his discretion about the enforcement of law as he can about custom. Law, unless it is permissive and relaxes the severity of another law, always carries penalties for its breach. Custom only has binding force by the sufferance and during the good pleasure of the sovereign prince, and so far as he is willing to authorize it. Thus the force of both statutes and customary law derives from the authorization of the prince…Included in the power of making and unmaking law is that of promulgating it and amending it when it is obscure, or when the magistrates find contradictions and absurdities…

All the other attributes and rights of sovereignty are included in this power of making and unmaking law, so that strictly speaking this is the unique attribute of sovereign power. It includes all other rights of sovereignty, that is to say of making peace and war, of hearing appeals from the sentences of all courts whatsoever, of appointing and dismissing the great officers of state; of taxing, or granting privileges of exemption to all subjects, of appreciating or depreciating the value and weight of the coinage, of receiving oaths of fidelity from subjects and liege-vassals alike, without exception of any other to whom faith is due…

But because law is an imprecise and general term, it is as well to specify the other attributes of sovereignty comprised in it, such as the making of war and peace. This is one of the most important rights of sovereignty, since it brings in its train either the ruin or the salvation of the state. This was a right of sovereignty not only among the ancient Romans, but has always been so among all other peoples...Sovereign princes are therefore accustomed to keep themselves informed of the smallest accidents and undertakings connected with warfare. Whatever latitude they may give to their representatives to negotiate peace or an alliance, they never grant the authority to conclude without their own express consent. This was illustrated in the negotiations leading up to the recent treaty of Cateaux-Cambresis, when the king's envoys kept him almost hourly informed of all proposals and counter-proposals...In popular states and aristocracies the difficulty of assembling the people, and the danger of making public all the secrets of diplomacy has meant that the people have generally handed responsibility over to the council. Nevertheless it remains true that the commissions and the orders that it issues in discharge of this function proceed from the authority of the people, and are despatched by the council in the name of the people...

The third attribute of sovereignty is the power to institute the great officers of state. It has never been questioned that the right is an attribute of sovereignty, at any rate as far as the great officers are concerned. I confine it however to high officials, for there is no commonwealth in which these officers, and many guilds and corporate bodies besides, have not some power of appointing their subordinate officials. They do this in virtue of their office, which carries with it the power to delegate. For instance, those who hold feudal rights of jurisdiction of their sovereign prince in faith and homage have the power to appoint the judges in their courts, and their assistants. But this power is devolved upon them by the prince...It is therefore not the mere appointment of officials that implies sovereign right, but the authorization and confirmation of such appointments. It is true however that in so far as the exercise of this right is delegated, the sovereignty of the prince is to that extent qualified, unless his concurrence and express consent is required.

The fourth attribute of sovereignty, and one which has always been among its principal rights, is that the prince should be the final resort of appeal from all other courts...Even though the prince may have published a law, as did Caligula, forbidding any appeal or petition against the sentences of his officers, nevertheless the subject cannot be deprived of the right to make an appeal, or present a petition, to the prince in person. For the prince cannot tie his own hands in this respect, nor take from his subjects the means of redress, supplication, and petition, notwithstanding the fact that all rules governing appeals and jurisdictions are matters of positive law, which we have shown does not bind the prince. This is why the Privy Council, including the Chancellor de l'Hopital, considered the action of the commissioners deputed to hold an enquiry into the conduct of the President l'Alemant irregular and unprecedented. They had forbidden him to approach within twenty leagues of the court, with the intention of denying him any opportunity of appeal. The king himself could not deny this right to the subject, though he is free to make whatsoever reply to the appeal, favourable or unfavourable, that he pleases...Were it otherwise, and the prince could acquit his subjects or his vassals from the obligation to submit their causes to him in the last instance, he would make of them sovereigns equal with himself...But if he would pre-serve his authority, the surest way of doing so is to avoid ever devolving any of the attributes of sovereignty upon a subject...

With this right is coupled the right of pardoning convicted persons, and so of overruling the sentences of his own courts, in mitigation of the severity of the law, whether touching life, property, honour, or domicile. It is not in the power of any magistrate, whatever his station, to do any of these things, or to make any revision of the judgement he has once given...In a well-ordered commonwealth the right should never be delegated either to a special commission, or to any high officer of state, save in those circumstances where it is necessary to establish a regency, either because the king is abroad in some distant place, or in captivity, or incapable, or under age. For instance, during the minority of Louis IX, the authority of the Crown was vested in his mother Blanche of Castile as his guardian...Princes however tend to abuse this right, thinking that to pardon is pleasing to God, whereas to exact the utmost punishment is displeasing to Him. But I hold, subject to correction, that the sovereign prince cannot remit any penalty imposed by the law of God, any more than he can dispense any one from the operation of the law of God, to which he himself is subject. If the magistrate who dispenses anyone from obedience to the ordinance of his king merits death, how much more unwarrantable is it for the prince to acquit a man of the punishment ordained by God's law? If a sovereign prince cannot deny a subject his civil rights, how can he acquit him of the penalties imposed by God, such as the death penalty exacted by divine law for treacherous murder?

Hugo Grotius,
selections from *On the Law of War and Peace*

Hugo Grotius (1583–1645 CE) was a Dutch jurist and legal scholar. Grotius's 1625 treatise, On the Law of War and Peace, is considered to be the founding and most comprehensive early work on modern inter-national law. In it, Grotius surveyed classical history and the Bible and argued that natural law established rules of conduct for nations and individuals, thereby constituting a legal foundation for international cooperation. Grotius studied law at the University of Leiden and wrote numerous theological and legal works, such as The Free Seas (1604), which advocated the unrestricted navigation of the seas for free trade.

Source: Hugo Grotius, *On the Law of War and Peace* (1625).

1. According to Grotius, does the principle of natural right depend on God and religion?

2. What does Grotius contend about natural law when he observes Aristotle's statement "that some things are no sooner named, than we discover their evil nature"?

BOOK I
Chapter 1: ON WAR AND RIGHT

X. Natural right is the dictate of right reason, shewing the moral turpitude, or moral necessity, of any act from its agreement or disagreement with a rational nature, and consequently that such an act is either forbidden or commanded by God, the author of nature. The actions, upon which such a dictate is given, are either binding or unlawful in themselves, and therefore necessarily understood to be commanded or forbidden by God. This mark distinguishes natural right, not only from human law, but from the law, which God himself has been pleased to reveal, called, by some, the voluntary divine right, which does not command or forbid things in themselves either binding or unlawful, but makes them unlawful by its prohibition, and binding by its command. But, to understand natural right, we must observe that some things are said to belong to that right, not properly, but, as the schoolmen say, by way of accommodation. These are not repugnant to natural right, as we have already observed that those things are called JUST, in which there is no injustice. Some times also, by a wrong use of the word, those things which reason shews to be proper, or better than things of an opposite kind, although not binding, are said to belong to natural right.

We must farther remark, that natural right relates not only to those things that exist independent of the human will, but to many things, which necessarily follow the exercise of that will. Thus property, as now in use, was at first a creature of the human will. But, after it was established, one man was prohibited by the law of nature from seizing the property of another against his will. Wherefore, Paulus the Lawyer said, that theft is expressly forbidden by the law of nature. Ulpian condemns it as infamous in its own nature; to whose authority that of Euripides may be added, as may be seen in the verse of Helena:

"For God himself hates violence, and will not have us to grow rich by rapine, but by lawful gains. That abundance, which is the fruit of unrighteousness, is an abomination. The air is common to men, the earth also where every man, in the ample enjoyment of his possession, must refrain from doing violence or injury to that of another."

Now the Law of Nature is so unalterable, that it cannot be changed even by God himself. For although the power of God is infinite, yet there are some things, to which it does not extend. Because the things so expressed would have no true meaning, but imply a contradiction. Thus two and two must make four, nor is it possible to be otherwise; nor, again, can what is really evil not be evil. And this is Aristotle's meaning, when he says, that some things are no sooner named, than we discover their evil nature. For as the substance of things in their nature and existence depends upon nothing but themselves; so there are qualities insepara-bly connected with their being and essence. Of this kind is the evil of certain actions, compared with the nature of a reasonable being. Therefore God himself suffers his actions to be judged by this rule, as may be seen in the xviiith chap. of Gen. 25. Isa. v. 3. Ezek. xviii. 25. Jer. ii. 9. Mich. vi. 2. From. ii. 6., iii. 6. Yet it some-times happens that, in those cases, which are decided by the law of nature, the undiscerning are imposed upon by an appearance of change. Whereas in reality there is no change in the unalterable law of nature, but only in the things appointed by it, and which are liable to variation. For example, if a creditor for-give me the debt, which I owe him, I am no longer bound to pay it, not because the law of nature has ceased to command the payment of a just debt, but because my debt, by a release, has ceased to be a debt. On this topic, Arrian in Epictetus argues rightly, that the bor-rowing of money is not the only requisite to make a debt, but there must be the additional circumstance of the loan remaining undis-charged. Thus if God should command the life, or property of any one to be taken away, the act would not authorise murder or robbery, words which always include a crime. But that cannot be murder or robbery, which is done by the express command of Him, who is the sovereign Lord of our lives and of all things. There are also some things allowed by the law of nature, not absolutely, but according to a certain state of affairs. Thus, by the law of nature, before prop-erty was introduced, every one had a right to the use of whatever he found unoc-cupied; and, before laws were enacted, to avenge his personal injuries by force.

XI. The distinction found in the books of the Roman Law, assigning one unchangeable right to brutes in common with man, which in a more limited sense they call the law of nature, and appropriating another to men, which they frequently call the Law of Nations, is scarcely of any real use. For no beings, except those that can form general maxims, are capable of possessing a right, which Hesiod has placed in a clear point of view, observing "that the supreme Being has appointed laws for men; but permitted wild beasts, fishes, and birds to devour each other for food." For they have nothing like justice, the best gift, bestowed upon men.

Cicero, in his first book of offices, says, we do not talk of the justice of hors-es or lions. In conformity to which, Plutarch, in the life of Cato the elder, observes, that we are formed by nature to use law and justice towards men only. In addition to the above, Lactantius may be cited, who, in his fifth book, says that in all animals devoid of reason we see a natural bias of self-love. For they hurt others to benefit themselves; because they do not know the evil of doing willful hurt. But it is not so with man, who, possessing the knowledge of good and evil, refrains, even with inconvenience to himself, from doing hurt. Polybius, relating the manner in which men first entered into society, concludes, that the injuries done to parents or benefactors inevitably provoke the indignation of mankind, giving an additional reason, that as understanding and reflection form the great difference between men and other animals, it is evident they cannot transgress the bounds of that difference like other animals, without exciting universal abhorrence of their conduct. But if ever justice is attributed to brutes, it is done improperly, from some shadow and trace of reason they may possess. But it is not material to the nature of right, whether the actions appointed by the law of nature, such as the care of our offspring, are common to us with other animals or not, or, like the worship of God, are peculiar to man.

XII. The existence of the Law of Nature is proved by two kinds of argument, a priori, and a posteriori, the former a more abstruse, and the latter a more popular method of proof. We are said to reason a priori, when we show the agreement or disagreement of any thing with a reasonable and social nature; but a posteriori, when without absolute proof, but only upon probability, any thing is inferred to accord with the law of nature, because it is received as such among all, or at least the more civilized nations. For a general effect can only arise from a general cause. Now scarce any other cause can be assigned for so general an opinion, but the common sense, as it is called, of mankind. There is a sentence of Hesiod that has been much praised, that opinions which have prevailed amongst many nations, must have some foundation. Heraclitus, establishing common reason as the best criterion of truth, says, those things are certain which generally appear so. Among other authorities, we may quote Aristotle, who says it is a strong proof in our favour, when all appear to agree with what we say, and Cicero maintains that the consent of all nations in any case is to be admitted for the law of nature. Seneca is of the same opinion, any thing, says he, appearing the same to all men is a proof of its truth. Quintilian says, we hold those things to be true, in which all men agree. We have called them the more civilized nations, and not without reason. For, as Porphyry well observes, some nations are so strange that no fair judgment of human nature can be formed from them, for it would be erroneous. Andronicus, the Rhodian says, that with men of a right and sound understanding, natural justice is unchangeable. Nor does it alter the case, though men of disordered and perverted minds think otherwise. For he who should deny that honey is sweet, because it appears not so to men of a distempered taste, would be wrong. Plutarch too agrees entirely with what has been said, as appears from a passage in his life of Pompey, affirming that man neither was, nor is, by nature, a wild unsociable creature. But it is the corruption of his nature which makes him so: yet by acquiring new habits, by changing his place, and way of living, he may be reclaimed to his original gentleness. Aristotle, taking a description of man from his peculiar qualities, makes him an animal of a gentle nature, and in another part of his works, he observes, that in considering the nature of man, we are to take our likeness from nature in its pure, and not in its corrupt state.

Thomas Hobbes,
The Leviathan

Thomas Hobbes, a philosopher and writer, published his political treatise, The Leviathan, in 1651 during the English Civil War (1642-1660), two years after the execution of King Charles I (r. 1625-1649). Hobbes lived and worked in England, but fled to Paris after the English Parliament condemned his book during the Civil War. In *The Leviathan*, Hobbes argued the best government was a "common-wealth," a government based on a covenant between a monarch and subjects. In this excerpt from chapter thirteen, Hobbes outlines his views regarding the natural state of man, or human nature in its most basic state. His views on the natural state of man served as a basis and justification for his ideas about government and the powers of a monarch.

Source: Thomas Hobbes, *The Leviathan, in Cambridge Texts in the History of Political Thought*, ed. by Richard Tuck (New York: Cambridge University Press, 1996), 86-90.

FOCUS QUESTIONS:

1. How did Hobbes describe the natural state of man? What was the best type of government given the natural state of man? What powers should a monarch or ruler have, according to Hobbes?

2. How did the English Civil War affect his views of government? What was his stance; did he support or oppose the end of the monarchy? Why or why not?

3. Compare Hobbes' views about a monarch's power to those by French advocates of "divine right" monarchy, such as Richelieu, Bossuet and Louis XIV. How were Hobbes's ideas similar? Different?

MEN BY NATURE EQUALL

Nature hath made men so equall, in the faculties of body, and mind; as that though there bee found one man sometimes manifestly stronger in body, or of quicker mind then another; yet when all is reckoned together, the difference between man, and man, is not so considerable, as that one man can thereupon claim to himselfe any benefit, to which another may not pretend, as well as he. For as to the strength of body, the weakest has strength enough to kill the strongest, either by secret machination, or by confederacy with others, that are in the same danger with himselfe.

And as to the faculties of the mind, (setting aside the arts grounded upon words, and especially that skill of proceeding upon generall, and infallible rules, called Science; which very few have, and but in few things; as being not a native faculty, born with us; nor attained, (as Prudence,) while we look after somewhat els,) I find yet a greater equality amongst men, than that of strength. For Prudence, is but Experience; which equall time, equally bestowes on all men, in those things they equally apply themselves unto. That which may perhaps make such equality incredible, is but a vain conceit of ones owne wisdome, which almost all men think they have in a greater degree, than the Vulgar; that is, than all men but themselves, and a few others, whom by Fame, or for concurring with themselves, they approve. For such is the nature of men, that howsoever they may acknowledge many others to be more witty, or more eloquent, or more learned; Yet they will hardly believe there be many so wise as themselves: For they see their own wit at hand, and other mens at a distance. But this proveth rather that men are in that point equall, than unequall. For there is not ordinarily a greater signe of the equall distribution of any thing, than that every man is contented with his share.

FROM EQUALITY PROCEEDS DIFFIDENCE

From this equality of ability, ariseth equality of hope in the attaining of our Ends. And therefore if any two men desire the same thing, which neverthelesse they cannot both enjoy, they become enemies; and in the way to their End, (which is principally their owne conservation, and sometimes their delectation only,) endeavour to destroy, or subdue one an other. And from hence it comes to passe, that where an Invader hath no more to feare, than an other mans single power; if one plant, sow, build, or possesse a convenient Seat, others may probably be expected to come prepared with forces united, to dispossesse, and deprive him, not only of the fruit of his labour, but also of his life, or liberty. And the Invader again is in the like danger of another.

FROM DIFFIDENCE WARRE

And from this diffidence of one another, there is no way for any man to secure himselfe, so reasonable, as Anticipation; that is, by force, or wiles, to master the persons of all men he can, so long, till he see no other power great enough to endanger him: And this is no more than his own conservation requireth, and is generally allowed. Also because there be some, that taking pleasure in contemplating their own power in the acts of conquest, which they pursue farther than their security requires; if others, that otherwise would be glad to be at ease within modest bounds, should not by invasion increase their power, they would not be able, long time, by standing only on their defence, to subsist. And by consequence, such augmentation of dominion over men, being necessary to a mans conservation, it ought to be allowed him.

Againe, men have no pleasure, (but on the contrary a great deale of griefe) in keeping company, where there is no power able to over-awe them all. For every man looketh that his companion should value him, at the same rate he sets upon himselfe: And upon all signes of contempt, or undervaluing, naturally endeavours, as far as he dares (which amongst them that have no common power to keep them in quiet, is far enough to make them destroy each other,) to extort a greater value from his contemners, by dommage; and from others, by the example.

So that in the nature of man, we find three principall causes of quarrell. First, Competition; Secondly, Diffidence; Thirdly, Glory.

The first, maketh men invade for Gain; the second, for Safety; and the third, for Reputation. The first use Violence, to make themselves Masters of other mens persons, wives, children, and cattell; the second, to defend them; the third, for trifles, as a word, a smile, a different opinion, and any other signe of undervalue, either direct in their Persons, or by reflexion in their Kindred, their Friends, their Nation, their Profession, or their Name.

OUT OF CIVIL STATES, THERE IS ALWAYS WARRE OF EVERYONE AGAINST EVERY ONE

Hereby it is manifest, that during the time men live without a common Power to keep them all in awe, they are in that condition which is called Warre; and such a warre, as is of every man, against every man. For WARRE, consisteth not in Bat-tell onely, or the act of fighting; but in a tract of time, wherein the Will to contend by Battell is sufficiently known: and therefore the notion of Time, is to be considered in the nature of WARRE; as it is in the nature of Weather. For as the nature of Foule weather, lyeth not in a showre or two of rain; but in an inclination thereto of many dayes together: So the nature of War, consisteth not in actuall fighting; but in the known disposition thereto, during all the time there is no assurance to the contrary. All other time is PEACE.

THE INCOMMODITIES OF SUCH A WAR

Whatsoever therefore is consequent to a time of Warre, where every man is Enemy to every man; the same is consequent to the time, wherein men live without other security, than what their own strength, and their own invention shall furnish them withall. In such condition, there is no place for Industry; because the fruit thereof is uncertain: and consequently no Culture of the Earth; no Navigation, nor use of the commodities that may be imported by Sea; no commodious Building; no Instruments of moving, and removing such things as require much force; no Knowledge of the face of the Earth; no account of Time; no Arts; no Letters; no Society; and which is worst of all, continuall feare, and danger of violent death; And the life of man, solitary, poore, nasty, brutish, and short.

It may seem strange to some man, that has not well weighed these things; that Nature should thus dissociate, and render men apt to invade, and destroy one another: and he may therefore, not trusting to this Inference, made from the

Passions, desire perhaps to have the same confirmed by Experience. Let him therefore consider with himselfe, when taking a journey, he armes himselfe, and seeks to go well accompanied; when going to sleep, he locks his dores; when even in his house he locks his chests; and this when he knowes there bee Lawes, and publike Officers, armed, to revenge all injuries shall bee done him; what opinion he has of his fellow subjects, when he rides armed; of his fellow Citizens, when he locks his dores; and of his children, and servants, when he locks his chests. Does he not there as much accuse mankind by his actions, as I do by my words? But neither of us accuse mans nature in it. The Desires, and other Passions of man, are in themselves no Sin. No more are the Actions, that proceed from those Passions, till they know a Law that forbids them: which till Lawes be made they cannot know: nor can any Law be made, till they have agreed upon the Person that shall make it.

It may peradventure be thought, there was never such a time, nor condition of warre as this; and I believe it was never generally so, over all the world: but there are many places, where they live so now. For the savage people in many places of America, except the government of small Families, the concord where-of dependeth on naturall lust, have no government at all; and live at this day in that brutish manner, as I said before. Howsoever, it may be perceived what man-ner of life there would be, where there were no common Power to feare; by the manner of life, which men that have formerly lived under a peacefull govern-ment, use to degenerate into, in a civill Warre.

But though there had never been any time, wherein particular men were in a condition of warre one against another; yet in all times, Kings, and Persons of Soveraigne authority, because of their Independency, are in continuall jealousies, and in the state and posture of Gladiators; having their weapons pointing, and their eyes fixed on one another; that is, their Forts, Garrisons, and Guns upon the Frontiers of their Kingdomes; and continuall Spyes upon their neighhours, which is a posture of War. But because they uphold thereby, the Industry of their Subjects; there does not follow from it, that misery, which accompanies the Liberty of particular men.

IN SUCH A WARRE, NOTHING IS UNJUST

To this warre of every man against every man, this also is consequent; that nothing can be Unjust. The notions of Right and Wrong, Justice and Injustice have there no place. Where there is no common Power, there is no Law: where no Law, no Injustice. Force, and Fraud, are in warre the two Cardinall vertues. Justice, and Injustice are none of the Faculties neither of the Body, nor Mind. If they were, they might be in a man that were alone in the world, as well as his Senses, and Passions. They are Qualities, that relate to men in Society, not in Solitude. It is consequent also to the same condition, that there be no Propriety, no Dominion, no Mineand Thinedistinct; but onely that to be every mans, that he can get; and for so long, as he can keep it. And thus much for the ill condition, which man by meer Nature is actually placed in; though with a possibility to come out of it, consisting partly in the Passions, partly in his Reason.

THE PASSIONS THAT ENCLINE MEN TO PEACE

The Passions that encline men to Peace, are Feare of Death; Desire of such things as are necessary to commodious living; and a Hope by their Industry to obtain them. And Reason suggesteth convenient Articles of Peace, upon which men may be drawn to agreement. These Articles, are they, which otherwise are called the Lawes of Nature: whereof I shall speak more particularly, in the two following Chapters.

The Treaty of Westphalia
1743

The Treaty of Westphalia (1743–1794 CE) was a treaty between the Holy Roman Emperor, Ferdinand III, and the King of France, Louis XIV. Part of a general European settlement that ended the Thirty Years' War and the Eighty Years' War between Spain and the Netherlands, the Treaty, negotiated in Westphalia, marked the beginning of the European state system based on the sovereignty of states. It ended the Holy Roman Empire's supremacy and witnessed France's rise as the major European power. Catholics, Lutherans ("Confession of Augsberg"), and, for the first time, Calvinists ("Reformed") were recognized and could be tolerated with the consent of the sovereign ruler of each territory.

Source: The Treaty of Westphalia, 1648.

FOCUS QUESTIONS:

1. Does the treaty appear to focus on general principles, specific issues, or both?

2. Does the treaty seem to focus mainly on the concerns of the Holy Roman Emperor or the King of France?

TREATY OF WESTPHALIA; OCTOBER 24, 1648

Peace Treaty between the Holy Roman Emperor and the King of France and their respective Allies.
I.

That there shall be a Christian and Universal Peace, and a perpetual, true, and sincere Amity, between his Sacred Imperial Majesty, and his most Christian

Majesty; as also, between all and each of the Allies, and Adherents of his said Imperial Majesty, the House of Austria, and its Heirs, and Successors; but chiefly between the Electors, Princes, and States of the Empire on the one side; and all and each of the Allies of his said Christian Majesty, and all their Heirs and Successors, chiefly between the most Serene Queen and Kingdom of Swedeland, the Electors respectively, the Princes and States of the Empire, on the other part. That this Peace and Amity be observ'd and cultivated with such a Sincerity and Zeal, that each Party shall endeavour to procure the Benefit, Honour and Advantage of the other; that thus on all sides they may see this Peace and Friendship in the Roman Empire, and the Kingdom of France flourish, by entertaining a good and faithful Neighbourhood.

III.

And that a reciprocal Amity between the Emperor, and the Most Christian King, the Electors, Princes and States of the Empire, may be maintain'd so much the more firm and sincere (to say nothing at present of the Article of Security, which will be mention'd hereafter) the one shall never assist the present or future Enemys of the other under any Title or Pretence whatsoever, either with Arms, Money, Soldiers, or any sort of Ammunition; nor no one, who is a Member of this Pacification, shall suffer any Enemy's Troops to retire thro' or sojourn in his Country.

XXVIII.

That those of the Confession of Augsburg, and particularly the Inhabitants of Oppenheim, shall be put in possession again of their Churches, and Ecclesiastical Estates, as they were in the Year 1624. as also that all others of the said Confession of Augsburg, who shall demand it, shall have the free Exercise of their Religion, as well in publick Churches at the appointed Hours, as in private in their own Houses, or in others chosen for this purpose by their Ministers, or by those of their Neighbours, preaching the Word of God.

XLVI.

As for the rest, Law and Justice shall be administer'd in Bohemia, and in all the other Hereditary Provinces of the Emperor, without any respect; as to the Catholicks, so also to the Subjects, Creditors, Heirs, or private Persons, who shall be of the Confession of Augsburg, if they have any Pretensions, and enter or prosecute any Actions to obtain Justice.

XLIX.

And since for the greater Tranquillity of the Empire, in its general Assemblys of Peace, a certain Agreement has been made between the Emperor, Princes and States of the Empire, which has been inserted in the Instrument and Treaty of

Peace, concluded with the Plenipotentiarys of the Queen and Crown of Swedeland, touching the Differences about Ecclesiastical Lands, and the Liberty of the Exercise of Religion; it has been found expedient to confirm, and ratify it by this present Treaty, in the same manner as the abovesaid Agreement has been made with the said Crown of Swedeland; also with those call'd the Reformed, in the same manner, as if the words of the abovesaid Instrument were reported here verbatim.

LXIV.

And to prevent for the future any Differences arising in the Politick State, all and every one of the Electors, Princes and States of the Roman Empire, are so establish'd and confirm'd in their antient Rights, Prerogatives, Libertys, Privileges, free exercise of Territorial Right, as well Ecclesiastick, as Politick Lordships, Regales, by virtue of this present Transaction: that they never can or ought to be molested therein by any whomsoever upon any manner of pretence.

LXV.

They shall enjoy without contradiction, the Right of Suffrage in all Deliberations touching the Affairs of the Empire; but above all, when the Business in hand shall be the making or interpreting of Laws, the declaring of Wars, imposing of Taxes, levying or quartering of Soldiers, erecting new Fortifications in the Territorys of the States, or reinforcing the old Garisons; as also when a Peace of Alliance is to be concluded, and treated about, or the like, none of these, or the like things shall be acted for the future, without the Suffrage and Consent of the Free Assembly of all the States of the Empire: Above all, it shall be free perpetually to each of the States of the Empire, to make Alliances with Strangers for their Preservation and Safety; provided, nevertheless, such Alliances be not against the Emperor, and the Empire, nor against the Publick Peace, and this Treaty, and without prejudice to the Oath by which every one is bound to the Emperor and the Empire.

LXX.

The Rights and Privileges of Territorys, water'd by Rivers or otherways, as Customs granted by the Emperor, with the Consent of the Electors, and among others, to the Count of Oldenburg on the Viserg, and introduc'd by a long Usage, shall remain in their Vigour and Execution. There shall be a full Liberty of Commerce, a secure Passage by Sea and Land: and after this manner all and every one of the Vassals, Subjects, Inhabitants and Servants of the Allys, on the one side and the other, shall have full power to go and come, to trade and return back, by Virtue of this present Article, after the same manner as was allowed before the Troubles of Germany; the Magistrates, on the one side and on the other, shall be oblig'd to protect and defend them against all sorts of

Oppressions, equally with their own Subjects, without prejudice to the other Articles of this Convention, and the particular laws and Rights of each place. And that the said Peace and Amity between the Emperor and the Most Christian King, may be the more corroborated, and the publick Safety provided for, it has been agreed with the Consent, Advice and Will of the Electors, Princes and States of the Empire, for the Benefit of Peace:

LXXVII.

The most Christian King shall, nevertheless, be oblig'd to preserve in all and every one of these Countrys the Catholick Religion, as maintain'd under the Princes of Austria, and to abolish all Innovations crept in during the War.

XC.

That all the Vassals, Subjects, Citizens and Inhabitants, as well on this as the other side the Rhine, who were subject to the House of Austria, or who depended immediately on the Empire, or who acknowledg'd for Superiors the other Orders of the Empire, notwithstanding all Confiscations, Transferrings, Donations made by any Captains or Generals of the Swedish Troops, or Confederates, since the taking of the Province, and ratify'd by the most Christian King, or decreed by his own particular Motion; immediately after the Publication of Peace, shall be restor'd to the possession of their Goods, immovable and stable, also to their Farms, Castles, Villages, Lands, and Possessions, without any exception upon the account of Expences and Compensation of Charges, which the modern Possessors may alledge, and without Restitution of Movables or Fruits gather'd in.

CIV.

As soon as the Treaty of Peace shall be sign'd and seal'd by the Plenipotentiarys and Ambassadors, all Hostilitys shall cease, and all Partys shall study immediately to put in execution what has been agreed to; and that the same may be the better and quicker accomplish'd, the Peace shall be solemnly publish'd the day after the signing thereof in the usual form at the Cross of the Citys of Munster and of Osnabrug. That when it shall be known that the signing has been made in these two Places, divers Couriers shall presently be sent to the Generals of the Armys, to acquaint them that the Peace is concluded, and take care that the Generals chuse a Day, on which shall be made on all sides a Cessation of Arms and Hostilitys for the publishing of the Peace in the Army; and that command be given to all and each of the chief Officers Military and Civil, and to the Governors of Fortresses, to abstain for the future from all Acts of Hostility: and if it happen that any thing be attempted, or actually innovated after the said Publication, the same shall be forthwith repair'd and restor'd to its former State.

CV.

The Plenipotentiarys on all sides shall agree among themselves, between the Conclusion and the Ratification of the Peace, upon the Ways, Time, and Securitys which are to be taken for the Restitution of Places, and for the Disbanding of Troops; of that both Partys may be assur'd, that all things agreed to shall be sincerely accomplish'd.

Done, pass'd and concluded at Munster in Westphalia, the 24th Day of October, 1648.

The Poor Laws

With vagrancy and poverty on the upswing at the end of the sixteenth century, the English Parliament and Queen Elizabeth I (r. 1533-1603) worked together to enact laws designed to address poverty. With Elizabeth's urging, the English Parliament passed a series of laws addressing poverty in England, collectively called the Poor Laws, beginning in 1597, that provided government assistance to those who could not provide for themselves including the sick, elderly, and young children. The Poor Laws also set up government workhouses for those who were able to work and designated which local officials were charged with instituting these programs. These laws remained in place long after Elizabeth's reign, providing the basis for government policies for the poor until the nineteenth century.

Source: G. W. Prothero, *Select Statutes and other Constitutional Documents Illustrative of the Reigns of Elizabeth and James I, 4th ed.,* (New York: Oxford at the Clarendon Press, 1934), 72-75, 96-103.

FOCUS QUESTIONS:

1. How did these laws define "the poor"? What did these laws mean for them?

2. How did these laws attempt to solve the problems associated with poverty? What groups or individuals were designated to implement these laws? Why?

3. What larger concerns or trends help to explain why these laws were enacted in this period?

AN ACT FOR THE RELIEF OF THE POOR

I. Be it enacted, That the churchwardens of every parish and four substantial householders there being subsidy men, or (for want of subsidy men) four other substantial householders of the said parish, who shall be nominated yearly in Easter week under the hand and seal of two or more justices of the peace in the same county, whereof one to be of the quorum, dwelling in or near the same parish, shall be called overseers of the poor of the same parish; and they... shall take order from time to time with the consent of two or more such justices of peace for setting to work of the children of all such [sic] whose parents shall not by the said persons be thought able to keep and maintain their children, and also all such persons, married or unmarried, as, having no means to maintain them, use no ordinary and daily trade of life to get their living by; and also to raise . . . by taxation of every inhabitant and every occupier of lands in the said parish... a convenient stock of flax, hemp, wool, thread, iron and other stuff to set the poor on work, and also competent sums of money for the necessary relief of the lame, impotent, old, blind and such other among them being poor and not able to work, and also for the putting out of such children to be apprentices... and to do all other things... concerning the premises as to them shall seem convenient:

* * *

II. And be it also enacted, That if the said justices of peace do perceive that the inhabitants of any parish are not able to levy among themselves sufficient sums of money for the purposes aforesaid, that then the said justices shall tax . . . any other of other parishes . . . within the hundred where the said parish is, to pay such sums of money . . . as the said justices shall think fit, according to the intent of this law; and if the said hundred shall not be thought to the said justices able to relieve the said several parishes . . . then the justices of peace at their general quarter sessions shall rate and assess as aforesaid any other of other parishes . . . within the said county for the purposes aforesaid as in their discretion shall seem fit.

III. And that it shall be lawful for the said churchwardens and overseers or any of them by warrant from any such two justices of peace to levy as well the said sums of money of every one that shall refuse to contribute... by distress and sale of the offender's goods, as the sums of money or stock which shall be behind upon any account to be made as aforesaid...; and in defect of such distress it shall be lawful for any such two justices of the peace to commit him to prison, there to remain... till payment of the said sum or stock; and the said justices of peace or any one of them to send to the house of correction such as shall not employ themselves to work being appointed thereunto as aforesaid; and also any two such justices of peace to commit to prison every one of the said churchwardens and overseers which shall refuse to account, there to remain... till he have made a true account and paid so much as upon the said account shall be remaining in his hands.

And be it further enacted, That it shall be lawful for the said churchwardens and overseers by the assent of any two justices of the peace to bind any such children as aforesaid to be apprentices when they shall see convenient, till such man-child shall come to the age of 24 years and such woman-child to the ahe of 21 years...

And be it further enacted, That... no person shall go wandering abroad and beg in any place whatsoever, by licence or without, upon pain to be taken and punished as a rogue: provided always that this present Act shall not extend to any poor people which shall ask relief of victuals only in the same parish where such poor people do dwell, so the same be... according to such order as shall be made by the churchwardens and overseers of the poor of the same parish...

XI. And be it further enacted, That all penalties and forfeitures before mentioned in this Act shall be employed to the use of the poor of the same parish, and towards a stock and habitation for them and other necessary uses and relief . . .

XIII. And be it also enacted, That the said justices of the peace at their general quarter sessions . . . shall set down what competent sum of money shall be sent quarterly out of every county or place corporate for the relief of the poor prisoners of the King's Bench and Marshalsea, and also of such hospitals and almshouses as shall be in the said county . . . so as there be sent out of every county yearly 20s. at the least to the prisoners of the King's Bench and Marshalsea;

XIV. And be it further enacted, That all the surplusage of money which shall be remaining in the said stock of any county shall by... the justices of peace in their quarter sessions be ordered and bestowed for the relief of the poor hospitals of that county, and of those that shall sustain losses by fire... or other casualties, and to such other charitable purposes... as to the said justices of peace shall seem convenient.

AN ACT FOR PUNISHMENT OF ROGUES, VAGABONDS AND STURDY BEGGARS

II. Be it further enacted, That all persons calling themselves scholars going about begging, all seafaring men pretending losses [&c.] shall be deemed rogues, vagabonds and sturdy beggars, and shall sustain such punishment as by this Act is in that behalf appointed.

III. And be it enacted, That every person which is by this present Act declared to be a rogue, vagabond or sturdy beggar, which shall be... taken begging, vagrant or misordering themselves . . . shall upon their apprehension ... be stripped naked from the middle upwards and shall be openly whipped until his or her body be bloody, and shall be forthwith sent from parish to parish... the next straight way to the parish where he was born, if the same may be known...., and if the same be not known, then to the parish where be last dwelt... one whole year, there to put himself to labour as a true subject ought to do; or not being known where he was born or last dwelt, then to the parish through which he last passed without punishment;... and the party so whipped and not known where he was born or last dwelt by the space of a year, shall by the officers of the said village where he

so last passed through without punishment be conveyed to the house of correction... or to the common gaol of that county or place, there to remain and be
employed in work until he shall be placed in some service, and so to continue by
the space of one whole year, or not being able of body,... to remain in some
almshouse in the same county or place.

IV. Provided, That if any of the said rogues shall appear to be dangerous... or
such as will not be reformed... it shall be lawful to the said justices . . . or any two
of them . . . to commit that rogue to the house of correction or to the gaol of that
county, there to remain until their next quarter sessions...; and then such of the
same rogues so committed, as by the justices of the peace... shall be thought fit
not to be delivered, shall... be banished out of this realm... and at the charge of
that county shall be conveyed unto such parts beyond the seas as shall be at any
time hereafter for that purpose assigned by the privy council... or by any six or
niore of them, whereof the Lord Chancellor or Lord Keeper of the Great Seal or
the Lord Treasurer to be one, or be judged perpetually to the galleys of this realm,
as by the same justices shall be thought fit; and if any such rogue so banished as
aforesaid shall return again into any part of this realm or dominion of Wales
without lawful licence... such offence shall be felony, and the party offending
therein suffer death as in case of felony...

XIV. Provided, That every seafaring man suffering shipwreck, not having
wherewith to relieve himself in his travels homewards, but having a testimonial
under the hand of some one justice of the peace of the place where he landed, .
. . may without incurring the penalty of this Act... ask to receive such 1 relief as
shall be necessary for his passage.

AN ACT FOR ERECTING OF HOSPITALS OR ABIDING AND WORK-ING HOUSES FOR THE POOR

I. Whereas at the last session of parliament provision was made as well as
for maimed soldiers, by collection in every parish, as for other poor, that it should
be lawful for every person, during twenty years next after the said parliament...,
to give and bequeath in fee-simple, as well to the use of the poor as for the provision or maintenance of any house of correction or abiding-houses, or of any
stocks or stores, all or any part of his lands [&c.]; her most excellent Majesty
understanding that the said good law hath not taken such effect as was intended, by reason that no person can erect or incorporate any hospital [&c.] but her
Majesty or by her Highness' special licence . . . , is of her princely care . . . for the
relief of maimed soldiers, mariners and other poor and impotent people pleased
that it be enacted... and be it enacted, That all persons seised of an estate in fee-
simple, their heirs, executors or assigns . . . shall have full power,... at any time
during the space of twenty yeals next ensuing, by deed enrolled in the High
Court of Chancery, to found and establish one or more hospitals, maisons de
dieu, abiding-places or houses of correction... to have continuance for ever, and

from time to time to place therein such head and members and such number of poor as to him [&c.] shall seem convenient...

V. Provided, That no such hospital [&c.] shall be erected, founded or incorporated by force of this Act, unless upon the foundation or erection thereof the same be endowed for ever with lands, tenements or hereditaments of the clear yearly value of £10.

AN ACT FOR THE SETTING OF THE POOR ON WORK, AND FOR THE AVOIDING OF IDLENESS

IV.... That in every city and town corporate within this realm a competent store and stock of wool, hemp, flax, iron or other stuff by order of the mayor... or other head officers... shall be provided; and that likewise in every other market-town or other place where (to the justices of peace in their general sessions yearly next after Easter shall be thought most meet) a like competent store and stock of wool [&c.] or other stuff as the country is most meet for... shall be provided, the said stores and stocks in such cities and towns corporate to be committed to the custody of such persons as shall by the mayor or other head officers in every such city or town corporate be appointed, and in other towns and places to such persons as by the said justices of peace in their said general sessions... shall be by them appointed; which said persons... shall from henceforth be called the collectors and governors of the poor, to the intent every such poor and needy person... able to do any work... shall not for want of work go abroad either begging or committing pilferings or other misdemeanours...; which collectors from time to time (as cause requireth) shall, of the same stock and store, deliver to such poor and needy person a competent portion to be wrought into yarn or other matter..., for which they shall make payment to them which work the same according to the desert of the work . . . ; which hemp [&c.] or other stuff, wrought from time to time, shall be sold by the said collectors... and with the money coming of the sale to buy more stuff...; and if hereafter any such person able to do any such work shall refuse to work . . . or taking such work shall spoil or embezzle the same... he, she or they shall be received into such house of correction, there to be straightly kept, as well in diet as in work, and also punished from time to time...

V. And moreover be it enacted, That within every county of this realm one, two or more abiding houses or places convenient in some market-town or corporate town or other place, by... order of the justices of peace in their said general sessions... shall be provided, and called houses of correction, and also stock and store and implements be provided for setting on work and punishing not only of those which by the collectors and governors of the poor for causes aforesaid to the said houses of correction shall be brought, but also of such as be inhabiting in no parish, or be taken as rogues... or for any other cause ought to be abiding and kept within the same county...

VI. And be it also further enacted, That the said justices of peace, in their said general sessions, shall appoint from time to time overseers of every such house of correction, which said persons shall be called the censors and wardens of the houses of correction...; and shall also appoint others for the gathering of such money as shall he taxed upon any persons within their several jurisdictions towards the maintenance of the said houses of correction, which shall be called the collectors for the houses of correction; and if any person refuse to be collector and governor of the poor or censor and warden or collector for any the houses of correction, that every person so refusing shall forfeit the sum of £5...

La Colonie,
"The Battle of Schellenberg"

L ouis XIV (r. 1643-1715) embarked on an ambitious policy to extend the borders of France and make it the most powerful country in Europe. This aggressive foreign policy meant almost constant war for France from the 1660s to 1715. The French crown borrowed heavily to fund these wars, leaving Louis XIV's successors with massive debts. The wars also tested the limits of the French military, both the army and the smaller naval forces. At this time, only nobles could be commanders or officers in the military while soldiers were often mercenaries, drawn from all over Europe. Wars also brought hardship and chaos to the areas where battles took place, as ill disciplined armies exacted food, supplies, and quarters from the peasants and townspeople around battle sites, often by force. In this excerpt, a French noble army commander, Monsieur de La Colonie, provides an account of his experiences during a battle in the War of Spanish Succession (1701-1714). This battle takes place in Schellenberg, between Switzerland and Austria, in the area that is present-day Liechtenstein.

Source: John Casey, *Eyewitness to History* (New York: Avon Books, 1997), 199-205.

Focus Questions:

1. What was the author's perspective and involvement in this event? What factors or issues likely influenced his account and version of events?
2. What does this tell us about the affects of warfare on those living in the areas where battles took place?
3. What does this account tell us about the affects of warfare on commanders? Soldiers?

I made a point of impressing upon my men the necessity of attention to orders, and of prompt obedience in carrying out any manoeuvres during the action with courage and in good order. I assured them that herein lay our safety and, perhaps, victory.

I had scarcely finished speaking when the enemy's battery opened fire upon us, and raked us through and through. They concentrated their fire upon us, and with their first discharge carried off Count de la Bastide, the lieutenant of my own company with whom at the moment I was speaking, and twelve grenadiers, who fell side by side in the ranks, so that my coat was covered with brains and blood. So accurate was the fire that each discharge of the cannon stretched some of my men on the ground. I suffered agonies at seeing these brave fellows perish without a chance of defending themselves, but it was absolutely necessary that they should not move from their post.

This cannonade was but the prelude of the attack that the enemy were developing, and I looked upon the moment when they would fling themselves against one point or another in our entrenchments as so instant that I would allow no man even to bow his head before the storm, fearing that the regiment would find itself in disorder when the time came for us to make the rapid movement that would be demanded of us. At last the enemy's army began to move to the assault, and still it was necessary for me to suffer this sacrifice to avoid a still greater misfortune, though I had five officers and eighty grenadiers killed on the spot before we had fired a single shot.

So steep was the slope in front of us that as soon almost as the enemy's column began its advance it was lost in view, and it came into sight only two hundred paces from our entrenchments. I noticed that it kept as far as possible from the glacis of the town and close alongside of the wood, but I could not make out whether a portion might not also be marching within the latter with the purpose of attacking that part of our entrenchments facing it, and the uncertainty caused me to delay movement. There was nothing to lead me to suppose that the enemy had such an intimate knowledge of our defences as to guide them to one point in preference to another for their attack.

Had I been able to guess that the column was being led by that scoundrel of a corporal who had betrayed us, I should not have been in this dilemma, nor should I have thought it necessary to keep so many brave men exposed to the perils of the cannonade, but my doubts came to an end two hours after midday, for I caught sight of the tips of the Imperial standards, and no longer hesitated. I changed front as promptly as possible, in order to bring my grenadiers opposite the part of our position adjoining the wood, towards which I saw that the enemy was directing his advance.

The regiment now left a position awkward in the extreme on account of the cannon, but we soon found ourselves scarcely better off, for hardly had our men lined the little parapet when the enemy broke into the charge, and rushed at full speed, shouting at the top of their voices, to throw themselves into our entrenchments.

The rapidity of their movements, together with their loud yells, were truly alarming, and as soon as I heard them I ordered our drums to beat the 'charge' so as to drown them with their noise, lest they should have a bad effect upon our people. By this means I animated my grenadiers, and prevented them hearing the shouts of the enemy, which before now have produced a heedless panic.

The English infantry led this attack with the greatest intrepidity, right up to our parapet, but there they were opposed with a courage at least equal to their own. Rage, fury, and desperation were manifested by both sides, with the more obstinacy as the assailants and assailed were perhaps the bravest soldiers in the world. The little parapet which separated the two forces became the scene of the bloodiest struggle that could be conceived. Thirteen hundred grenadiers, of whom seven hundred belonged to the Elector's Guards, and six hundred who were left under my command, bore the brunt of the enemy's attack at the forefront of the Bavarian infantry.

It would be impossible to describe in words strong enough the details of the carnage that took place during this first attack, which lasted a good hour or more. We were all fighting hand to hand, hurling them back as they clutched at the parapet; men were slaying, or tearing at the muzzles of guns and the bayonets which pierced their entrails; crushing under their feet their own wounded comrades, and even gouging out their opponents' eyes with their nails, when the grip was so close that neither could make use of their weapons. I verily believe that it would have been quite impossible to find a more terrible representation of Hell itself than was shown in the savagery of both sides on this occasion.

At last the enemy, after losing more than eight thousand men in this first onslaught, were obliged to relax their hold, and they fell back for shelter to the dip in the slope, where we could not harm them. A sudden calm now reigned amongst us, our people were recovering their breath, and seemed more determined even than they were before the conflict. The ground around our parapet was covered with dead and dying, in heaps almost as high as our fascines, but our whole attention was fixed on the enemy and his movements; we noticed that the tops of his standards still showed at about the same place as that from which they had made their charge in the first instance, leaving little doubt but that they were reforming before returning to the assault. As soon as possible we set vigorously to work to render their approach more difficult for them than before, and by means of an increasing fire swept their line of advance with a torrent of bullets, accompanied by numberless grenades, of which we had several wagon loads in rear of our position. These, owing to the slope of the ground, fell right amongst the enemy's ranks, causing them great annoyance and doubtless added not a little to their hesitation in advancing the second time to the attack. They were so disheartened by the first attempt that their generals had the greatest difficulty in bringing them forward again, and indeed would never have succeeded in this, though they tried every other means, had they not dismounted and set an example by placing themselves at the head of the column, and leading them on foot.

Their devotion cost them dear, for General Stirum and many other generals and officers were killed. They once more, then, advanced to the assault, but with nothing like the success of their first effort, for not only did they lack energy in their attack, but after being vigorously repulsed, were pursued by us at the point of the bayonet for more than eighty paces beyond our entrenchments, which we finally re-entered unmolested.

After this second attempt many efforts were made by their generals, but they were never able to bring their men to the assault a third time...

But I noticed all at once an extraordinary movement on the part of our infantry, who were rising up and ceasing fire withal. I glanced around on all sides to see what had caused this behaviour, and then became aware of several lines of infantry in greyish white uniforms on our left flank. From lack of movement on their part, their dress and bearing, I verily believed that reinforcements had arrived for us, and anybody else would have believed the same. No information whatever had reached us of the enemy's success, or even that such a thing was the least likely, so in the error I laboured under I shouted to my men that they were Frenchman, and friends, and they at once resumed their former position behind the parapet.

Having, however, made a closer inspection, I discovered bunches of straw and leaves attached to their standards, badges the enemy are in the custom of wearing on the occasion of battle, and at that very moment was struck by a ball in the right lower jaw, which wounded and stupefied me to such an extent that I thought it was smashed. I probed my wound as quickly as possible with the tip of my finger, and finding the jaw itself entire, did not make much fuss about it; but the front of my jacket was so deluged with the blood which poured from it that several of our officers believed that I was dangerously hurt. I reassured them, however, and exhorted them to stand firmly with their men. I pointed out to them that so long as our infantry kept well together the danger was not so great, and that if they behaved in a resolute manner, the enemy, who were only keeping in touch with us without daring to attack us, would allow us to retire without so much as pursuing. In truth, to look at them it would seem that they hoped much more for our retreat than any chance of coming to blows with us. I at once, therefore, shouted as loudly as I could that no one was to quit the ranks, and then formed my men in column along the entrenchments facing the wood, fronting towards the opposite flank, which was the direction in which we should have to retire. Thus, whenever I wished to make a stand, I had but to turn my men about, and at any moment could resume the retirement instantaneously, which we thus carried out in good order. I kept this up until we had crossed the entrenchments on the other flank, and then we found ourselves free from attack. This retreat was not made, however, without loss, for the enemy, although they would not close with us when they saw our column formed for the retirement, fired volleys at close range into us, which did much damage.

My men had no sooner got clear of the entrenchments than they found that the slope was in their favour, and they fairly broke their ranks and took to flight, in order to reach the plain that lay before them before the enemy's cavalry could get upon their track. As each ran his hardest, intending to reform on the further side, they disappeared like a flash of lightning without ever looking back, and I, who was with the rearguard ready to make a stand if necessary against our opponents, had scarcely clambered over the entrenchments when I found myself left entirely alone on the height, prevented from running by my heavy boots.

I looked about on all sides for my drummer, whom I had warned to keep at hand with my horse, but he had evidently thought fit to look after himself, with the result that I found myself left solitary to the mercy of the enemy and my own sad thoughts, without the slightest idea as to my future fate. I cudgelled my brains in vain for some way out of my difficulty, but could think of nothing the least certain; the plain was too wide for me to traverse in my big boots at the necessary speed, and to crown my misfortunes, was covered with cornfields. So far the enemy's cavalry had not appeared on the plain, but there was every reason to believe that they would not long delay their coming; it would have been utter folly on my part to give them the chance of discovering me embarrassed as I was, for as long as I was hampered with my boots, a trooper would always find it an easy affair to catch me.

I noticed, however, that the Danube was not so very far away, and determined to make my way towards it at all risk, with the hope of finding some beaten track or place where there would be some chance of saving my life, as I saw it was now hopeless to think of getting my men together. As a matter of fact, I found a convenient path along the bank of the river, but this was not of much avail to me, for, owing to my efforts and struggles to reach it through several fields of standing corn, I was quite blown and exhausted and could only just crawl along at the slowest possible pace. On my way I met the wife of a Bavarian soldier, so distracted with weeping that she travelled no faster than I did. I made her drag off my boots, which fitted me so tightly about the legs that it was absolutely impossible for me to do this for myself. The poor woman took an immense time to effect this, and it seemed to me at least as if the operation would never come to an end. At last this was effected, and I turned over in my mind the best way to profit by my release, when, raising my head above the corn at the side of the road, I saw a number of the enemy's troopers scattered over the country, searching the fields for any of our people who might be hidden therein, with the intention, doubtless, of killing them for the sake of what plunder might be found upon them. At this cruel prospect all my hopes vanished, and the exultation I felt at my release from the boots died at the moment of its birth. My position was now more perilous than ever; nevertheless, I examined under the cover afforded by the corn the manoeuvres of these cavaliers to see if I could not find some way out of the difficulty. A notion came into my head which, if it could have been carried out, might have had a curious ending. It was that if one trooper only should approach me, and his comrades remained sufficiently distant, I should keep hidden and wait until he got near enough for me to kill him with a shot from my pistol, for I had two on my belt; I would then take his uniform, mount his horse, and make my escape in this disguise, a plan which would be favoured by the approaching darkness. But not seeing any chance of being able to carry out this idea, I thought of another, namely, to get into the river up to my chin in the water under the bushes on the bank, wait for nightfall and the return of the troopers to their camp, and then to escape in the dark. But there were more difficulties to contend with in risking this even than in the other case, and as a last resource it struck me I might save myself by crossing the river, for happily I knew how to swim, although the risk here was very great owing to the breadth and rapidity of the Danube. I hurriedly determined on this plan, as I now saw a number of troopers approaching ever nearer to my hiding place, who were refusing to give quarter to the unhappy wounded they found hidden in the corn, whom they ruthlessly despatched the more easily to despoil them. There was no reason to suppose that they were likely to show any more mercy to me, particularly as I was worth more in the shape of plunder than a private soldier, nor was there time to lose in making up my mind, so I then and there determined to swim the river. Before taking to the water I took the precaution of leaving on the bank my richly embroidered uniform, rather spoiled as it was by the events of the late action. I scattered in a similar manner my hat, wig, pistols, and sword, at one point and another, so that if the troopers came up before I had got well away, they would devote their attention to collecting these articles instead of looking in the water, and it turned out just as I thought. I kept on my stockings, vest, and breeches, simply buttoning the sleeves of the vest and tucking the pockets within my breeches for safety; this done, I threw myself upon the mercy of the stream. I had hardly got any distance when up came the troopers, who, as I had hoped, dismounted as quickly as they could to lay hands on the spoil lying before them; they even set to work to quarrel over it, for I distinctly heard them shouting and swearing in the most delightful manner. Others apparently got no share, and they amused themselves by saluting me with several musket shots, but the current of the river which carried me on my way soon put me out of their range. Finally, after a very long and hard swim, I was lucky enough to reach the other bank, in spite of the strength of the stream.

Peter the Great, "Correspondence with Alexis"

Peter the Great, Tsar of Russia (r. 1672-1725) established greater links between his country and Western Europe, and introduced important reforms in the military and government with the goal of making Russia a European power. Borrowing from Western European shipbuilding techniques, Peter oversaw the construction of the first Russian naval fleet. He also made significant changes in the army, for example, putting in place programs to better train and organize the Russian nobles who served as government and military officers. Peter's ambitions for Russian territorial expansion led to numerous wars with Sweden, Poland, and the Ottoman Empire. His son Alexis, born in 1690, was his heir to the throne, but around 1715 Peter changed the terms of this succession so it passed over Alexis to Peter's grandson (Alexis's son). Alexis attempted to flee Russia in 1716, eventually returned, but his father, who believed he was plotting to assassinate him, ordered Alexis's arrest. Alexis died in 1718 as a result of his imprisonment and torture. When Peter died in 1725, a succession crisis and period of instability followed that finally ended with when Catherine the Great (r. 17291796), Peter's second wife, came to the throne.

Source: *The Global Experience,* Vol. 2, by Philip F. Riley, et. al. (Upper Saddle River, NJ: Prentice Hall, 1998), pp. 44–46.

FOCUS QUESTIONS:

1. What were Peter the Great's views regarding war? What beliefs or ideas informed his views?

2. How did Peter the Great hope to increase the power and prestige of Russia in Europe?

3. What did this letter say about the succession issue? What was Peter's view about who would inherit the Russian throne after his death? His son's response?

A LETTER TO ALEXEI
October 11, 1715
Declaration to My Son,

You cannot be ignorant of what is known to all the world, to what degree our people groaned under the oppression of the Swedes before the beginning of the present war.

By the usurpation of so many maritime places so necessary to our state. they had cut us off from all commerce with the rest of the world, and we saw with regret that besides they had cast a thick veil before the eyes of the clear-sighted. You know what it has cost us in the beginning of this war (in which God alone has led us, as it were, by the hand. and still guides us) to make ourselves experienced in the art of war, and to put a stop to those advantages which our implacable enemies obtained over us.

We submitted to this with a resignation to the will of God, making no doubt but it was he who put us to that trial, till he might lead us into the right way, and we might render ourselves worthy to experience, that the same enemy who at first made others tremble, now in his turn trembles before us, perhaps in a much greater degree. These are the fruits which, next to the assistance of God, we owe to our own toil and to the labour of our faithful and affectionate children. our Russian subjects.

But at the time that I am viewing the prosperity which God has heaped on our native country, if I cast an eye upon the posterity that is to succeed me, my heart is much more penetrated with grief on account of what is to happen, then I rejoice at those blessings that are past, seeing that you, my son, reject all means of making yourself capable of well-governing after me. I say your incapacity is voluntary. because you cannot excuse yourself with want of natural parts and strength of body, as if God had not given you a sufficient share of either: and though your constitution is none of the strongest, yet it cannot be said that it is altogether weak.

But you even will not so much as hear warlike exercises mentioned; though it is by them that we broke through that obscurity in which we were involved, and that we made ourselves known to nations, whose esteem we share at present.

I do not exhort you to make war without lawful reasons: I only desire you to apply yourself to learn the art of it: for it is impossible well to govern without knowing the rules and discipline of it, was it for no other end than for the defense of the country.

I could place before your eyes many instances of what I am proposing to you. I will only mention to you the Greeks, with whom we are united by the same profession of faith. What occasioned their decay but that they neglected arms? Idleness and repose weakened them, made them submit to tyrants, and brought them to that slavery to which they are now so long since reduced. You mistake, if you think it is enough for a prince to have good generals to act under his order. Everyone looks upon the head; they study his inclinations and conform themselves to them: all the world owns this. My brother during his reign loved magnificence in dress, and great equipages of horses. The nation were not much inclined that way, but the prince's delight soon became that of his subjects. for they are inclined to imitate him in liking a thing as well as disliking it.

If the people so easily break themselves of things which only regard pleasure, will they not forget in time, or will they not more easily give over the practice of arms, the exercise of which is the more painful to them, the less they are kept to it?

You have no inclination to learn war. you do not apply yourself to it, and consequently you will never learn it: And how then can you command others, and judge of the reward which those deserve who do their duty. or punish others who fail of it? You will do nothing, nor judge of anything but by the eyes and help of others. like a young bird that holds up his bill to be fed.

You say that the weak state of your health will not permit you to undergo the fatigues of war: This is an excuse which is no better than the rest. I desire no fatigues, but only inclination, which even sickness itself cannot hinder. Ask those who remember the time of my brother. He was of a constitution weaker by far than yours. He was not able to manage a horse of the least mettle, not could he hardly mount it: Yet he loved horses. hence it came, that there never was, nor perhaps is there actually now in the nation a finer stable than his was.

By this you see that good success does not always depend on pain, but on the will.

If you think there are some, whose affairs do not fail of success, though they do not go to war themselves; it is true: But if they do not go themselves, yet they have an inclination for it, and understand it.

For instance, the late King of France did not always take the field in person; but it is known to what degree he loved war, and what glorious exploits he performed in it, which made his campaigns to be called the theatre and school of the world. His inclinations were not confined solely to military affairs, he also loved mechanics, manufactures and other establishments, which rendered his kingdom more flourishing than any other whatsoever.

After having made to you all those remonstrances, I return to my former subject which regards you.

I am a man and consequently I must die. To whom shall I leave after me to finish what by the grace of God I have begun, and to preserve what I have partly recovered? To a man, who like the slothful servant hides his talent in the earth, that is to say, who neglects making the best of what God has entrusted to him?

Remember your obstinacy and ill-nature, how often I reproached you with it, and even chastised you for it, and for how many years I almost have not spoke to you; but all this has availed nothing, has effected nothing. It was but losing my time: it was striking the air. You do not make the least endeavors. and all your pleasure seems to consist in staying idle and lazy at home: Things of which you ought to be ashamed (forasmuch as they make you miserable) seem to make up your dearest delight, nor do you foresee the dangerous consequences of it for yourself and for the whole state. St. Paul has left us a great truth when he wrote: If a man know not how to rule his own house, how shall he take of the church of God?

After having considered all those great inconveniences and reflected upon them, and seeing I cannot bring you to good by any inducement, I have thought fit to give you in writing this act of my last will, with this resolution however to wait still a little longer before I put it in execution to see if you will mend. If not, I will have you to know that I will deprive you of the succession, as one may cut off a useless member.

Do not fancy, that, because I have no other child but you, I only write this to terrify you. I will certainly put it in execution, if it please God; for whereas I do not spare my own life for my country and the welfare of my people, why should I spare you who do not render yourself worthy of either? I would rather choose to transmit them to a worthy stranger, than to my own unworthy son.

Peter

ALEXEI'S REPLY
Most Clement Lord and Father,

I have read the paper your Majesty gave me on the 27th of October, 1715, after the funeral of my late consort.

I have nothing to reply to it, but, that if your Majesty will deprive me of the succession to the Crown of Russia by reason of my incapacity, your will be done; I even most instantly beg it of you, because I do not think myself fit for the government. My memory is very much weakened, and yet it is necessary in affairs. The strength of my mind and of my body is much decayed by the sicknesses which I have undergone, and which have rendered me incapable of governing so many nations; this requires a more vigorous man than I am.

Therefore I do not aspire after you (whom God preserve many years) to the succession of the Russian Crown, even if I had no brother as I have one at present, whom I pray God preserve. Neither will I pretend for the future to that succession, of which I take God to witness, and swear it upon my soul, in testimony whereof I write and sign this present with my own hand.

I put my children into your hands, and as for myself, I desire nothing of you but a bare maintenance during my life, leaving the whole to your consideration and to your will.

Your most humble servant and son. Alexei

CHAPTER 12

Expanding Worlds

Letters from the Kings of Portugal to the King of Kongo

In the 1400s and early 1500s, the Portuguese led the way in European exploration and expansion, first in Africa and later in the Atlantic world. Portuguese Prince Henry "The Navigator" (1394-1460), a member of the Portuguese royal family, was an important patron and supporter for early expeditions to Africa, beginning in 1418 under his father King John I (r.1383-1433) and brother King Duarte (r. 1433-1438) and continuing after Henry's death under the reign of Afonso V (r.1438-1481). By the 1480s, during the reign of John II (r. 14811495), Portuguese expeditions had reached into the sub-Saharan. In 1484, the Portuguese formed an alliance with the Bantu speaking Kongo kingdom, along the Congo River in West-Central Africa. Their ruler, Nzinga Mbemba (r. c. 1506-43), converted to Christianity, adopted the name Afonso I, and made an alliance with the Portuguese that allowed land and trading privileges, including the right to conduct raids to supply the slave trade. The Kongo slid into decline after 1570, as a result of warring factions within their loosely knit kingdom. The letters that follow were exchanges between the ruler of the Kongo kingdom, Nzinga Mbemba (or Alfonso I) and Portuguese kings Manuel I (r. 1495-1521) and John III (r.1521-1557).

Source: "Letters from the Kings of the Kongo to the King of Portugal," MonumentaMissionaria Africana, ed. Antonio Brasio, (Lisboa: Agencia Geral do Ultramar, 1952), vol. 1: 262–63, 294–95, 335, 404, 470, 488, trans. Linda Wimmer; reprinted in The Global Experience: Readings in World History,ed. Stuart B. Schwartz, et al., (New York: Addison Wesley, Longman, Inc., 1997), 240–42.

Focus Questions:

1. How does the African king use language and imagery that would appeal to a European monarch?

2. How successful do you imagine Alfonso was in his petitions to the Portuguese crown?

PORTUGUESE MILITARY AID DURING CIVIL WAR

And our brother who usurped us, and without justice occupied us, with arms and a great number of people... became empowered in all of our kingdom, and lordships, with which when we saw the only solution for our person we feigned sickness; and it being so with us, by a divine inspiration of our Lord, we raised and strengthened ourself, and called up our 36 men, and with them we appeared, and went with them to the main square of the city, where our Father died, and where people of infinite number were with our said brother, and... for our Lord Jesus Christ, and we began to fight with our adversaries... our 36 men, inspired by grace, and aided by God, our adversaries quickly fled... and chaos ensued, and with them witnessing... there appeared in the air a white Cross, and the blessed Apostle St. James with many men armed and on horseback, and dressed in white battle garments, and killed them, and so great was the chaos, and mortality, that it was a thing of great wonder.

In this defeat our brother was taken prisoner and with justice condemned to die, as he died, for having rebelled against us; and finally we made peace in our kingdoms... as it is today, with the Grace of God... and through the miracle made by our Lord, and we send word to the King Dom Emanuel of Portugal... and we send to him Dom Pedro our brother, who was one of the 36 men with us... and with the letters that the king sent of great works given....

And as the King of Portugal saw the good example... followed... for the greater growth of our Holy Catholic Faith, he sent by our cousin Dom Pedro and by Simao da Sylva noblemen of your house who came with him, the arms pictured in this card, and the shields with insignias... [A]nd as these weapons arrived a cross was seen in the sky, and so the Apostle St. James and all the other Saints fought with us, and with the help of our Lord God we were given victory, and so also as by the King sent us his [men] took part with the said arms....

PROBLEMS IN CONVERSION EFFORTS (1515)

Very High and Powerful Lord,

We the King Dom Alfonso... Lord, much holy grace and praise I give to the Holy God the Father and the Son and the Holy Spirit... all good and holy things are done through the will of God, without which we can do nothing... our faith is still like glass in this kingdom, due to the bad examples of the men who come here to teach it, because through worldly greed for a few riches truth is destroyed, as through greed the Jews crucified the Son of God, my brother, until today he is crucified through bad examples and bad deeds... in our time by us who walk crying in this real valley of misery and tears.

... [I]n teaching the word of Our Lord [these bad priests] become bad examples and so take the key to the Celestial Kingdom that is the Doctrine of our Holy Catholic Faith, to open the hearts of our simple people... and by entering into a life of sin take the key to Hell... due to the greed of this world, do not merely take their own bodies and souls to Hell, but guide those most blind with them through their bad examples. I ask of you, Brother, to aid me in establishing our Holy Catholic Faith, because, Lord my Brother, for us it were better... that the souls of our relatives and brothers and cousins and nephews and grandchildren who are innocent, to see... good examples.

... I ask you to send stonemasons and house carpenters to build a school to teach our relatives and our people, because Lord, although greedy and jealous men still give bad examples... with the Holy Sacred Scripture we may change that, because the world of the Holy Spirit is contrary to the world, the flesh and the devil....

ATTEMPTS TO BUY A CARAVEL (1517)

Very Powerful and Very High Prince and King My Brother

... I have several times written you of the necessity of having a ship, telling you to make me one to buy, and I don't know why Your Highness does not want to consent, because I want nothing more than... to use it in God's service....

EFFECTS OF PORTUGUESE TRADE (1526)

Lord,

... [Y]our factors and officials give to the men and merchants that come to this Kingdom... and spread... so that many vassals owing us obedience... rebel because they have more goods [through trade with Portuguese] than us, who before had been content and subject to our... jurisdiction, which causes great damage....

... And each day these merchants take our citizens, native to the land and children of our nobles and vassals, and our relations, because they are thieves and men of bad conscience, steal them with the desire to have things of this kingdom... take them to sell... our land is all spoiled... which is not to your service.... For this we have no more necessity for other than priests and educators, but [send] no more merchandise... nor merchants....

EXPANSION AND REGULATION OF THE SLAVE TRADE (1526)

[M]any of our subjects, through the desire for merchandise and things of this Kingdoms which you bring... to satisfy their appetite, steal many of our free and exempt subjects. And nobles and their children and our relatives are often stolen to be sold to white men... hidden by night.... And the said white men are so powerful... they embark and... buy them, for which we want justice, restoring them to liberty....

And to avoid this great evil, by law all white men in our kingdom who buy slaves... must make it known to three nobles and officials of our court... to see these slaves....

Bartolomé de Las Casas, *Very Brief Report on the Destruction of the Indians*

In his accounts of Spanish conquests in the Americas, Bartolomé de Las Casas (1475-1566) emphasized the brutal and cruel treatment of Amerindians by Spanish conquistadors. Las Casas wrote his accounts of Spanish conquest of the Americas for a European audience, hoping that the vivid accounts of excessive violence used against the Amerindians and their subsequent enslavement would result in significant changes in Spanish colonial policies. As a Dominican monk, Las Casas's religious ideas and beliefs significantly influenced his arguments and approach to these issues.

Sources: Bartolomé de Las Casas, *His Life, His Apostolate, and His Writings*, trans. by Francis Augustus McNutt (New York, 1909), 314-315 and Bartolomé de Las Casas, *Very Brief Report on the Destruction of the Indians*, trans. Francis Augusts Mac Nutt [need publishing info and date here], 319-20.

FOCUS QUESTIONS:

1. How did Las Casas describe Amerindians in this passage? What ideas or sources did he draw on for this description? Why?
2. How did Las Casas' background and beliefs shape his account of Spanish colonial policies and actions?
3. How did Las Casas portray the Spanish conquistadors? To what extent was this account reliable (why or why not)?

God has created all these numberless people to be quite the simplest, without malice or duplicity, most obedient, most faithful to their natural Lords, and to the Christians, whom they serve; the most humble, most patient, most peaceful, and calm, without strife nor tumults; not wrangling, nor querulous, as free from uproar, hate and desire of revenge, as any in the world.

They are likewise the most delicate people, weak and of feeble constitution, and less than any other can they bear fatigue, and they very easily die of whatsoever infirmity; so much so, that not even the sons of our Princes and of nobles, brought up in royal and gentle life, are more delicate than they; although there are among them such as are of the peasant class. They are also a very poor people, who of worldly goods possess little, nor wish to possess: and they are therefore neither proud, nor ambitious, nor avaricious.. . .They are likewise of a clean, unspoiled, and vivacious intellect, very capable, and receptive to every good doctrine; most prompt to accept our Holy Catholic Faith, to be endowed with virtuous customs; and they have as little difficulty with such things as any people created by God in the world.

Once they have begun to learn of matters pertaining to faith, they are so importunate to know them, and in frequenting the sacraments and divine service of the Church, that to tell the truth, the clergy have need to be endowed of God with the gift of preeminent patience to bear with them: and finally, I have heard many lay Spaniards frequently say many years ago, (unable to deny the goodness of those they saw) certainly these people were the most blessed of the earth, had they only knowledge of God.

The Christians, with their horses and swords and lances, began to slaughter and practise strange cruelty among them. They penetrated into the country and spared neither children nor the aged, nor pregnant women, nor those in child labour, all of whom they ran through the body and lacerated, as though they were assaulting so many lambs herded in their sheepfold.

They made bets as to who would slit a man in two, or cut off his head at one blow: or they opened up his bowels. They tore the babes from their mothers' breast by the feet, and dashed their heads against the rocks. Others they seized by the shoulders and threw into the rivers, laughing and joking, and when they fell into the water they exclaimed:"boil body of so and so!"They spitted the bodies of other babes, together with their mothers and all who were before them, on their swords.

They made a gallows just high enough for the feet to nearly touch the ground, and by thirteens, in honour and reverence of our Redeemer and the twelve Apostles, they put wood underneath and, with fire, they burned the Indians alive....

And because all the people who could flee, hid among the mountains and climbed the crags to escape from men so deprived of humanity, so wicked, such wild beasts, exterminators and capital enemies of all the human race, the Spaniards taught and trained the fiercest boar-hounds to tear an Indian to pieces as soon as they saw him, so that they more willingly attacked and ate one, than if he had been a boar. These hounds made great havoc and slaughter.

Jamestown Charter

The colony at Jamestown, on the coast of Virginia, was the first permanent English colony in North America. The charter for the colony, drafted in 1606 by the English government under King James I (r. 1603-1625) provided for its founding in May of 1607. The charter set up the land rights, institutions, and government for the colony. The colony at Jamestown experienced many difficulties, including a high death rate from disease, poor crop yields, attacks from Native American groups, and a major fire in 1608. In 1610, it was saved when Thomas West arrived from England with new settlers and supplies.

Source: "Letters patent to Sir Thomas Gates and others, April 10, 1606" in *The Jamestown Voyages Under the First Charter, 1606-1609*, vol. 1, ed. by Philip L Barbour (Cambridge: Cambridge University Press, 1969), 24-34.

FOCUS QUESTIONS:

1. What plans did this charter make for the physical layout of the settlement and for its supplies or support?
2. Who were to be its leaders, and how was the government to be organized?
3. What motivated the English to establish colonial settlements in the Americas?

II..10 April 1606

Letters Patent to Sir Thomas Gates and Others

James by the grace of God &c Whereas our loving and well disposed subiects Sir Thomas Gates and Sir George Somers Knightes Richard Hackluit Clarke prebendarie of Westminster and Edwarde Maria Winghfeilde Thomas Hannam and Raleighe Gilberde Esquiers William Parker and George Popham Gentlemen and divers others of our loving subiects haue been humble sutors vnto vs that wee woulde vouchsafe vnto them our licence to make habitacion plantaion and to deduce a Colonie of sondrie of our people into that parte of America commonly called Virginia and other parts and territories in America either appertaining vnto vs or which are not nowe actuallie possessed by anie Christian Prince or people scituate lying and being all along the sea Coastes

* * *

and to that ende and for the more speedy accomplishemente of theire saide intended plantacion and habitacion there are desirous to devide themselues into two severall Colonies and Companies the one consisting of certaine Knightes Gentlemen marchauntes and other Adventurers of our Cittie of London and elsewhere

* * *

and the other consisting of sondrie Knightes Gentlemen merchauntes and other Adventurers of our Citties of Bristoll and Exeter and of our towne of Plymouthe and of other places which doe ioyne themselues vnto that Colonie

* * *

wee greatly commending and graciously accepting of theire desires to the furtherance of soe noble a worke which may be the providence of Almightie God hereafter tende to the glorie of hys divyne maiestie in propagating of Christian religion to suche people as yet live in darkenesse and myserable ignorance of the true knowledge and worshippe of god and may in tyme bring the infidels and salvages lyving in those partes to humane civilitie and to a setled and quiet govermente doe by theise our lettres Patentes graciously accepte of and agree to theire humble and well intended desires

* * *

And that they shall haue all the landes woodes soyle Groundes havens portes Ryvers Mynes Myneralls Marshes waters Fyshings Commodities and hereditamentes whatsoever from the said first seate of theire plantacion and habytacion by the space of Fyftie miles of Englishe statute measure all alongest the saide Coaste of Virginia and

* * *

America towardes the Weste and southeweste as the Coaste lyeth with all the Islandes within one hundred myles directlie over againste the same sea Coaste

* * *

and towardes the Easte and Northeaste

* * *

And directly into the mayne lande by the space of One hundred like Englishe myles and shall and may inhabyt and remaine there and shall and may alsoe buylde and fortifie within anie the same for theire better safegarde and defence according to theire best discrecions and the direction of the Counsell of that Colonie and that noe other of our subiects shalbe permitted or suffered to plante or inhabyt behinde or on the backside of them towardes the mayne lande without the expresse lycence or consente of the Counsell of that Colonie thereunto in writing firste had or obtained

* * *

And wee doe alsoe ordaine establishe and agree for vs our heires and successors that eache of the saide Colonies shall haue a Counsell which shall governe and order all matters and Causes which shall arise growe or happen to or within the same severall Colonies according to such lawes ordynaunces and Instructions as shalbe in that behalfe given and signed with our hande or signe manuell and passe vnder the privie seale of our Realme of Englande Eache of which Counsells shall consist of Thirteene parsons [i.e., persons] and to be ordained made and removed from tyme to tyme according as shalbe directed and comprised in the same Instructions and shall haue a severall seale for all matters that shall passe or concerne the same severall Counsells Eache of which seales shall haue the Kinges Armes engraven on the one syde thereof and hys pourtraiture on the other

* * *

And that alsoe ther shalbe a Counsell established here in Englande which shall in like manner consist of thirteene parsons to be for that purpose appointed by vs our heires and successors which shalbe called our Counsell of Virginia And shall from tyme to tyme haue the superior managing and direction onelie of and for all matters that shall or may concerne the govermente aswell of the said seuerall Colonies as of and for anie other parte or place within the aforesaid preinctes

* * *

And moreover wee doe graunte and agree for vs our heires and successors that the saide severall Counsells of and for the saide severall Colonies shall and lawfully may by vertue hereof from tyme to tyme without intervpcion of vs our heires or successors giue and take order to digg myne and searche for all manner of Mynes of Goulde Silver and Copper aswell within anie parte of theire saide severall Colonies as of the saide Mayne landes on the backeside of the same Colonies and to haue and enjoy the Goulde Silver and Copper to be gotten thereof to the vse and behoofe of the same Colonies and the plantacions thereof yielding therefore yerelie to vs our heires and successors the Fifte parte onelie of all the same Goulde and Silver and the Fifteenth parte of all the same Copper soe to be gotten or had as ys aforesaide without anie other manner of profytt or Accompte to be given or yeilded to vs our heires or successors for or in respecte of the same And that they shall or lawfullie may establishe and cawse to be made a coyne to passe currant there betweene the people of those severall Colonies for the more ease of traffique and bargaining betweene and amongst them and the natives there of such mettall and in suche manner and forme as the same severall Counsells there shall lymitt and appointe

* * *

Moreover wee doe by theise presentes for vs our heires and successors giue and graunte licence vnto the said Sir Thomas Gates Sir George Sumers Richarde Hackluite Edwarde Maria Winghfeilde Thomas Hannam Raleighe Gilberde William Parker and George Popham and to everie of the said Colonies that they and everie of them shall and may from tyme to tyme and at all tymes for ever hereafter for their severall defences incounter or expulse repell and resist as well by sea as by lande by all waies and meanes whatsoever all and everie suche

* * *

parson and parsons as without especiall licence of the said severall Colonies and plantacions shall attempt to inhabit within the saide seuerall precinctes and lymittes of the saide severall Colonies and plantacions or anie of them or that shall enterprise or attempt at anie tyme hereafter the hurte detrymente or annoyance of the saide severall Colonies or plantacions

* * *

Alsoe wee doe vor vs our heires and successor declare by theise presentes that all and everie the parsons being our subiectes which shall dwell and inhabit within everie or anie of the saide severall Colonies and plantacions and everie of theire children which shall happen to be borne within the lymittes and precinctes of the said severall Colonies and plantacyons shall haue and enioy all liberties Franchises and Immunities within anie of our other domynions to all intentes and purposes as yf they had been abyding and borne within this our Realme of Englande or anie other of our saide Domynions

* * *

Prouided alwaies and our will and pleasure ys and wee doe hereby declare to all Christian Kings Princes and estates that yf anie parson or parsons which shall hereafter be of anie of the said severall Colonies and plantacions or anie other by his theire or anie of theire licence or appointement shall at anie tyme or tymes hereafter robb or spoile by sea or by lande or doe anie Acte of vniust and vnlawfull hostilitie to anie the subiectes of vs our heires or successors or anie of the subiects of anie King Prince Ruler Governor or State being then in league or Amitie with vs our heires or successors and that vpon suche Iniurie or vpon iuste complainte of such Prince Ruler Governor or State or theire subiects wee our heires or successors shall make open proclamacion within anie the portes of our Realme of Englande commodious for that purpose that the saide parson or parsons having committed anie such Robberie or spoyle shall within the tearme to be lymitted by suche Proclamacions make full restitucion or satisfactin of all suche Iniuries done soe as the saide Princes or others soe complained may houlde themselues fully satisfied and contented and that yf the saide parson or parsons having comitted such robberie or spoyle shall not make or cause to be made satisfaction accordingly with[in] such tyme soe to be lymitted That then yt shalbe lawfull to vs our heires and successors to put the saide parson or parsons having comitted such robberie or spoyle and theire procurers Abbettors or Comfortors out of our allegeaunce and protection and that yt shalbe lawfull and free for all Princes and others to pursue with hostilitie the saide Offenders and everie of them and theire and everie of theire procurors Ayders Abbettors and comforters in that behalfe

Richard Frethorne,
"Letter to Father and Mother"

The European settlements were often multicultural communities with societies that evolved differently from those in Europe, allowing more class mobility for Europeans who came and became permanent settlers. Nevertheless, class and economic differences persisted, even in the colonies. One way to fund the costly voyage from Europe to the New World colonies was to sign on as an indentured servant. Under the terms of such contracts, workers agreed to several years of service, usually about seven, in return for the payment of their passage to North America. The work done by indentured servants varied according to their skills and gender. Some, especially women, served as domestic servants while men usually worked in the fields, or if they had skills, as artisans. This letter, written by Richard Frethorne to his parents, provides a first hand account of what conditions were like for indentured servants in the early English colony of Jamestown, in Virginia.

Source: Richard Frethorne, "Letter to his father and mother, March 20, April 2 and 3, 1623" in *The Records of the Virginia Company of London*, ed. by Susan Kingsbury (Washington D.C.: Government Printing Office, 1935), 4: 58-62.

FOCUS QUESTIONS:

1. Given Frethorne's account, what was life like for an indentured servant?

2. How did Frethorne, in general terms, describe life in the colony and how did his own situation or status inform his view?

3. What does this tell us about early English colonial settlements in the Americas?

LOVING AND KIND FATHER AND MOTHER:

My most humble duty remembered to you, hoping in god of your good health, as I myself am at the making hereof. This is to let you understand that I you child am in a most heavy case by reason of the country, [which] is such that it causeth much sic kness, [such] as the sccurvy and the bloody flux and diverse other diseases, which maketh the body very poor and weak. And when we are sick there is nothing to comfort us; for since I came out of the ship I never ate anything but peas, and loblollie (that is, water gruel). As for deer or venison I never saw any since I came into this land. There is indeed some fowl, but we are not allowed to go and get it, but must work hard both early and late for a mess of water gruel and a mouthful of bread and beef. A mouthful of bread for a penny loaf must serve for four men which is most pitiful. [You would be grieved] if you did know as much as I [do], when people cry out day and night—Oh! That they were in England without their limbs—and would not care to lose any limb to be in England again, yea, though they beg from door to door. For we live in fear of the enemy every hour, yet we have had a combat with them... and we took two alive and made slaves of them. But it was by policy, for we are in great danger; for our plantation is very weak by reason of the death and sickness of our company. For we came but twenty for the merchants, and they are half dead just; and we look every hour when two more should go. Yet there came some four other men yet to live with us, of which there is but one alive; and our Lieutenant is dead, and [also] his father and his brother. And there was some five or six of the last year's twenty, of which there is but three left, so that we are fain to get other men to plant with us; and yet we are but 32 to fight against 3000 if they should come. And the nighest help that we have is ten mile of us, and when the rogues overcame this place [the] last [time] they slew 80 persons. How then shall we do, for we lie even in their teeth? They may easily take us, but [for the fact] that God is merciful and can save with few as well as with many, as he showed to Gilead. And like Gilead's soldiers, if they lapped water, we drink water which is but weak.

And I have nothing to comfort me, nor is there nothing to be gotten here but sickness and death, except [in the event] that one had money to lay out in some things for profit. But I have nothing at all—no, not a shirt to my back but two rags (2), nor clothes but one poor suit, nor but one pair of shoes, but one pair of stockings, but one cap, [and] but two bands [collars]. My cloak is stolen by one of my fellows, and to his dying hour [he] sould not tell me what he did with it; but some of my fellows saw him have butter and beef out of a ship, which my cloak, I doubt [not], paid for. So that I have not a penny, nor a penny worth, to help me too either spice or sugar or strong waters, without the which one cannot live here. For as strong beer in England doth fatten and strengthen them, so water here doth wash and weaken these here [and] only keeps [their] life and soul together. But I am not half [of] a quarter so strong as I was in England, and all is for want of victuals; for I do protest unto you that I have eaten more in [one] day at home than I have allowed me here for a week. You have given more than my day's allowance to a beggar at the door; and if Mr. Jackson had not relieved me,

I should be in a poor case. But he like a father and she like a loving mother doth still help me.

For when we go to Jamestown (that is 10 miles of us) there lie all the ships that come to land, and there they must deliver their goods. And when we went up to town [we would go], as it may be, on Monday at noon, and come there by night, [and] then load the next day by noon, and go home in the afternoon, and unload, and then away again in the night, and [we would] be up about midnight. Then if it rained or blowed never so hard, we must lie in the boat on the water and have nothing but a little bread. For when we go into the boat we [would] have a loaf allowed to two men, and it is all [we would get] if we stayed there two days, which is hard; and [we] must lie all that while in the boat. But that Goodman Jackson pitied me and made me a cabin to lie in always when I [would] come up, and he would give me some poor jacks [fish] [to take] home with me, which comforted me more than peas or water gruel. Oh, they be very godly folks, and love me very well, and will do anything for me. And he much marvelled that you would send me a servant to the Company; he saith I had been better knocked on the head. And indeed so I find it now, to my great grief and misery; and [I] saith that if you love me you will redeem me suddenly, for which I do entreat and beg. And if you cannot get the merchants to redeem me for some little money, then for God's sake get a gathering or entreat some good folks to lay out some little sum of money in meal and cheese and butter and beef. Any eating meat will yield great profit. Oil and vinegar is very good; but, father, there is great loss in leaking. But for God's sake send beef and cheese and butter, or the more of one sort and none of another. But if you send cheese, it must be very old cheese; and at the cheesemonger's you may buy very food cheese for twopence farthing or halfpenny, that will be liked very well. But if you send cheese, you must have a care how you pack it in barrels; and you must put cooper's chips between every cheese, or else the heat of the hold will rot them. And look whatsoever you send me—be in never so much—look, what[ever] I make of it, I will deal truly with you. I will send it over and beg the profit to redeem me; and if I die before it come, I have entreated Goodman Jackson to send you the worth of it, who hath promised he will. If you send, you must direct your letters to Goodman Jackson, at Jamestown, a gunsmith. (You must set down his freight, because there be more of his name there.) Good father, do not forget me, but have mercy and pity my miserable case. I know if you did but see me, you would weep to see me; for I have but one suit. (But [though] it is a strange one, it is very well guarded.) Wherefore, for God's sake, pity me. I pray you to remember my love to all my friends and kindred. I hope all my brothers and sisters are in good health, and as for my part I have set down my resolution that certainly will be; that is, that the answer of this letter will be life or death to me. Therefore, good father, send as soon as you can; and if you send me any thing let this be the mark.

Christopher Columbus
"The Letters of Columbus to Ferdinand and Isabel"

While he may not have been the first European to explore the Atlantic, Christopher Columbus initiated a new era of European voyages to the Atlantic world as a result of his voyages. Columbus was an experienced map maker from the port city of Genoa in the Italian states. The Spanish rulers, King Ferdinand and Queen Isabella (r.1479-1504) commissioned his voyage in 1492 with the goal of seeking a new Western route to Asia from Europe. Instead, Columbus landed on several islands in the Caribbean just off the Americas, including San Salvador, Cuba and Hispaniola. Columbus and his small crew encountered people on the island, and called them "Indians," mistakenly believing that they had found a route to Asia and; reached islands just off of India. Columbus's voyages helped establish Spain as a leader in the early era of European exploration and settlement of the Americas.

Source: Christopher Columbus, *The Journal of Christopher Columbus*, trans. By Cecil Jane (London: Anthony Blond, 1968), 191, 194, 196-198, 200-201.

Focus Questions:

1. For whom was Columbus writing this account? What was his main goal in writing the letter?
2. What does Columbus' account of the lands he sees tell us about what Europeans hoped to find in the "new world" and their motivations for going to those areas?
3. What did Columbus's account of the people he encountered there, whom he called "Indians," tell us about early European attitudes about these people? What ideas or beliefs informed these views?

SIR: Since I know that you will be pleased at the great victory with which Our Lord has crowned my voyage, I write this to you, from which you will learn how in thirty-three days I passed from the Canary Islands to the Indies, with the fleet which the most illustrious King and Queen, our Sovereigns, gave to me. There I found very many islands, filled with innumerable people, and I have taken possession of them all for their Highnesses, done by proclamation and with the royal standard unfurled, and no opposition was offered to me.

To the first island which I found I gave the name "San Salvador," in remembrance of the Divine Majesty, Who had marvellously bestowed all this; the Indians call it "Guanahani." To the second, I gave the name the island of "Santa Maria de Concepcion," to the third, "Fernandina," to the fourth, "Isabella," to the fifth island, "Juana," and so each received from me a new name....

Española is a marvel. The sierras and the mountains, the plains, the champaigns, are so lovely and so rich for planting and sowing, for breeding cattle of every kind, for building towns and villages. The harbours of the sea here are such as cannot be believed to exist unless they have been seen, and so with the rivers, many and great, and of good water, the majority of which contain gold. In the trees, fruits and plants, there is a great difference from those of Juana. In this island, there are many spices and great mines of gold and of other metals.

The people of this island and of all the other islands which I have found and of which I have information, all go naked, men and women, as their mothers bore them, although some of the women cover a single place with the leaf of a plant or with a net of cotton which they make for the purpose. They have no iron or steel or weapons, nor are they fitted to use them. This is not because they are not well built and of handsome stature, but because they are very marvellously timorous. They have no other arms than spears made of canes, cut in seeding time, to the ends of which they fix a small sharpened stick. Of these they do not dare to make use, for many times it has happened that I have sent ashore two or three men to some town to have speech with them, and countless people have come out to them, and as soon as they have seen my men approaching, they have fled, a father not even waiting for his son. This is not because ill has been done to any one of them; on the contrary, at every place where I have been and have been able to have speech with them, I have given to them of that which I had, such as cloth and many other things, receiving nothing in exchange. But so they are, incurably timid. It is true that, after they have been reassured and have lost this fear, they are so guileless and so generous with all that they possess, that no one would believe it who has not seen it. They refuse nothing that they possess, if it be asked of them; on the contrary, they invite any one to share it and display as much love as if they would give their hearts.

They are content with whatever trifle of whatever kind that may be given to them, whether it be of value or valueless. I forbade that they should be given things so worthless as fragments of broken crockery, scraps of broken glass and lace tips, although when they were able to get them, they fancied that they possessed the best jewel in the world. So it was found that for a thong a sailor received gold to the weight of two and a half Castellanos, and others received much more for other things which were worth less. As for new blancas, for them they would give everything which they had, although it might be two or three castellanos' [gold coins] weight of gold or an arroba or two of spun cotton. They took even the pieces of the broken hoops of the wine barrels and, like savages, gave what they had, so that it seemed to me to be wrong and I forbade it. I gave them a thousand handsome good things, which I had brought, in order that they might conceive affection for us and, more than that, might become Christians and be inclined to the love and service of Your Highnesses and of the whole Castilian nation, and strive to collect and give us of the things which they have in abundance and which are necessary to us.

They do not hold any creed nor are they idolaters; but they all believe that power and good are in the heavens and were very firmly convinced that I, with these ships and men, came from the heavens, and in this belief they everywhere received me after they had mastered their fear. This belief is not the result of ignorance, for they are, on the contrary, of a very acute intelligence and they are men who navigate all those seas, so that it is amazing how good an account they give of everything. It is because they have never seen people clothed or ships of such a kind.

As soon as I arrived in the Indies, in the first island which I found, I took some of the natives by force, in order that they might learn and might give me information of whatever there is in these parts. And so it was that they soon understood us, and we them, either by speech or signs, and they have been very serviceable. At present, those I bring with me are still of the opinion that I come from Heaven, for all the intercourse which they have had with me. They were the first to announce this wherever I went, and the others went running from house to house, and to the neighbouring towns, with loud cries of, "Come! Come! See the men from Heaven!" So all came, men and women alike, when their minds were set at rest concerning us, not one, small or great, remaining behind, and they all brought something to eat and drink, which they gave with extraordinary affection....

In all these islands, I saw no great diversity in the appearance of the people or in their manners and language. On the contrary, they all understand one another, which is a very curious thing, on account of which I hope that their Highnesses will determine upon their conversion to our holy faith, towards which they are very inclined. I have already said how I went one hundred and seven leagues in a straight line from west to east along the seashore of the island of Juana, and as a result of this voyage I can say that this island is larger than England and Scotland together, for, beyond these one hundred and seven leagues, there remain to the westward two provinces to which I have not gone. One of these provinces they call "Avan," and there people are born with tails. These provinces cannot have a length of less than fifty or sixty leagues, as I could understand from those Indians whom I have and who know all the islands.

The other island, Española, has a circumference greater than all Spain from Collioure by the seacoast to Fuenterabia in Vizcaya, for I voyaged along one side for one hundred and eighty-eight great leagues in a straight line from west to east. It is a land to be desired and, when seen, never to be left. I have taken possession of all for their Highnesses, and all are more richly endowed than I know how or am able to say, and I hold all for their Highnesses, so that they may dispose of them as they do of the kingdoms of Castile and as absolutely. But especially, in this Española, in the situation most convenient and in the best position for the mines of gold and for all trade as well with the mainland here as with that there, belonging to the Grand Khan, where will be great trade and profit, I have taken possession of a large town, to which I gave the name "Villa de Navidad," and in it I have made fortifications and a fort, which will now by this time be entirely completed. In it I have left enough men for such a purpose with arms and artillery and provisions for more than a year, and a fusta, and one, a master of all seacraft, to build others, and I have established great friendship with the king of that land, so much so, that he was proud to call me "brother" and to treat me as such....

In conclusion, to speak only of what has been accomplished on this voyage, which was so hasty, their Highnesses can see that I will give them as much gold as they may need, if their Highnesses will render me very slight assistance; presently, I will give them spices and cotton, as much as their Highnesses shall command; and mastic, as much as they shall order to be shipped and which, up to now, has been found only in Greece, in the island of Chios, and the Seignory sells it for what it pleases; and aloe, as much as they shall order to be shipped; and slaves, as many as they shall order, and who will be from the idolaters. I believe also that I have found rhubarb and cinnamon, and I shall find a thousand other things of value, which the people whom I have left there will have discovered, for I have not delayed at any point, so far as the wind allowed me to sail, except in the town of Navidad, in order to leave it secured and well established, and in truth I should have done much more if the ships had served me as reason demanded....

This is an account of the facts, thus abridged. Done in the caravel, off the Canary Islands, on the fifteenth day of February, in the year one thousand four hundred and ninety-three.

Cieza de León
"The Chronicle of Peru"

Pedro Cieza de León went to South America from Spain as a solider when he was only 14 years old. He remained in South America for most of his life, traveling throughout the continent and participating in military battles for Spain, primarily against the Inca. The Inca Empire in that period covered a vast stretch of Western South America, and was comprised of over 12 million people, including many different ethnic groups. In 1532, the Spanish wiped out what remained of the crumbling Incan Empire. Cieza de León was involved in the military campaigns that destroyed it, and immediately after 1532, he interviewed those who survived them, both Spanish and Inca alike. He then wrote one of the most important and reliable chronicles for that period.

Source: Pedro Cieza de León, "The Chronicle of Peru: The Incas," reprinted in *Primary Source Document Workbook to Accompany Western Civilizations,* *by Philip J. Adier; prepared* by Robert Welborn (New York: West Publishing Company, 1996), 35-36.

Focus Questions:

1. Why did the author write this account? What did he hope to accomplish by doing so?

2. What does the author say about the Inca people? What informs his account and views?

3. What does this account tell us about Spanish attitudes and actions in relation to the Inca?

It should be well understood that great prudence was needed to enable these kings to govern such large provinces, extending over so vast a region, parts of it rugged and covered with forests, parts mountainous, with snowy peaks and ridges, parts consisting of deserts of sand, dry and without trees or water. These regions were inhabited by many different nations, with varying languages, laws, religions, and the kings had to maintain tranquility and to rule so that all should live in peace and in friendship towards their lord. Although the city of Cuzco was the head of the empire,... yet at certain points, as we shall also explain, the king stationed his delegates and governors, who were the most learned, the ablest, and the bravest men that could be found, and none was so youthful that he was not already in the last third part of his age. As they were faithful and none betrayed their trusts,... none of the natives, though they might be more power-ful, attempted to rise in rebellion; or if such a thing ever did take place, the town where the revolt broke out was punished, and the ringleaders were sent prison-ers to Cuzco....

All men so feared the king, that they did not dare to speak evil even of his shadow. And this was not all. If any of the king's captains or servants went forth to visit a distant part of the empire on some business, the people came out on the road with presents to receive them, not daring, even if one came alone, to omit to comply with all his commands.

So great was the veneration that the people felt for their princes, through-out this vast region, that every district was as well regulated and governed as if the lord was actually present to chastise those who acted contrary to his rules. This fear arose from the known valor of the lords and their strict justice. It was felt to be certain that those who did evil would receive punishment without fail, and that neither prayers nor bribes would avert it. At the same time, the Incas always did good to those who were under their sway, and would not allow them to be ill-treated, nor that too much tribute should be exacted from them. Many who dwelt in a sterile country where they and their ancestors have lived with dif-ficulty, found that through the orders of the Inca their lands were made fertile and abundant, the things being supplied which before were wanting. In other districts, where there was scarcity of clothing, owing to the people having no flocks, orders were given that cloth should be abundantly provided. In short, it will be understood that these lords knew how to enforce service and the payment of tribute, so they provided for the maintenance of the people, and took care that they should want for nothing. Through these good works, and because the lord always gave women and rich gifts to his principal vassals, he gained so much on their affections that he was most fondly loved....

One of the things which I admired most, in contemplating and noting down the affairs of this kingdom, was to think how and in what manner they can have made such grand and admirable roads as we now see, and what a number of men would suffice for their construction, and with what tools and instruments they can have leveled the mountains and broken through the rocks to make them so broad and good as they are. For it seems to me that if the King of Spain should desire to give orders for another royal road to be made, like that which goes from Quito to Cuzco,... with all his power I believe that he could not get it done; nor could any force of men achieve such results unless there was also the perfect order by means of which the commands of the Incas were carried into execution....

Anonymous,
"The English Describe Pawatah's People"

The first permanent English settlement in North America, at Jamestown on the coast of Virginia in 1607, brought the English into contact with Native Americans already inhabiting the area, including the Powhatan group described in this passage. Written by one of the settlers at Jamestown, this description of the Powhatan reflects early English impressions of Native Americans. The English settlers did not speak the Algonquian language of the Powhatan tribe and had only limited contact with them.

Source: "Description of the People, Letter on May 21-June 21, 1607" in *The Jamestown Voyages Under the First Charter, 1606-1609*, vol. 1, ed. by Philip L Barbour (Cambridge: Cambridge University Press, 1969), 102-104.

FOCUS QUESTIONS:

1. What was the audience for this account and how did that shape it?

2. What ideas or beliefs informed this Englishman's impressions of the Powhatan?

3. What does this account tell us about European encounters with Native Americans in this period?

21 May-21 June 1607.
Description of the People.
A Brief discription of the People.

There is a king in this land called great Pawatah, vnder whose dominions are at least 20th several kingdomes, yet each king potent as a prince in his owne territory. these have their Subiectes at so quick Comaund, as a beck bringes obedience, even to the resticucion of stolne goodes which by their naturall inclinac[i]on they are loth to leave. They goe all naked save their privityes, yet in coole weather they were deare skinns, with the hayre on loose: some have leather stockinges vp to their twisties,[1] & sandalls on their feet, their hayre is black generally, which they weare long on the left side, tyed vp on a knott, about which knott the kinges and best among them have a kind of Coronett of deares hayre coloured redd, some have chaines of long linckt copper about their neckes, and some chaines of pearle, the comon sort stick long fethers in this knott, I found not a grey eye among them all. their skynn is tawny not so borne, but with dying and paynting them selues, in which they delight greatly. The wemen are like the men, onely this difference; their hayre groweth long al over their heades save clipt somewhat short afore, these do all the labour and the men hunt and goe at their plesure. They live commonly by the water side in litle cottages made of canes and reedes, covered with the barke of trees; they dwell as I guesse by families of kindred & allyance some 40 tie or 50 ti in a Hatto[2] or small village; which townes are not past a myle or half a myle asunder in most places. They live vpon sodden wheat beanes & peaze for the most part, also they kill deare take fish in their weares, & kill fowle aboundance, they eate often and that liberally; they are proper lusty streight men very strong runn exceeding swiftly, their feight is alway in the wood with bow & arrowes, & a short wodden sword, the celerity they vse in skirmish is admirable. the king directes the batle & is always in front. Their manner of entertainment is vpon mattes on the ground vnder some tree, where they sitt themselues alone in the midst of the matt, & two mattes on each side, on which they[r] people sitt, then right against him (making a square forme) satt we alwayes. when they came to their matt they have an vsher goes before them, & the rest as he sittes downe give a long showt. The people steale any thing comes neare them, yea are so practized in this art that lookeing in our face they would with their foot betwene their toes convey a chizell knife, percer or any indifferent light thing: which having once conveyed they hold it an iniury to take the same from them; They are naturally given to trechery, howbeit we could not …

---

1 'The junction of the thighs' (OED)

2 'Hatto' possibly represents and element cognate with modern Cree *otanow*, 'town', which appears as the second element in the village name Kecoughtan. It may have been pronounced with a glottal stop or other initial throaty sound which the author recorded with an 'h'.

"The Code Noir"

By the early eighteenth century, Europeans had established permanent colonies on Caribbean islands and in North and South America. Europeans began the forced migration of Africans to colonies for slave labor in the 1500s and, by 1700, slavery had become an institution in European colonies in the Atlantic. In the Caribbean islands, the Dutch, English and the French colonies all relied on slaves as the main source of the backbreaking labor needed for the cultivation crops grown for export to Europe: sugar cane, tobacco, and indigo (a dye for cloth). Issued by King Louis XIV (r. 1643-1715) in 1685, the *Code Noir* (or Black Laws) attempted to dictate every aspect of the lives of the enslaved in the French colonies. Initially, the edict was designed for the French colony of Saint-Domingue (present day Haiti), but was later applied in all other French colonies, including Louisiana. The *Code Noir* remained in effect, with some additions and changes, until the abolition of slavery in French holdings in the nineteenth century. What follows here are excerpts from the 60 articles of the *Code Noir* promulgated by Louis XIV in 1685

Source: Long, Edward. *The History of Jamaica* London: T. Lowndes, 1774). Reprint, Edward Long, *The History of Jamaica*, vol. 3. New York: Arno Press, 1972, 921-934.

Focus Questions:

1. According to these laws, to what extent were enslaved people in the French colonies classified as people with rights or were they considered property?
2. What ideas, issues, traditions and beliefs influenced these laws?
3. How were these laws enforced? How successfully?

    Edict of the King, Concerning the People of the islands of the French Americas March 1685. Registered by the Sovereign Council of Saint Domingue May 6, 1687

1 We will and intend, that the edict of the late king of glorious memory, our lord and father, of the 23rd of April 1615, should be executed in our islands. To which end, we enjoin our officers, in every department, to banish all Jews whatsoever who have taken up their residence there; which Jews (being avowed enemies to the name of Christ) we hereby command to retire from the fame within the space of three months, to be counted from the day of publication of these presents, on pain of forfeiting their lives and goods.

3 We forbid the public exercise of any other than the Catholic, Apostolic, and Roman religion*. We will that all persons, who act contrary to this prohibition,

*The Catholic Church

shall be punished as rebels against our authority. In this view, we forbid all heretical assemblies; declaring the same to be illegal and seditious conventions, subject to the like punishment; which also shall be inflicted upon those masters who permit their slaves to attend such assemblies.

6 We enjoin all our subjects, of what quality or condition soever, to observe the Lord's-day [Sunday], and the holidays that are kept by our subjects of the Catholic, Apostolic, and Roman religion. We forbid them to labour, or cause their salves to labour on those days, from the hour of midnight to the following midnight, whether it be in the culture of land, or manufacture of sugar, or any other kind of work; on penalty that the masters so offending shall be subject to a fine, and arbitrary punishment, and the forfeiture of all such sugar, as well as of the slaves, detected at work by our officers.

9 Free men who have one or more children born during concubinage with their slaves, as well as masters of slaves who suffer such concubinage, shall be condemned each in a fine of two thousand pounds weight of sugar. And, if any master shall have children by his own slave, we will, that, over and above the like fine, he shall be deprived of such slave and children; and that both she and they shall be forfeited to the use and benefit of the hospital, with disability of their becoming enfranchised. We mean not, however, that the present article take effect, in case the father, not being a married man at the time of such his concubinage with his slave, shall afterwards intermarry with his said slave (according to the forms observed by the church); in consequence whereof, she shall become enfranchised, and the children free and legitimate.

11 We forbid clergymen to solemnize the marriage of slaves, unless they can produce the consent of their master. And we likewise forbid masters to use any constraint toward their slaves, to make them marry involuntarily.

12 The children produced from the marriage of one slave with another shall be slaves, and belong to the master of the wife, and not of the husband, if the husband and wife have different masters.

13 We will, that, if a male slave shall intermarry with a free woman, the issue of such marriage, as well male as female, shall follow the condition of the mother, and be free like her not withstanding the slavery of the father; but, if the father be free, and the mother a slave, her children shall in like manner be slaves.

18. We forbid salves to sell sugar-canes on any account or pretence whatsoever, and notwithstanding any permission from their master, on penalty that such slaves shall be whipped; and the master so permitting shall be fined in the amount of ten French livres; and the buyer of such canes in the same sum.

19. We likewise forbid them to expose at public sale, or to carry into any private houses for the purpose of sale, any kind of commodity, not even fruits, pulse, fire wood, pot herbs, or salads and cattle, without leave of their masters

expressed by a ticket, or some known token, on penalty that their masters may claim the things so sols, without making and restitution of the price paid by the purchasers thereof, and receive also from such purchasers a fine of six French livres, to be appropriated to their own use.

22 Masters shall be obliged to furnish, every week, to their slaves of ten years old, or upwards, for their subsistence, three pots (of the country measure) of cassava meal or three bunches of cassava roots, weighing each two livres** and a half at the least; or some other vegetable food equivalent; together with two livres of salted beef or three livres of fish, or some other animal food in proportion; and to children, from the time of the weaning to the age of ten, half the aforesaid quantity of like provisions.

25 Masters shall be obliged to furnish each and every of their slaves, yearly, with two suits of linen cloth, or five yards of light cloths, whichsoever the said masters shall judge most proper.

26. Slaves that are not subsisted, clothed, and maintained, in the manner we have directed by these presents, may give notice thereof to our attorney, and put their case into his hands; in consequence of which, or even without them, of the cause of complaint shall come to his knowledge by any other means, the masters shall be prosecuted at his instance, and without any expense; which process we would also have observed in regard to those masters who abuse or treat their slaves in a barbarous and inhuman manner.

33 The slave that strikes his master, or the wife of his master, his mistress, or any of the children, so as to cause an effusion of blood; or that gives them, or any of them, a blow upon the face; shall be punished with death.

35 Certain kinds of theft, as of horses, mares, mules, oxen, and cows, committed by slaves, or by others who have been made free, shall be punished effectually; and even with death, if the case require it.

36 Slaves, guilty of stealing sheep, goats, hogs, poultry, sugar canes, cassava, peas, or other kinds of pulse, shall, according to the nature and quality of their crime, be punished by the judges; who may, if they think fit, order them to be whipped by the common hangman, and branded on the shoulder with a fleur-de-lis.***

38 A fugitive slave that shall continue out for a month, computing from the day of his being publicly advertised by his master, shall have both his ears cut off, and shall be branded on one of his shoulders with a fleur-de-lis. In case of his repetition of the same offence, computing in like manner from the day of his being publicly advertised, he shall be hamstrung, and be branded on the other shoulder. But for the third offence, he shall be punished with death.

**Approximately equivalent to an English pound.
***The fleur-de-lis was the symbol of the French Bourbon dynasty, and a prominent royal insignia.

CHAPTER 13

Thought and Culture in Early Modern Europe

Francis Bacon,
from *Novum Organum*

Francis Bacon (1561–1626) was a prophet of the scientific revolution of the seventeenth century—a revolution that transformed the foundations of thought and ushered in the Age of Science. Like the prophets of the Old Testament, Bacon concentrated first on the evils around him. Although for him these evils were intellectual rather than moral or religious, he couched his criticism of the science of his day in biblical terms. Like the medieval schoolmen, the leading thinkers of his age, he argued, had wandered from the path of truth into the worship of idols. In the selection that follows he lists four such idols, to which he gives the picturesque titles of idols of the *Tribe*, the *Cave*, the *Marketplace*, and the *Theatre*. To avoid falling prey to these idols, people must turn their backs on scholastic philosophy and develop a new science based on a true knowledge of the workings of nature. Such knowledge, Bacon held, was to be derived from careful and continued observation of specific natural occurrences. This observational method, which he called induction, is explained and illustrated in his major work, the *Instauratio Magna* (Great Renewal). In his opinion, this treatise represented a "total reconstruction of the sciences, arts, and all human knowledge."

Although he was a prophet of the new science, Bacon himself did not fully grasp the nature of the method that men like Galileo and Newton were to employ in their work. His concept of induction fails to take adequate account of two other basic elements of the modern scientific method—the formulation of hypotheses and the deduction and verification of their consequences.

Living at the height of the English Renaissance (which followed by a hundred years the Italian Renaissance), Bacon exemplified many of the attitudes found in previous Renaissance writers: the rejection of the medieval worldview as pernicious error, the somewhat naïve optimism about his ability to take the whole of human knowledge as his sphere of activity, and the faith that he stood on the thresh-old of a new intellectual era. Finally, in his assertion that "knowledge is power," Bacon repeated a central concept of Machiavelli, but with a significant difference—Machiavelli was concerned with the power that a prince could wield over his subjects, but Bacon was concerned with the power (derived from scientific understanding), that all humans could wield over nature.

The following selection is from *Novum Organum* (the *New Organon* written in 1620), which forms a part of *Instauratio Magna*.

Source: J. Spedding, trans., Francis Bacon, *Novum Organum* (1620).

FOCUS QUESTIONS:

1. How does Bacon propose to find truth?
2. What are the strengths and weaknesses of his inductive method?

NOVUM ORGANUM
Aphorisms Concerning the Interpretation of Nature and the Kingdom of Man

I. Man, being the servant and interpreter of Nature, can do and understand so much and so much only as he has observed in fact or in thought in the course of nature: beyond this he neither knows anything nor can do anything.

II. Neither the naked hand nor the understanding left to itself can effect much. It is by instruments and helps that the work is done, which are as much wanted for the understanding as for the hand. And as the instruments of the hand either give motion or guide it, so the instruments of the mind supply either suggestions for the understanding or cautions.

III. Human knowledge and human power meet in one; for where the cause is not known the effect cannot be produced. Nature to be commanded must be obeyed; and that which in contemplation is as the cause is in operation as the rule.

IV. Towards the effecting of works, all that man can do is to put together or put asunder natural bodies. The rest is done by nature working within.

* * *

VI. It would be an unsound fancy and self-contradictory to expect that things which have never yet been done can be done except by means which have never yet been tried.

* * *

XI. As the sciences which we now have do not help us in finding out new works, so neither does the logic which we now have help us in finding out new sciences.

XII. The logic now in use serves rather to fix and give stability to the errors which have their foundations in commonly received notions than to help the search after truth. So it does more harm than good.

XVIII. The discoveries which have hitherto been made in the sciences are such as lie close to vulgar notions, scarcely beneath the surface. In order to penetrate into the inner and further recesses of nature, it is necessary that both notions and axioms be derived from things by a more sure and guarded way; and that a method of intellectual operation be introduced altogether better and more certain.

* * *

XIX. There are and can be only two ways of searching into and discovering truth. The one flies from the senses and particulars to the most general axioms, and from these principles, the truth of which it takes for settled and immovable, proceeds to judgment and to the discovery of middle axioms. And this way is now in fashion. The other derives axioms from the senses and particulars, rising by a gradual and unbroken ascent, so that it arrives at the most general axioms last of all. This is the true way, but as yet untried.

* * *

XXII. Both ways set out from the senses and particulars, and rest in the highest generalities; but the difference between them is infinite. For the one just glances at experiment and particulars in passing, the other dwells duly and orderly among them. The one, again, begins at once by establishing certain abstract and useless generalities, the other rises by gradual steps to that which is prior and better known in the order of nature.

* * *

XXXI. It is idle to expect any great advancement in science from the superinducing and engrafting of new things upon old. We must begin anew from the very foundations, unless we would revolve forever in a circle with mean and contemptible progress.

* * *

XXXV. It was said by Borgia of the expedition of the French into Italy, that they came with chalk in their hands to mark out their lodgings, not with arms to force their way in. I in like manner would have my doctrine enter quietly into the minds that are fit and capable of receiving it; for confutations cannot be employed, when the difference is upon first principles and very notions and even upon forms of demonstration.

XXXVI. One method of delivery alone remains to us; which is simply this: we must lead men to the particulars themselves, and their series and order; while men on their side must force themselves for awhile to lay their notions by and begin to familiarize themselves with facts.

XXXVII. The doctrine of those who have denied that certainty could be attained at all, has some agreement with my way of proceeding at the first setting out; but they end in being infinitely separated and opposed. For the holders of that doctrine assert simply that nothing can be known; I also assert that not much can be known in nature by the way which is now in use. But then they go on to destroy the authority of the senses and understanding; whereas I proceed to devise and supply helps for the same.

XXXVIII. The idols and false notions which are now in possession of the human understanding, and have taken deep root therein, not only so beset men's minds that truth can hardly find entrance, but even after entrance is obtained, they will again in the very instauration of the science meet and trouble us, unless men being forewarned of the danger fortify themselves as far as may be against their assaults.

XXXIX. There are four classes of Idols which beset men's minds. To these for distinction's sake I have assigned names, calling the first class Idols of the Tribe; the second, Idols of the Cave; the third, Idols of the Marketplace; the fourth, Idols of the Theatre.

* * *

XL. The formation of ideas and axioms by true induction is no doubt the proper remedy to be applied for the keeping off and clearing away of idols. To point them out, however, is of great use; for the doctrine of Idols is to the Interpretation of Nature what the doctrine of the refutation of Sophisms is to common Logic.

XLI. The Idols of the Tribe have their foundation in human nature itself, and in the tribe or race of men. For it is a false assertion that the sense of man is the measure of things. On the contrary, all perceptions as well of the sense as of the mind are according to the measure of the universe. And the human under-standing is like a false mirror, which, receiving rays irregularly, distorts and discolours the nature of things by mingling its own nature with it.

XLII. The Idols of the Cave are the idols of the individual man. For every one (besides the errors common to human nature in general) has a cave or den of his own, which refracts and discolors the light of nature; owing either to his own proper and peculiar nature; or to his education and conversation with others; or to the reading of books, and the authority of those whom he esteems and admires; or to the differences of impressions, accordingly as they take place in a mind preoccupied and predisposed or in a mind indifferent and settled; or the like. So that the spirit of man (according as it is meted out to different individuals) is in fact a thing variable and full of perturbation, and governed as it were by chance. Whence it was observed by Heraclitus that men look for sciences in their own lesser worlds, and not in the greater or common world.

XLIII. There are also Idols formed by the intercourse and association of men with each other, which I call Idols of the Marketplace, on account of the commerce and consort of men there. For it is by discourse that men associate; and words are imposed according to the apprehension of the vulgar. And therefore the ill and unfit choice of words wonderfully obstructs the understanding. Nor do the definitions or explanations wherewith in some things learned men are wont to guard and defend themselves, by any means set the matter right. But words plainly force and overrule the understanding, and throw all into confusion, and lead men away into numberless empty controversies and idle fancies.

XLIV. Lastly, there are Idols which have immigrated into men's minds from the various dogmas of philosophies, and also from wrong laws of demonstration. These I call Idols of the Theatre; because in my judgment all the received systems are but so many stage-plays, representing worlds of their own creation after an unreal and scenic fashion. Nor is it only of the systems now in vogue, or only of the ancient sects and philosophies, that I speak; for many more plays of the same kind may yet be composed and in like artificial manner set forth; seeing that errors the most widely different have nevertheless causes for the most part alike. Neither again do I mean this only of entire systems, but also of many principles and axioms in science, which by tradition, credulity, and negligence have come to be received.

William Harvey,
Address to the Royal College of Physicians
1628

William Harvey has been termed the father of modern physiology. He was heir to a legacy of interest in the internal workings of the human body that had most recently been evidenced among artists during the Renaissance, but, whereas Michelangelo studied the body to better represent the human form, Harvey sought to discover the internal workings for their own scientific merit. In this, he was more closely akin to the earlier scientific studies of Leonardo da Vinci. Harvey built upon the work of the Greek physician Galen (fl. 150 CE), who demonstrated that the arteries carried blood instead of air, and his exacting methods set the pattern of scientific research for generations. In the following selection, which was an address to the Royal College of Physicians in 1628, he gives the results of his methodical dissections and experiments.

Source: R. Willis, trans.,"I Learn and Teach from the Fabric of Nature," *The Works of William Harvey* (London: Sydenham Society, 1847), pp. 5–7, 31–32, 45–47.

FOCUS QUESTIONS:

1. Why did William Harvey want to present his findings in an address before the Royal College of Physicians?
2. What was he afraid of?
3. Why were his discoveries about the heart and circulation of blood so important and perhaps so threatening?

As this book alone declares the blood to course and revolve by a new route, very different from the ancient and beaten pathway trodden for so many ages, and illustrated by such a host of learned and distinguished men, I was greatly afraid lest I might be charged with presumption did I lay my work before the public at home, or send it beyond seas for impression, unless I had first proposed its subject to you, had confirmed its conclusions by ocular demonstrations in your presence, had replied to your doubts and objections, and secured the assent and support of our distinguished President. For I was most intimately persuaded, that if I could make good my proposition before you and our College...I had less to fear from others...For true philosophers, who are only eager for truth and knowledge, never regard themselves as already so thoroughly informed, but that they welcome further information from whomsoever and from whencesoever it may come; nor are they so narrow-minded as to imagine any of the arts or sciences transmitted to us by the ancients, in such a state of forwardness or completeness, that nothing is left for the ingenuity and industry of others...Neither do they swear such fealty to their mistress Antiquity, that they openly, and in sight of all, deny and desert their friend Truth...

My dear colleagues...I profess both to learn and to teach anatomy, not from books, but from dissections; not from the positions of philosophers, but from the fabric of nature...

From these and other observations of the like kind, I am persuaded it will be found that the motion of the heart is as follows:

First of all, the auricle contracts, and in the course of its contraction throws the blood, (which it contains in ample quantity as the head of the veins, the store-house and cistern of the blood,) into the ventricle, which being filled, the heart raises itself straightway, makes all its fibers tense, contracts the ventricles, and performs a beat, by which beat it immediately sends the blood supplied to it by the auricle into the arteries; the right ventricle sending its charge into the lungs by the vessel which is called vena arteriosi, but which, in structure and function, and all things else, is an artery; the left ventricle sending its charge into the aorta, and through this by the arteries to the body at large...

Thus far I have spoken of the passage of the blood from the veins into the arteries, and of the manner in which it is transmitted and distributed by the action of the heart...But what remains to be said upon the quantity and source of the blood which thus passes, is of so novel and unheard-of character, that I not only fear injury to myself from the envy of a few, but I tremble lest I have mankind at large for my enemies...Still, the die is cast, and my trust is in my love of truth, and the candor that inheres in cultivated minds. And when I surveyed my mass of evidence...I revolved in my mind, what might be the quantity of blood which was transmitted, in how short a time its passage might be effected, and the like...I began to think whether there might not be A MOTION, AS IT WERE, IN A CIRCLE. Now this I afterwards found to be true; and I finally saw that the blood, forced by the action of the left ventricle into the arteries, was distributed to the body at large...impelled by the right ventricle...through the veins, and so round to the left ventricle in the manner already indicated...

The heart, consequently, is the beginning of life; the sun of the microcosm, even as the sun in his turn might well be designated the heart of the world; for it is the heart by whose virtue and pulse the blood is moved, perfected, made apt to nourish, and is preserved from corruption and coagulation; it is the household divinity which, discharging its function, nourishes, cherishes, quickens the whole body, and is indeed the foundation of life, the source of all action.

René Descartes,
The Discourse on Method and Metaphysical Meditations,
"I Think, Therefore I Am"

René Descartes was born in 1596 in western France but lived primarily in Holland for the last twenty years of his life. He attended Jesuit schools and graduated in law from the university in Poitiers. He was not attracted to a legal career, however, and became a soldier in the German wars of the time. It was while he was billeted in a German town that he had an intellectual revelation akin, as he later maintained, to a religious conversion. He had a vision of the great potential for progress, if mathematical method were to be applied to all fields of knowledge. He thus pursued a career devoted to the propagation of a strict method, best exemplified by his invention of analytical geometry. Descartes believed that human beings were endowed by God with the ability to reason and that God served as the guarantor of the correctness of clear ideas. The material world could thus be understood through adherence to mathematical laws and methods of inquiry. Descartes championed the process of deductive reasoning whereby specific information could be logically deduced from general information. His method was influential well into the eighteenth century, when it was supplanted by the method of scientific induction, whereby generalizations could be drawn from the observation of specific data.

The following selection is drawn from Descartes' most famous work, *Discourse on the Method of Rightly Conducting the Reason* (1636).

Source: G. B. Rawlings, trans., René Descartes, "I Think, Therefore I Am," in The *Discourse on Method and Metaphysical Meditations* (London: Walter Scott, 1901), pp. 32–35, 60–61, 75–76.

Focus Questions:

1. What did Descartes mean by the phrase "I think, therefore I am"? Why was this so fundamental to his method?
2. Reconstruct his logic for the existence of God. Do you find it compelling?

As a multitude of laws often furnishes excuses for vice, so that a state is much better governed when it has but few, and those few strictly observed, so in place of the great number of precepts of which logic is composed, I believed that I should find the following four sufficient, provided that I made a firm and constant resolve not once to omit to observe them.

The first was, never to accept anything as true when I did not recognize it clearly to be so, that is to say, to carefully avoid precipitation and prejudice, and to include in my opinions nothing beyond that which should present itself so clearly and so distinctly to my mind that I might have no occasion to doubt it.

The second was, to divide each of the difficulties which I should examine into as many parts as were possible, and as should be required for its better solution.

The third was, to conduct my thoughts in order, by beginning with the simplest objects, and those most easy to know, so as to mount little by little, as if by steps, to the most complex knowledge, and even assuming an order among those which do not naturally precede one another.

And the last was, to make everywhere enumerations so complete, and reviews so wide, that I should be sure of omitting nothing...

I had long remarked that, in conduct, it is sometimes necessary to follow opinions known to be very uncertain, just as if they were indisputable, as has been said above; but then, because I desired to devote myself only to the research of truth, I thought it necessary to do exactly the contrary, and reject as absolutely false all in which I could conceive the least doubt, in order to see if afterwards there did not remain in my belief something which was entirely indisputable. Thus, because our senses sometimes deceive us, I wanted to suppose that nothing is such as they make us imagine it; and because some men err in reasoning...and judging that I was as liable to fail as any other, I rejected as false all the reasons which I had formerly accepted as [true]...I resolved that everything which had ever entered into my mind was no more true than the illusions of my dreams. But immediately afterwards I observed that while I thus desired everything to be false, I, who thought, must of necessity [exist]; and remarking that this truth, I think, therefore I am, was so firm and so assured that all the most extravagant suppositions of the skeptics were unable to shake it, I judged that I could unhesitatingly accept it as the first principle of the philosophy I was seeking...

After this, and reflecting upon the fact that I doubted, and that in consequence my being was not quite perfect (for I saw clearly that to know was a greater perfection than to doubt), I [wondered where] I had learned to think of something more perfect than I; and I knew for certain that it must be from some nature which was in reality more perfect. [And I clearly recognized that] this idea...had been put in me by a nature truly more perfect than I, which had in itself all perfections of which I could have any idea; that is, to explain myself in one word, God...

Finally, whether awake or asleep, we ought never to allow ourselves to be persuaded of the truth of anything unless on the evidence of our Reason. And it must be noted that I say of our Reason, and not of our imagination or of our senses: thus, for example, although we very clearly see the sun, we ought not therefore to determine that it is only of the size which our sense of sight presents; and we may very distinctly imagine the head of a lion joined to the body of a goat, without being therefore shut up to the conclusion that a chimaera exists; for it is not a dictate of Reason that what we thus see or imagine is in reality existent; but it plainly tells us that all our ideas or notions contain in them some truth; for otherwise it could not be that God, who is wholly perfect and veracious, should have placed them in us.

Charles Perrault,
Little Red Riding-Hood

Charles Perrault was a French nobleman as well as an accomplished scholar and writer. Perrault initially trained to be a member of the Parliament (French law court) but with the support of King Louis XIV's (r.16431715), he became the supervisor of royal buildings, an important government post. As a member of the Royal Academy of Arts and Sciences, Perrault became embroiled in a lively public debate, the quarrel of the ancients and moderns, an argument over the merit of works by new authors versus those of Ancient scholars, such as Aristotle. Perrault passionately argued on behalf of the "moderns," claiming the contributions of contemporary authors and artists were as important as those of the ancient scholars. This excerpt is taken from Perrault's collection of stories first published in 1697. For these stories, Perrault drew on oral story telling traditions, or stories that had been passed down through word of mouth through many generations, by the French peasantry whose stories, while humorous, also reflected the sometimes harsh realities of their lives. Perrault wrote them down and published them for the first time just as they had been told to him, by his nursemaid, a peasant woman, the original "Mother Goose." To increase the appeal of these stories to his audience, literate nobles at the royal Court, he added short poems at the end of each tale.

Source: Jacques Barchilon and Henry Pettit eds., *The Authentic Mother Goose. Fairy Tales and Nursery Rhymes* (Denver: Swallow, 1960), reprint of Charles Perrault, *Mother Goose's Tales*, trans. by Robert Samber (London: Pote, 1729), 1-8.

FOCUS QUESTIONS:

1. Who was Perrault's audience for this story and how does he adapt the story to his audience?
2. What was the overall message or point of this story?
3. What does this story suggest about the realities of peasants' lives in this period?

There was once upon a time a little country girl, born in a village, the prettiest little creature that ever was seen. Her mother was beyond reason excessively fond of her, and her grandmother yet much more. This good woman caused to be made for her a little red Riding Hood which made her look so very pretty, that every body call'd her, The little red Riding Hood.

One day, her mother having made some custards, said to her, Go my little biddy, for her Christian name was Biddy, go and see how your grandmother does, for I can hear she has been ill, carry her a custard, and this little pot of butter. The little red Riding Hood sets out immediately to go to her grandmother, who lived in another village. As she was going through the wood, she met with Gossop Wolfe, who had a good mind to eat her up, but he did not dare, because of some faggot-makers that were in the forest.

He asked of her wither she was going: The poor child, who did not know how dangerous a thing it is to stay and hear a Wolfe talk, said to him, I am going to see my grandmamma, and carry her a custard pie, and a little pot of butter my mamma sends her. Does she live far off? Said the Wolfe. Oh! Ay, said the little red Riding Hood, on the other side of the mill below yonder, at the first house in the village. Well, said the Wolfe, and I'll go and see her too; I'll go this way, and go you that, and we shall see who will be there soonest.

The Wolfe began to run as fast as he was able, the shortest way; and the little girl went the longest, diverting her self in gathering nuts, running after butterflies, and making nose-gays of all the little flowers she met with. The Wolfe was not long before he came to the grandmother's house; he knocked at the door toc, toc. Whose There Your grand-daughter, the little red Riding Hood, said the Wolfe, counterfeiting her voice, who had brought you a custard pie, and a little pot of butter mamma sends you.

The good grandmother, who was in bed, because she found herself somewhat ill, cried out, Pull the bobbin, and the latch will go up. The Wolfe pull'd the bobbin, and the door open'd; upon which he fell upon the good woman, and eat her up in the tenth part of a moment; for he had eaten nothing for above three days before. After that, he shut the door, and went into the grandmother's bed, expecting the little red Riding Hood, who came some time afterwards, and knock'd at the door toc toc, Who's there? The little red Riding Hood, who hearing the big voice of the Wolfe, was at first afraid; but believing her grandmother had got a cold and was grown hoarse, said, it is your granddaughter, The little red Riding Hood, who has brought you custard pie, and a little pot of butter mamma sends you. The Wolfe cried out to her softening his voice as much as he could, Pull the bobbin, and the latch will go up. The little red Riding Hood, pull'd the bobbin, and the door opened.

The Wolfe seeing her come in, said to her, hiding himself under the clothes. Put the custard, and the little pot of butter upon the stool, and come into bed to me. The little red Riding Hood, undressed herself, and went into bed, where she was very much astonished to see how her grandmother looked in her night clothes: So he said to her,

Grandmamma what great arms you have got! It is the better to embrace thee my pretty child. Grandmamma, what great legs you have got! It is to run the better my child. Grandmamma, what great ears you have got! It is to hear the better, my child. Grandmamma, what great eyes you have got! It is to see thee better, my child. Grandmamma, what great teeth you have got! It is to eat thee up. And, upon saying these words, the wicked Wolfe fell upon poor Little Red Riding Hood, and ate her up.

The Moral

From this short story easy we discern,
What conduct all young people ought to learn.
But above all, the growing ladies fair,
Whose orient rosy blooms begin t'appear
Who, beauties in the fragrant spring of age
With pretty airs young hearts are apt t'engage.
Ill do they listen to all sorts of tongues,
Since some enchant and lure like Sirens songs.
No wonder therefore 'tis, if overpower'd.
So many of them has the wolf devour'd.
The Wolfe, I say, for Wolves too sure there are
Of every sort, and of every character.
Some of them mild and gentle humour'd be,
Of noise and gall, and rancour wholly free.
Who, tame, familiar, full of complaisance
Ogle and leer, languish, cajole and glance,
With luring tongues, and language sweet,
Follow young ladies as they walk in the street,
E'en to their very houses, nay, beside
And artful, tho' their true designs they bide
Yet all! These simpering fools who does not see
Most dangerous of all wolves in fact to be?

Isaac Newton,
from *Opticks*

Isaac Newton (1642–1727) had formulated his theory of universal gravitation by the time he was twenty-four, but it was not until several years later, in 1687, that he published it, at the insistence of friends, under the title *The Mathematical Principles of Natural Philosophy*—the culmination of a scientific development that had been in progress for well over a hundred years and had included such names as Copernicus, Kepler, and Galileo. But Newton was the heir of other thinkers in an even broader sense. The selection from his *Opticks* (1704) begins with a reaffirmation of the atomistic theory of matter, which was first developed by Democritus, an ancient Greek.

Source: Issac Newton, *Opticks, or A Treatise of the Reflections, Refractions, Inflections and Colours of Light*, 4ᵗʰ ed. (London, 1730). [Capitalization and spelling have been modernized—Ed.]

FOCUS QUESTIONS:

1. Describe Newton's method. How does he arrive at his conclusions?
2. According to rule four, what can we imply about scientific conclusions? Are they definite? Why or why not?

All these things being considered, it seems probable to me, that God in the beginning formed matter in solid, massy, hard, impenetrable, moveable particles, of such sizes and figures, and with such other properties, and in such proportion to space, as most conduced to the end for which he formed them; and that these primitive particles, being solids, are incomparably harder than any porous bodies compounded of them; even so very hard, as never to wear or break in pieces; no ordinary power being able to divide what God himself made one in the first creation. While the particles continue entire, they may compose bodies of one and the same nature and texture in all ages: But should they wear away, or break in pieces, the nature of things depending on them would be changed. Water and earth, composed of old worn particles and fragments of particles, would not be of the same nature and texture now, with water and earth composed of entire particles in the beginning. And therefore, that nature may be lasting, the changes of corporeal things are to be placed only in the various separations and new associations and motions of these permanent particles; compound bodies being apt to break, not in the midst of solid particles, but where those particles are laid together, and only touch in a few points.

It seems to me farther, that those particles have not only a force of inertia accompanied with such passive laws of motion as naturally result from that force, but also that they are moved by certain active principles, such as is that of gravity, and that which causes fermentation, and the cohesion of bodies. These principles I consider, not as occult qualities, supposed to result from the specific forms of things, but as general laws of nature, by which the things themselves are formed; their truth appearing to us by phenomena, though their causes be not yet discovered. For these are manifest qualities, and their causes only are occult. And the Aristotelians gave the name of occult qualities, not to manifest qualities, but to such qualities only as they supposed to lie hid in bodies, and to be the unknown causes of manifest effects: Such as would be the causes of gravity, and of magnetic and electric attractions, and of fermentations, if we should suppose that these forces or actions arose from qualities unknown to us, and incapable of being discovered and made manifest. Such occult qualities put a stop to the improvement of natural philosophy, and therefore of late years have been rejected. To tell us that every species of things is endowed with an occult specific quality by which it acts and produces manifest effects, is to tell us nothing: But to derive two or three general principles of motion from phenomena, and afterwards to tell us how the properties and actions of all corporeal things follow from those manifest principles, would be a very great step in philosophy, though the causes of those principles were not yet discovered: And therefore I scruple not to propose the principles of motion above-mentioned, they being of very general extent, and leave their causes to be found out.

Now by the help of these principles, all material things seem to have been composed of the hard and solid particles above-mentioned, variously associated in the first creation by the counsel of an intelligent agent. For it became him who created them to set them in order. And if he did so, it's unphilosophical to seek for any other origin of the world, or to pretend that it might arise out of a chaos by the mere laws of nature; though being once formed, it may continue by those laws for many ages. For while comets move in very eccentric orbs in all manner of positions, blind fate could never make all the planets move one and the same way in orbs concentric, some inconsiderable irregularities excepted, which may have risen from the mutual actions of comets and planets upon one another, and which will be apt to increase, till this system wants a reformation. Such a wonderful uniformity in the planetary system must be allowed the effect of choice. And so much the uniformity in the bodies of animals, they having generally a right and a left side shaped alike, and on either side of their bodies two legs behind, and either two arms, or two legs, or two wings before their shoulders, a neck running down into a backbone, and a head upon it; and in the head two ears, two eyes, a nose, a mouth, and a tongue, alike situated. Also the first contrivance of those very artificial parts of animals, the eyes, ears, brain, muscles, heart, lungs, midriff, glands, larynx, hands, wings, swimming bladders, natural spectacles, and other organs of sense and motion; and the instinct of brutes and insects, can be the effect of nothing else than the wisdom and skill of a powerful ever-living agent, who being in all places, is more able by his will to move the bodies within his boundless uniform sensorium, and thereby to form and reform the parts of the universe, than we are by our will to move the parts of our bodies. And yet we are not to consider the world as the body of God, or the several parts thereof, as the parts of God. He is a uniform being, void of organs, members, or parts, and they are his creatures subordinate to him, and subservient to his will; and he is no more the soul of them, than the soul of man is the soul of the species of things carried through the organs of sense into the place of its sensation, where it perceives them by means of its immediate presence, with-out the intervention of any third thing. The organs of sense are not for enabling the soul to perceive the species of things in its sensorium, but only for conveying them thither; and God had no need of such organs, he being everywhere present to the things themselves. And since space is divisible in infinitum, and matter is not necessarily in all places, it may be also allowed that God is able to create particles of matter of several sizes and figures, and in several proportions to space, and perhaps of different densities and forces, and thereby to vary the laws of nature, and make worlds of several sorts in several parts of the universe. At least, I see nothing of contradiction in all this.

As in mathematics, so in natural philosophy, the investigation of difficult things by the method of analysis, ought ever to precede the method of composition. This analysis consists in making experiments and observations, and in drawing general conclusions from them by induction and admitting of no objections against the conclusions, but such as are taken from experiments, or other certain truths. For hypotheses are not to be regarded in experimental philosophy. And although the arguing from experiments and observations by induction be no demonstration of general conclusions; yet it is the best way of arguing which the nature of things admits of, and may be looked upon as so much the stronger, by how much the induction is more general. And if no exception occur from phenomena, the conclusion may be pronounced generally. But if at any time afterwards any exception shall occur from experiments, it may then begin to be pronounced with such exceptions as occur. By this way of analysis we may proceed from compounds to ingredients, and from motions to the forces producing them; and in general, from effects to their causes, and from particular causes to more general ones, till the argument ends in the most general. This is the method of analysis: And the synthesis consists in assuming the causes discovered, and established as principles, and by them explaining the phenomena proceeding from them, and proving the explanations.

THE MATHEMATICAL PRINCIPLES OF NATURAL PHILOSOPHY

The Rules of Reasoning in Philosophy

Rule I. We are to admit no more causes of natural things, than such as are both true and sufficient to explain their appearances.

To this purpose the philosophers say, that Nature does nothing in vain, and more is in vain, when less will serve; for Nature is pleased with simplicity, and affects not the pomp of superfluous causes.

Rule II. Therefore to the same natural effects we must, as far as possible, assign the same causes. As to respiration in a man, and in a beast; the descent of stones in Europe and in America; the light of our culinary fire and of the sun; the reflection of light in the earth, and in the planets.

Rule III. The qualities of bodies, which admit neither intension nor remission of degrees, and which are found to belong to all bodies within reach of our experiments, are to be esteemed the universal qualities of all bodies whatsoever.

For since the qualities of bodies are only known to us by experiments, we are to hold for universal, all such as universally agree with experiments; and such as are not liable to diminution, can never be quite taken away. We are certainly not to relinquish the evidence of experiments for the sake of dreams and vain fictions of our own devising; nor are we to recede from the analogy of Nature, which is wont to be simple, and always consonant to itself. We no other way know the extension of bodies, than by our senses, nor do these reach it in all bodies; but because we perceive extension in all that are sensible, therefore we ascribe it universally to all others, also. That abundance of bodies are hard we learn by experience. And because the hardness of the whole arises from the hardness of the parts, we therefore justly infer the hardness of the undivided particles not only of the bodies we feel but of all others. That all bodies are impenetrable, we gather not from reason, but from sensation. The bodies which we handle we find impenetrable, and thence conclude impenetrability to be a universal property of all bodies whatsoever. That all bodies are moveable, and endowed with certain powers (which we call the forces of inertia) or persevering in their motion or in their rest, we only infer from the like properties observed in the bodies which we have seen. The extension, hardness, impenetrability, mobility, and force of inertia of the whole, result from the extension, hardness, impenetrability, mobility, and forces of inertia of the parts: and thence we conclude that the least particles of all bodies to be also all extended, and hard, and impenetrable, and moveable, and endowed with their proper forces of inertia. And this is the foundation of all philosophy. Moreover, that the divided but contiguous particles of bodies may be separated from one another, is a matter of observation; and, in the particles that remain undivided, our minds are able to distinguish yet lesser parts, as is mathematically demonstrated. But whether the parts so distinguished, and not yet divided, may, by the powers of nature, be actually divided and separated from one another, we cannot certainly determine. Yet had we the proof of but one experiment, that any undivided particle, in breaking a hard and solid body, suffered a division, we might by virtue of this rule, conclude, that the undivided as well as the divided particles, may be divided and actually separated into infinity.

Lastly, if it universally appears, by experiments and astronomical observations, that all bodies about the earth, gravitate toward the earth; and that in proportion to the quantity of matter which they severally contain; that the moon likewise, according to the quantity of its matter, gravitates toward the earth; that on the other hand our sea gravitates toward the moon; and all the planets mutually one toward another; and the comets in like manner towards the sun; we must, in consequence of this rule, universally allow, that all bodies whatsoever are endowed with a principle of mutual gravitation. For the argument from the appearances concludes with more force for the universal gravitation of all bodies, than for their impenetrability, of which among those in the celestial regions, we have no experiments, nor any manner of observation. Not that I affirm gravity to be essential to all bodies. By their inherent force I mean nothing but their force of inertia. This is immutable. Their gravity is diminished as they recede from the earth.

Rule IV. In experimental philosophy we are to look upon propositions collected by general induction from phenomena as accurately or very nearly true, notwithstanding any contrary hypotheses that may be imagined, till such time as other phenomena occur, by which they may either be made more accurate, or liable to exceptions.

This rule we must follow that the argument of induction may not be evaded by hypotheses.

John Bunyan,
Pilgrim's Progress

John Bunyan (1628-1688) came from the ranks of artisans. He was a tinker who also became a writer and well-known preacher in England. He was a Puritan, a Protestant movement in England that grew out of the teachings of Protestant reformer John Calvin, and a prominent advocate of their beliefs. Bunyan spent twelve years in prison, for holding Puritan church services despite laws banning them. He was also involved in the English Civil War (1642-1660). He wrote *Pilgrim's Progress* in 1678. It was widely read in Europe after its publication.

Source: *The Pilgrim's Progress*, by John Bunyan, Penguin Classics, ed. Roger Sharrock (New York: Penguin Books, 1987) 43–49.

FOCUS QUESTIONS:

1. What audience was Bunyan writing for? What reasons did he give for writing this book?
2. What was Bunyan's view of humankind? What ideas or beliefs informed his view?
3. How were Bunyan's ideas tied to the Puritan movement in England at the time?

THE AUTHOR'S APOLOGY FOR HIS BOOK

When at the first I took my pen in hand,
Thus for to write, I did not understand
That I at all should make a little book
In such a mode; nay, I had undertook
To make another, which when almost done,
Before I was aware, I this begun.

And thus it was: I writing of the way
And race of saints in this our Gospel-day,
Fell suddenly into an allegory
About their journey, and the way to glory,
In more than twenty things, which I set down;
This done, I twenty more had in my crown,
And they again began to multiply,

Like sparks that from the coals of fire do fly.
Nay then, thought I, if that you breed so fast,
I'll put you by yourselves, lest you at last
Should prove ad infinitum, and eat out
The book that I already am about.

Well, so I did; but yet I did not think
To show to all the world my pen and ink
In such a mode; I only thought to make
I knew not what, nor did I undertake
Thereby to please my neighbour; no, not I,
I did it mine own self to gratify.
Neither did I but vacant seasons spend
in this my scribble, nor did I intend

But to divert myself in doing this,
From worser thoughts which make me do amiss.

Thus I set pen to paper with delight,
And quickly had my thoughts in black and white.
For having now my method by the end,
Still as I pulled it came, and so I penned
It down, until it came at last to be
For length and breadth the bigness which you see.

Well, when I had thus put mine ends together,
I show'd them others that I might see whether
They would condemn them, or them justify:
And some said, 'let them live'; some, 'let them die':
Some said, 'John, print it'; others said, 'not so':
Some said, 'It might do good'; others said, 'no'.
Now was I in a strait, and did not see
Which was the best thing to be done by me:
At last I thought, since you are thus divided,
I print it will, and so the case decided.

For, thought I, some I see would have it done,
Though others in that channel do not run.
To prove then who advised for the best,
Thus I thought fit to put it to the test.

I further thought, if now I did deny
Those that would have it thus, to gratify,

I did not know, but hinder them I might,
Of that which would to them be great delight.

For those that were not for its coming forth,
I said to them, offend you I am loth;
Yet since your brethren pleased with it be,
Forbear to judge, to you do further see.

If that thou wilt not read, let it alone;
Some love the meat, some love to pick the bone:
Yea, that I might them better palliate,
I did too with them thus expostulate.

May I not write in such a style as this?
In such a method too, and yet not miss
Mine end, thy good? why may it not be done?
Dark clouds bring waters, when the bright bring none;
Yea, dark, or bright, if they their silver drops
Cause to descend, the earth by yielding crops
Gives praise to both, and carpeth not at either,
But treasures up the fruit they yield together:
Yea, so commixes both, that in her fruit
None can distinguish this from that, they suit
Her well when hungry, but if she be full
She spews out both, and makes their blessings null.

You see the ways the fisherman doth take
To catch the fish, what engines doth he make?

Behold! how he engageth all his wits
Also his snares, lines, angles, hooks and nets.
Yet fish there be, that neither hook, nor line,
Nor snare, nor net, nor engine can make thine;
They must be groped for, and be tickled too,
Or they will not be catched, what e'er you do.
How doth the fowler seek to catch his game?
By divers means, all which one cannot name.
His gun, his nets, his lime-twigs, fight and bell:
He creeps, he goes, he stands; yea, who can tell
Of all his postures? Yet there's none of these
Will make him master of what fowls he please.
Yea, he must pipe, and whistle to catch this,
Yet if he does so, that bird he will miss.

If that a pearl may in a toad's head dwell,
And may be found too in an oyster-shell;
If things that promise nothing, do contain
What better is than gold, who will disdain
(That have an inkling of it) there to look,
That they may find it? Now my little book
(Though void of all those paintings that may make
It with this or the other man to take)
Is not without those things that do excel,
What do in brave but empty notions dwell.

'Well, yet I am not fully satisfied,
That this your book will stand, when soundly tried.

Why, what's the matter? 'It is dark', What tho'? '
But it is feigned', What of that I trow?
Some men by feigning words as dark as mine,
Make truth to spangle, and its ray to shine.

'But they want solidness.' Speak man thy mind.
'They drowned the weak; metaphors make us blind.'
Solidity, indeed becomes the pen
Of him that writeth things divine to men:
But must I needs want solidness, because
By metaphors I speak; was not God's laws,
His Gospel-laws in olden time held forth
By types, shadows and metaphors? Yet loth
Will any sober man be to find fault
With them, lest he be found for to assault
The highest wisdom. No, he rather stoops,
And seeks to find out what by pins and loops,
By calves, and sheep, by heifers, and by rams,
By birds and herbs, and by the blood of lambs
God speaketh to him: and happy is he
That finds the light, and grace that in them be.

Be not too forward therefore to conclude
That I want solidness, that I am rude:
All things solid in show not solid be;
All things in parables despise not we
Lest things most hurtful lightly we receive;
And things that good are, of our souls bereave.

My dark and cloudy words they do but hold
The truth, as cabinets enclose the gold.
The prophets used much by metaphors
To set forth truth; yea, who so considers
Christ, his Apostles too, shall plainly see,
That truths to this day in such mantles be.

Am I afraid to say that Holy Writ,
Which for its style and phrase puts down all wit,
Is everywhere so full of all these things,
(Dark figures, allegories), yet there springs
From that same book that lustre and those rays
Of light that turns our darkest nights to days.

Come, let my carper to his life now look,
And find there darker lines than in my book
He findeth any. Yea, and let him know
That in his best things there are worse lines too.

May we but stand before impartial men,
To his poor one, I durst adventure ten
That they will take my meaning in these lines
Far better than his lies in silver shrines.
Come, truth, although in swaddling-clouts,
I find Informs the judgement, rectifies the mind,
Pleases the understanding, makes the will
Submit; the memory too it doth fill
With what doth our imagination please,
Likewise, it tends our troubles to appease.

Sound words I know Timothy is to use,
And old wives' fables he is to refuse,
But yet grave Paul him nowhere doth forbid
The use of parables; in which lay hid
That gold, those pearls, and precious stones that were
Worth digging for, and that with greatest care.

Let me add one word more, O man of God!
Art thou offended? Dost thou wish I had

Put forth my matter in another dress,
Or that I had in things been more express?

Three things let me propound, then I submit
To those that are my betters (as is fit).

1. I find not that I am denied the use
Of this my method, so I no abuse
Put on the words, things, readers, or be rude
In handling figure, or similitude,
In application; but all that I may
Seek the advance of Truth this or that way.
Denied did I say? Nay, I have leave
(Example too, and that from them that have
God better please by their words or ways
Than any man that breatheth nowadays),
Thus to express my mind, thus to declare
Things unto thee that excellentest are.

2. I find that men (as high as trees) will write
Dialogue-wise; yet no man doth them slight
For writing so: indeed if they abuse
Truth, cursed be they, and the craft they use
To that intent: but yet let truth be free
To make her sallies upon thee, and me,
Which way it pleases God. For who knows how,
Better than he that taught us first to plough,
To guide our mind and pens for his design?
And he makes base things usher in divine.

3. I find that Holy Writ in many places
Hath semblance with this method, where the cases
Doth call for one thing to set forth another:
Use it I may then, and yet nothing smother
Truth's golden beams, nay, by this method may
Make it cast forth its rays as light as day.

And now, before I do put up my pen,
I'll show the profit of my book, and then
Commit both thee, and it unto that hand
That pulls the strong down, and makes weak ones stand.

This book it chalketh out before thine eyes
The man that seeks the everlasting prize:
It shows you whence he comes, whither he goes,
What he leaves undone, also what he does:

It also shows you how he runs, and runs,
Till he unto the Gate of Glory comes.

It shows too who sets out for life amain,
As if the lasting crown they would attain:
Here also you may see the reason why
They lose their labour, and like fools do die.

This book will make a traveller of thee,
If by its counsel thou wilt ruled be;
It will direct thee to die Holy Land,
If thou wilt its directions understand:
Yea, it will make the slothful active be,
The blind also delightful things to see.

Art thou for something rare, and profitable?
Would'st thou see a truth within a fable?
Art thou forgetful? Wouldest thou remember
From New Year's Day to the last of December?
Then read my fancies, they will stick like burrs,
And may be to the helpless, comforters.

This book is writ in such a dialect
As may the minds of listless men affect:

It seems a novelty, and yet contains
Nothing but sound and honest gospel-strains.

Would'st thou divert thyself from melancholy?
Would'st thou be pleasant, yet be far from folly?
Would'st thou read riddles and their explanation,
Or else be drownded in they contemplation?
Dost thou love picking-meat? Or would'st thou see
A man i' the clouds, and hear him speak to thee?
Would'st thou be in a dream, and yet not sleep?
Or would'st thou in a moment laugh and weep?
Wouldest thou lose thyself, and catch no harm
And find thyself again without a charm?
Would'st read thyself, and read thou know'st not what
And yet know whether thou art blest or not,
By reading the same lines? O then come hither,
And lay may book, thy head and heart together.

JOHN BUNYAN